BROTHER
BROTHER
A MEMOIR

DAN DUFFY

MAY DAY
PUBLISHERS

Brother, Brother is mostly truth, part fiction. I have tried to recreate events, locales and conversations from my memories of them. In some instances, I have changed the names of individuals and places.

May Day Publishers
Rockport, Massachusetts

Editors: Helene Schwalje & Sandra Williams

Cover Design by Phil Poole, www.99designs.com

Audiobook Narration by Braden Wright

DEDICATION

I will forever be indebted to my wife, Helene for her unwavering support and assistance throughout the writing and rewriting process. Her capable editing abilities and suggestions for improvement strengthened the coherence of my story.

This book is dedicated to those who died or became Missing In Action during the Vietnam War and to those, like my brother, who may still be Missing In America.

A portion of the proceeds from the sale of this book will be donated to the Vietnam Veterans Memorial Fund www.vvmf.org in the names of Richard E Duffy and Truman J McManus

"The thing about a story is that you dream it as you tell it, hoping that others might then dream along with you, and in this way memory and imagination and language combine to make spirits in the head. There is the illusion of aliveness."

Tim O'Brien
The Things They Carried

"Be patient toward all that is unsolved in your heart and try to love the questions themselves, like locked rooms and like books that are now written in a very foreign tongue. Do not now seek the answers, which cannot be given you because you would not be able to live them. And the point is, to live everything. Live the questions now. Perhaps you will then gradually, without noticing it, live along some distant day into the answer."

Rainer Maria Rilke
Letters to a Young Poet

Author Comments

December 2015 marked the 45th anniversary of my older brother Rich's disappearance. I've lived with so many questions about his fate. Though, the most important one still remains unanswered: If I had acted could I have changed the outcome?

The story I've chosen to write is a fictionalized memoir. This is a recollection, fragments of distant memories of my brother's life, our shared eighteen years, and my mental images of his Vietnam and post-Vietnam experiences. An important outcome of my reflection is that, although my brother is the focus of my story, it's really about the impact of his life on mine.

The fictional aspect revolves around my yearning to understand Rich's war experiences, which rendered him partially disabled. I've also used my imagination in reconstructing his '70 cross-country trip to a commune in New Mexico. My 2015 version of his journey is comprised of equal parts myth and reality, as my college girlfriend and I had our own cross-country experience in the Summer of '72.

I have endeavored to capture what I believe to be my own personal truth with the hope that, once written, I would be free of it. Rich's disappearance has stalked me too long.

Now it's time to lay his story to rest.

Chapter One

"What's this all about?" I murmured, standing in front of EZ Storage garage door #105. I inserted the key and heard the mechanism click. My fingers quivered as I struggled with the lock. I raised the door, and the rollers screeched as if a car were skidding through an intersection just before impact.

What the hell? There rested a candy apple red Pontiac GTO convertible, just like my brother's 66' classic muscle car. The last time I saw Rich's GTO was in the driveway where he abandoned it in favor of his thumb. When he came back from Vietnam he hitchhiked everywhere he needed to go or bummed a ride from me or one of my friends.

I walked around the dust-covered car. All four tires were flat. Cragar alloy wheels supported it. I bumped my head on the door frame as I hunched over to sit in the driver's seat. I saw a key in the ignition and two below dangling on a ring. I turned the ignition—silence.

I pulled down the visor and a Polaroid snapshot fell in my lap—Rich and Diane on their wedding day in '65. I picked it up with my left hand and my right floated above, tracing, but not touching the image. Rich was in his Marine Corps dress blues and Diane wore a simple white wedding gown with a pillbox veil. They were so young and happy, standing on the threshold of their dreams, unaware of how their circumstances would transform them over the next few years.

There was no question that their blissful image matched the one I've cloistered in my mind for decades. *You both ruined it, though. Didn't you? Whose fault was it? Rich's because he went to war or Diane's because she wouldn't wait for him?* I shook my head and sighed before tucking the photo in my shirt pocket.

1

I reached to open the glove box. After inserting two different keys, I found the one that fit. Inside was a '66 GTO Owner's Manual along with registration and insurance cards. I raised them to the windshield for more light. My brother's name was on both documents. They had expired in May 1970, one month before he left for Corrales, New Mexico. Beads of sweat began to form on my forehead, and my hands felt clammy. Then a voice came out of nowhere.

It took you long enough to get here. What did ya expect? Mom's '51 Merc?

I was supercharged, as if I had just chugged a can of Red Bull. I grabbed the handle and shoved the door wide open, banging it with my shoulder. I was halfway out when I heard, *Where you going bro? It's only me.*

"Only you? What the fuck!" My heart was pounding. *Where the hell was his voice coming from?* I fell back into the driver's seat as if I had plunged into salt water, ten feet below the surface and sinking fast. *Just breathe. Underwater?* I took a deep breath, uncertain if it would be my last. *Just keep breathing.* I pressed the heels of my palms into my eyes and rubbed. *Can that really be my brother's voice? After all these years, do I really want to dredge up "wreckage" from the depths of a sea called "Rich's life"?* Hoping to insulate myself from any further infiltration from the past I squeezed my eyes shut and covered them with my hands. I reminded myself to focus on the present, the here and now.

I know you're here, Danny. So, you can open your eyes.

I spread my fingers apart and peered between them hoping that I'd wake up from this freaky dream.

It's not a dream, man. It's for real.

I turned and saw his silhouette in the passenger seat. I squinted and his profile came into focus. He wore a red and blue Indian bead headband. His unruly long brown hair framed his face and exploded into curls, some grazing his shoulders. When he turned and gave me his gap-toothed smile, I knew it was Rich. He looked exactly like he had the last time I saw him in the summer of '70.

This can't be happening. So many years have passed. "It can't be you."

Yeah, it's me. Glad to see you, too. You know I've been stuck here for a long, long time.

"You've been stuck?" I banged my fist against the steering wheel scraping my knuckles. "You don't know what stuck is because I've been knee deep in mud, or more like horse shit, for years trying to figure out what happened to you."

Just chill, little bro'. It's cool.

"Chill? When it comes to you, I can't chill. You left Mom and me and everyone else wondering what we did wrong to have you run away and never return. There are too many loose ends, too many questions."

Question after question flooded my mind all demanding answers. *Where've you been for forty-five years? Why haven't you kept in touch? Why'd you leave without saying goodbye?*

We'll have an eternity to discuss 'em.

What the hell. Now he's reading my mind? My legs felt like rubber as I stood and almost lost my balance. I shuffled to the back of the car and leaned against the trunk. It was a beautiful spring day with bright sunshine against a brilliant blue backdrop. Looking at the sky helped me to momentarily gain my composure. Since I opened the door nothing had changed outside, yet, everything inside me was now in a state of chaos. *Is it possible I just talked to Rich?*

Why don't ya open the trunk?

I fumbled with the key ring, found a key that fit and exposed a jam packed mess. It looked like everything Rich owned had been stuffed inside. Several large cardboard boxes were pushed together along the back; two smaller ones were wedged side-by-side in front. One was overflowing with 8-track tapes of sixties rock and roll bands. There was outdoor equipment strewn all over: a tent, sleeping bag, lantern, hiking boots, an aluminum frame backpack, a road atlas, and national park guide. Next to the spare tire were about a half dozen paperbacks, squeezed together like soldiers marching in formation.

"Wow. It looks like I've uncovered a lost tomb."

Maybe you have. Now what are ya gonna do?

"I really don't know. I stopped here to see what Mom had in storage. I didn't count on finding your car or dealing with you after all this time. I just don't know how to handle it."

It was getting late. There was not enough time for me to search through all of Rich's belongings, and I wasn't sure I really wanted to anyway. I took a deep breath and slowly exhaled. With my arms outstretched, I regained my grip on the bottom lip of the trunk and began to close it.

Wait! Hold on. You're not gonna leave me here by myself. Are you, little bro'?

"Hell, I don't know what I'm going to do. I guess I'll be back tomorrow."

Do you pinky swear?

"Yeah, I pinky swear."

Don't worry. I'll be here. I've got nowhere to go.

I closed the trunk, returning my brother's possessions to darkness.

Chapter Two

Unsure of what I had just discovered, I sat in my SUV, staring at the closed garage door. I mulled over the scene trying to make sense of it. *What have I found? Can this be the key that unlocks answers to my questions? Do I really want to find out the truth?*

Since I was a young man I had imagined possible scenarios surrounding Rich's disappearance. Sometimes I've wondered if he could be living "off the grid," leaving no paper trail for me to follow. More often, I was haunted by the scene of him drowning in the Rio Grande River, gone without a trace. However, I never found evidence of one or the other.

Yet, one fact remained—the brother I knew who left for Vietnam, didn't return the same. Perhaps his drastic change was attributed to stress he endured as a Forward Observer or from shock when his young wife deserted him. Like a movie editor striving to create a coherent film, he was conflicted, attempting to assemble the discordant elements of his former life. But, he couldn't. Too many images were out of focus and scenes of his past had faded in meaning and relevance.

To fill the void, he created a new identity as a flower child and Jesus freak. He referred to himself as a born again Christian. I was encouraged to see his sense of self change for the positive, as he embraced peace, love, and spirituality. Maybe that's why I stood by passively even though he engaged in the negative behaviors associated with the counter-culture— namely, drug experimentation and abuse.

During the spring of '70, Rich met several kindred spirits and together they embarked on an adventure of driving cross-country from the Jersey Shore to Corrales, New Mexico to form a commune. *What was he seeking? Was he running away from or toward something?*

Hearing his voice again brought me back to that dreadful day in December of '70 when Mom received a cryptic postcard from his girlfriend Ginny. "Rich and I went to the Rio Grande, took LSD, and when I woke up he was gone."

Mom seemed in denial, interpreting Ginny's message to mean, "Maybe Rich smartened up and walked away from those people." She could have asked a cop or detective she knew from working at the Old Time Tavern to make a few phone calls to New Mexico on her behalf. But, she didn't, and we never discussed it as a family. I guess she was too consumed with more immediate concerns as a single-parent raising four other kids.

What was I supposed to have done? I had felt helpless. At the time I was a freshman at a community college determined to change the cycle I'd grown up with of living from paycheck to paycheck. With little money, I didn't know what to do or how to do it from 2,000 miles away. I thought that just because we hadn't heard from him since Mom received the post card didn't mean he wasn't living his life the way he wanted. *Hell, he survived a year in Vietnam, hadn't he?* I assumed he was OK somewhere.

A year and a half later in the summer of '72, I traveled cross-country with my college girlfriend. Ever since, I had regretted not visiting the Corrales, New Mexico commune where Rich had lived. I really don't remember it as a conscious decision to visit or not. But, hindsight tells me that I missed an irretrievable opportunity. It was only a few years after his disappearance and maybe I could have found and spoken with the only eye witness—Ginny. All I can say about my decision not to visit Rich's commune is if I could turn back time to undo it, I would.

Within the first five years of his disappearance, I was busy finishing college, beginning my career, getting married and buying a home at the Jersey Shore. Yet, thoughts of Rich nagged me. So, over the course of the next few decades I made numerous attempts to locate him.

I drafted a letter including a description of Rich and the circumstances of his disappearance. It was the pre-internet age, so I contacted a mailing list company, sending letters to over 100 men who shared his name. No luck. I used his social security number to inquire about any recent activity. No luck. I used his military service number to have the Veteran's Administration forward a letter to his last known address. No luck. I conducted driver's license searches of his name in four Western states. No luck.

Most recently, I filed a Missing Persons Case with the FBI in Albuquerque and Special Agent Parker told me that the only record she could find about Rich was an early June '70 drug arrest. I also spoke with the Manager of Archives at the Albuquerque Public Library. She reviewed copies of the *Journal* and *Tribune* from June 1st to December 31st 1970 but didn't find any articles about a Rio Grande drowning victim.

Concurrently, I conducted an online people search and was able to locate and speak with a few members of his former communal family. No one was able to shed any light on his disappearance. They told me that Rich cared deeply for Ginny and loved his lifestyle. That contradicted what Mom liked to think. I also queried them further about Ginny. None of them could remember her last name or current whereabouts. Perhaps it was because acid had burnt out the synapses of their brain cells, or maybe they just wanted to forget a painful time in their young lives.

Once, after an LSD trip, Rich had told them he saw a spiral staircase and pledged that he'd take it if it ever reappeared. Consequently, they all shared a belief that Rich transcended time and space by ascending Jacob's Ladder when it appeared to him over the Rio Grande River.

I couldn't think about it anymore. I rolled down my window and spit on the ground. "Dammit!" I yelled. I've been repeatedly disheartened, trying to piece together what became of Rich. *Now he mysteriously resurfaces? What am I supposed to do now? Do I want to stir up the past again? Do I really want to spend time and energy looking through his stuff? What good would it do?* Sometimes it's best not to know what you don't know.

I needed time to think about what all this meant.

Chapter Three

When I went to bed that night after "seeing" Rich, my head was spinning. Someone was using me for a punching bag. Bam! I was hit in the head when Mom died. Bam! I took a body blow, discovering Rich's car and possessions. Bam! I was jabbed with a right to the skull, seeing Rich. Bam! I was slammed with an uppercut. *He and I were talking?* Bam! I was on the ropes, my legs were buckling. *Hold on, Dan. Wait for the bell. I can handle it, right?* Ding! I was startled awake, as if smelling salts had been jammed up my nose. I shook my head, hoping to be splashed with water before the next round.

I sat up in bed. Things were moving too fast, and everything was hazy. It seemed like only yesterday that Mom died. Yet it had already been a week since I went to her lawyer's office as executor, hearing her will read and getting her key to the EZ Storage unit. I didn't even know she had anything in long term storage, let alone Rich's '66 GTO. *Now, I had to root through all of his shit?*

I could hear Mom's raspy voice say, "Of course you're gonna look through Rich's stuff. Haven't you spent your whole life wondering about his disappearance?"

I leaned back against the headboard. A beam of moonlight shined through the window as I thought about Mom's words. "I'll go back in the morning."

∞

My pulse quickened as I backed up to the EZ Storage unit for the second time. Once again, I raised the garage door. This time I felt a potent connection with my brother. My tension eased a bit when I saw the bright red GTO. I remembered being with him at Trenery Pontiac the day he bought it. Hell, I loaned him the down payment.

Memory after memory flooded over me. I saw visions of our early years playing together as kids. Then, thought about choices Rich made during his teens; one poor choice after another—smoking, drinking, dropping out of school, stealing, and getting into trouble with the police. Gradually, his behavior eroded my big brother image of him. Until finally, he was standing before a judge and given the option: go to jail or join the Marine Corps. Now, I was faced with searching through remnants of another life he had lived.

I was anxious to examine Rich's possessions, hopeful that I might find a clue to a puzzle. First, I'd study each piece. Then, I'd look for nuances shared by two or more. Finally, I'd try to find connections linking each segment into a unified whole. *Who am I kidding?* Jigsaw puzzles weren't my strong suit. The pieces I had to work with didn't appear to fit together. Like an archeologist, I hoped to find meaning amid fragments of a long-lost life. What I had was a mess of disparate articles. The only place I knew to start from was where I was at. I took a deep breath and began in earnest.

I unloaded several archive boxes from my trunk and began filling one with books. They compiled a cross-section of the counter-culture bestseller list of the sixties and seventies: *Stranger in a Strange Land, The Electric Kool-Aid Acid Test, Walden, On the Road, Bury My Heart at Wounded Knee* and *Catch 22.*

I opened Heinlein's *Stranger in a Strange Land* and saw that Rich and I shared the same habit of underlining passages. He had circled "Grok," printing in the margin: "drink, love, understand and to be one with."

The next thing I knew Rich was back.

Can you Grok that bro'?

"Grok, what?"

Grok everything about me?

"I can't do that right now and not sure I'll ever be able to. I didn't get much sleep last night thinking about what happened yesterday. One moment I was pissed at you for not keeping in touch with us all these years. And the next, I just wanted to spend time with you."

Yesterday was far-out! You don't have to Grok me all at once. We'll have time to rap.

"OK, I guess. I can try, but in small doses. Can you help me do what I have to do?"

What's that?

"Well, start by going through all your stuff."

Sure. That's cool.

My mind wandered, remembering Rich's transformation, from U.S. Marine to Jesus freak. Shortly after his return home, he began wearing a mop haired Beatles wig to hide his shaved head. He shed his former clothes and created a robe out of an old Army blanket by cutting a hole in the middle for his head. He tied it around his waist with a piece of rope and called it his Moses robe. In place of shoes, he wore open-toe, leather sandals. Within a matter of months, his hair had grown longer, so he stopped wearing the wig and didn't shave. His beard completed his transformation into a "hippie."

I picked up a black, leather-bound Bible. Recognizing it immediately, I didn't need to open it. But, I did. There on the title page, my mother's crooked script inscribed our family name. The Bible confirmed that these possessions were indeed Rich's. I suspected that he had taken the Bible with him to New Mexico. After his discharge, he had carried it with him wherever he went.

You found my Bible.

"I did. It's good to know that you carried a part of your family with you out West."

It was sacred and as a hippie I rejected everything about materialism and the middle-class.

Rich and I were talking, but it seemed like we were standing on either side of an impenetrable wall. I thought about what he had said and didn't agree with any of it. I couldn't reject middle-class values. I aspired to embrace them, not push them away. Achieving them meant everything to me—proof that I could break through economic and social barriers previously unavailable to me and my family.

As I placed the Bible in the box, I pictured him, his peaceful ear-to-ear smile, quoting scripture from the Book of Revelations, predicting the second coming of Christ.

That's right. Do you remember me spreading the word of the Lord? Jesus will come again. Just read Revelations.

"I don't have to read it. You told me about it, again and again and again. In fact, I don't remember you talking about anything else but the Bible." I shook my head and rolled my eyes remembering Rich immersed in his alternate universe.

It was the Lord's word. It got me through sleepless nights in 'Nam. I promised Jesus that if he spared me, I'd walk in his footsteps. He did. I was blessed and became one of his disciples. But, guess what? There's other stuff for you to find.

I picked up a brown leather journal with the initials R.D. in the corner. Grasping its smooth surface, I held it to my face and whiffed its earthly scent. My fingers traced each hand-carved letter and the words "Live Free or Die" carved across the cover. I visualized Rich's hands gripping a sharp blade, rendering his imprint for eternity.

You found my journal. Everything's in there.

My knees buckled and I fell back onto the bumper. I shook my head in doubt. *Have I found the mother lode?*

I opened the back inside cover where he had drawn a peace sign in the form of a heart with tiny dots. The words PEACE and LOVE were written above and below it. They looked like the tattoo he had given himself. He had wrapped thread around a needle, dunked it in India ink and pierced the letters MOM into his left arm. I turned to the front inside cover and saw another drawing of a peace sign. Within each of

12

the sign's three segments were the words—Sex, Drugs and Rock n' Roll.

I thumbed through page after page of Rich's tiny printing. His entries began on the first day of summer, June 21, 1970 at a campground in Pennsylvania and continued along his route through Indiana and Illinois. I skimmed the next entries from The Badlands National Park and Pine Ridge Indian Reservation in South Dakota, Yellowstone and The Grand Tetons in Wyoming. His next stops included San Francisco's Haight Ashbury District, Yosemite National Park in California, The Grand Canyon and the town of Jerome in Arizona and Zion National Park in Utah.

I flipped to the back, hoping to find clues about what happened to him in Corrales, New Mexico. I snapped Rich's journal shut and wacked myself on the knee with it. "Fuck!" I shouted, hearing my voice echo off the walls of the storage unit. I couldn't believe that the last pages were torn out.

Where the hell was I now? I tossed his journal onto the driver's seat of my car, vowing not to let it out of my sight until I could read it more carefully. I continued rummaging around his trunk. As I lifted two large books, a US Road Atlas and a National Park Guide, out dropped a map of the forty-eight contiguous states.

I see you found something else. Why don't you open it?

I noticed that someone had used a marker, tracing a path across the map. It looked like it followed some of Rich's journal entries.

"Are these your markings? Is this your cross-country route?"

Now you're getting somewhere.

"Getting somewhere? I don't think so."

Sure, you are. It was bitchin'. A trip of a lifetime. I was free, like never before.

I tossed his comment around in my mind. It released a memory of Janis Joplin singing about freedom and having nothing left to lose. I slipped the Atlas and the National Park Guide under Rich's journal on my front seat and crammed the archive boxes into the trunk of the GTO.

You're not gonna take everything?

"I have to get out of here."

Where are you going?

"I can't stay right now."

Don't worry. I'm not going anywhere.

"I didn't think so."

Closing the overhead door I thought, *Why is this happening to me?*

Chapter Four

I turned east and drove to the ocean where I've always done my best thinking. It was low tide, and Seaside Park beach in springtime was barren, like a desert, with no one visible in sight. Seagulls floated in the updraft above the breakers along miles of dunes with clam shells strewn along the wet sand.

I tore off my shoes and socks, rolled up my jeans and ran to the water's edge. I was enveloped in a salty mist from the waves crashing to shore. Before me, the cobalt sea and sky seemed infinite.

For about an hour I walked along the jagged tidal line that separated the wet sand from the dry, picking up and examining shells and pieces of sea glass. "Wait up," I heard someone shout from the boardwalk as two cyclists rode by on their beach cruisers.

∞

Rich was running behind me holding the seat of my two-wheeler as we went up and down the alley next to our apartment. "Don't worry, Danny. I'll hold you 'til you're ready." I didn't think I was ready. *What five-year old kid ever is?* When I balanced, Rich let go and kept running behind me. Each time I fell, he helped me up and said, "You can do it." Rich was the only male role model I had as a kid. He was there for me in Dad's absence, and Dad was absent a lot from our young lives.

∞

I bolted for the boardwalk and ran back to the 7th Avenue beach entrance where I had parked my car. Within twenty minutes I found myself again in front of the storage

15

compartment. I pulled up the garage door, popped the trunk and heard, *Back so soon?*

I tried to ignore it as I quickly tossed the rest of Rich's stuff into my SUV. But, then I found myself saying, "Yeah. I decided to bring it all home."

Wanna take her for a ride? It would be cool to get the GOAT on the road again.

∞

Rich was on the ground, looking up at me, chanting, "Just jump! Hold on tight!" I was balancing on the edge of our second floor apartment rooftop with Dad's big black umbrella open over my head. I didn't think it would work, but I jumped anyway. I hit the ground hard and discovered that umbrellas allowed someone to float only in cartoons. Nothing was broken, but, I limped for a week. I told Mom I fell off my bike when she asked me about it.

∞

No, I've been down that road too many times, and all it ever leads to is trouble. I have to get out of here. I slammed the trunk, pulled down the door and ran to my SUV.

Chapter Five

I looked at the clock on my bedside table for the third time—2:12 a.m. I slipped my pillow from under my head, and stuffed it over my face to keep from staring at the ceiling fan all night. "Relax," I mouthed. But snippets of my childhood with Rich continued to bounce around in my mind.

∞

It was the 4th of July. Mom let Rich and me walk two blocks to the park, bordered on one side by the train tracks. We must have walked to the park and back at least three times that day. We ate ice cream and cotton candy and wove colorful potholders for Mom at an "arts and crafts" picnic table. Rich boosted me up in the saddle and I rode a pony for the first time. When we returned to the midway at dusk, we played "Pop the Balloon" and "Catch a Fish."

Rich spotted cat tails growing in the marshy soil beside the tracks. "Let's get some punks." Mom had told us to stay away from the tracks, but I followed Rich anyway, my feet squishing in his sunken footsteps. He reached a cluster of cat tails, bent them over and began cutting with a pocket knife.

"Does Dad know you have his knife?"

"Don't tell him."

As darkness fell we sat on the tracks holding our punks, waiting for the fireworks to begin. "Let's have some fun." Rich reached into his jacket pocket and pulled out a silver Zippo lighter.

"Is that Mom's?"

Rich looked at me with a sly smile as he flicked the lighter, igniting a blue-yellow flame. He held it next to the punk and it emitted acrid fumes. He threw it to the ground and took a pack of firecrackers out of his other pocket and flicked the lighter again. I sat there, watching in amazement as he lit the fuse and threw the sizzling pack into the air shouting, "Happy Fourth of July!"

∞

Next, Rich and I were standing beside an old ringer washing machine. Someone from a neighborhood apartment had abandoned it in no-man's-land, behind the string of stores and apartments and the shopping center parking lot. That relic sat there with weeds all around it, like a tombstone in a neglected graveyard. We examined it closely, twisting and turning the agitator back and forth.

"It moves," Rich said. "Get inside. I'll push you."

Rich offered me a boost and I climbed inside the basin. Crossing my legs around the center post, I put my hands against the sides for balance. He spit on his hands, gripped the rim and ran around in circles. "Faster, Rich, faster." I held on tight. He pushed as fast as he could then fell down laughing, watching my head spin round and round. I spun a half-dozen more times before it finally stopped. I put my leg over the side and fell to the ground beside Rich—laughing. When I tried to stand I couldn't, so he helped me up. I just stood there trying to regain my balance. Rich put my arm around his shoulder and tried to get me walking. My legs were wobbly and sweat poured from my brow. Then, my stomach gurgled, and I burped. I put my hands on my knees and barfed remnants of my lunch all over the ground.

∞

Some might say I bore the brunt of Rich's shenanigans because I was young and gullible. But, in reality, I loved being with him. He was larger than life. Sure he was the instigator, but I had learned early on not to snitch on him because he made me pinky-swear not to tell. *What were a few bruises and a little tarnished pride when it came to being blood* brothers? Didn't that imply we'd be committed to each other through life's highs and lows?

Had I finally found Rich? I really couldn't say. But, I did feel a powerful connection with him and was willing to keep an open mind.

It was 5:00 a.m. when I left a voicemail message for Gus, my Auto Tech asking him to give me a call about restoring the GTO.

Chapter Six

"Beep. Beep. Beep."

I circled my hands in front of me and shouted to the tow truck driver, "Come on back." He got out of the cab, walked around the GTO and shook his head.

"I'll have to jack up the front bumper to get my dolly under the flat tires. You'll have to sign a release 'cause I'm not responsible for damage."

"No problem."

He held a clipboard and took out a pen. "I'll need to see the registration and insurance cards."

"Sure. But they expired forty-five years ago."

"Don't matter to me. Just following procedures."

I *opened the door, sat in the driver's seat and reached to open the glove box.*

What's happening?

"I'm towing the car to my mechanic."

It'll be cool to get it back on the road again. Maybe even follow my route?

"Follow your route?"

Yeah, man. My cross-country route.

"Jeez. How the hell can I do that?"

You'll take it one mile at a time. Just like I did.

"There you go again stirring things up for me." The idea of a cross-country trip enticed me, but I wasn't sure.

Why not, bro'? It'll be an awesome trip, just the three of us—you, me and all our fears.

"You'd be coming too?"

You'll need someone to show you the way, won't you?

I laughed. *Show me the way? Sure, that's what you've always done so well. Right?* I was still pissed about him abandoning me and our family so long ago. One thing I knew for certain. For most of my life, I had heard the words, "What if?" echoing in my mind. I had missed other opportunities and shouldn't miss this one. Now that I was retired, I really didn't have an excuse.

Who knows what will happen? Anything's possible.

"I'm in."

Chapter Seven

Having spent eight weeks in Gus's garage, the GTO looked like it had just been driven off the showroom floor. Gus knew exactly what to do, restoring the engine and all its components. He recommended a "shake-down" period before beginning my trip. A week later, he gave me the go ahead.

It was June 21st, Summer Solstice, my scheduled day of departure. The gloomy morning clouds cast an ominous shadow. Rich's US Road Atlas, National Park Guide, and journal were on the passenger seat. The trunk was repacked with several of his original boxes, some of his outdoor equipment, plus a new backpack and camp stove.

When I turned the ignition, the 389 under the hood with dual exhaust emitted a deep guttural sound—vroom. I pressed the pedal up and down and the engine came to life, like the sixties muscle car it was.

Put the pedal to the metal, man.

I turned, and seated beside me was brother Rich. He grinned, a wide toothy smile. His chaotic beard and mustache consumed his face, as if he were a mountain man just out of the wilderness.

"You're back?"

Of course. I'm going with you. It took you so long to find me. You better not leave me behind.

"That's the last thing I'd want to do. You know why? Because, you and I have a lot of distance to cover."

Don't worry. We'll get it covered. How about if you drive, and I'll just chill.

"That's the only option we have, right? Besides, driving will give me a chance to think."

Hearing the engine purr, I inserted one of Rich's favorites into the 8-track tape deck, the driving blues-rock band, Canned Heat. "On The Road Again" began playing. I sensed something quite profound about someone not wanting to travel a road alone. Maybe that someone was Rich and perhaps me. As I listened to Alan Wilson's hypnotic harmonica playing, tears came to my eyes, and a lump formed in my throat.

I recalled hearing those kings of boogie for the first time at the Atlantic City Pop Festival in the summer of '69. Rich was also there that weekend, having returned from Vietnam a few months earlier. We experienced the festival from two different worlds, me straight and Rich stoned.

"Remember hearing Canned Heat play this song live?"

Sure do. The band jammed at that outdoor concert. At least you're not traveling alone on this trip.

"No. I'm not," I replied, still unsure whether or not it were true.

Chapter Eight

Since Gus installed cruise control, all I had to do was feather the steering wheel to keep heading west. I had been driving 65 mph for hours. But, internally, I was traveling at warp speed. My mind replayed scenes of our young lives like I was looking at old 8mm family movie clips.

∞

Rich and I were on our way to redeem bottles at Grand Union for deposit refunds. A 12-ounce Coke was worth two cents, a 32-ounce a nickel. The word recycling hadn't been invented yet. I knew it as candy money; sugar-coated gum drops were my favorite. Rich called it spending money because he didn't have a sweet tooth, like I did.

We stopped at the corner of Queen Anne Road and West Englewood Avenue to put our paper bags down to count our bottles. There was a pile of cinderblocks obstructing the sidewalk, next to a deep hole, about a half a block long. A guy stood in the sandy hole and shouted to us, "Hey, kids, wanna make some money?"

Rich didn't waste any time grabbing a block, shuffling over to the edge of the sidewalk and dropping it with a thud. It looked like fun. I wanted to try it, too. He handed me one. It scratched my fingers as I held it. I waddled like a duck, inching my way to the sidewalk's edge before letting go. We worked for what seemed like hours. Perhaps, it was a mere thirty minutes. My pace was always one block less than every two Rich threw down.

The mason told us to stop and climbed up the ladder to the sidewalk. He reached into his pocket, pulled out a handful of change. My eyes lit up seeing no pennies—just nickels, dimes and quarters. He put two quarters in Rich's hand and gave me thirty-five cents. I looked at my palm, then Rich's. My watery eyes met the mason's. I sniffled as I held back tears. "Mister, I did a good job, too."

∞

Rich squinted from the midday sun in his eyes. "You embarrassed the poor guy into putting another fifteen cents in your hand."

"Well, I deserved it, didn't I?"

"Sure, Danny. I'm not gonna argue with you. Sometimes it's just easier to give in than to put up a fight."

"Really? Was I that hard-nosed?"

Rich paused. He looked at me, shook his head and rolled his eyes. "There are other words to describe what you can be. To you it's always someday this...someday that... Your head is somewhere far away in the future. That's not real. What's real is right now, not in another day or hour or minute. Right now. We've got nothing else. Do you get it?"

I heard Rich's words, but really wasn't listening. If all I ever had to do was focus on the present, wouldn't I be bounced around like a pin ball, not knowing when I'd be hit next or where I'd be going?

"Life isn't about being in control of everything or trying to predict the future. Don't be like some people who miss what's right in front of them because their eyes are always on the horizon."

I thought about Rich's perspective but disagreed. I didn't tell him. My focus on planning for the future had served me well. I wasn't interested in making compromises at that point in my life.

∞

Honk! Honk! I was startled from my musing when a trucker blasted his air horn. He motioned to the driver ahead of me to pull over. The right wheel of the guy's pop up camper was wobbling.

But, Rich? Rich? Where are you? Where'd you go? Come back! *Wasn't he sitting right beside me?* He sure was. There was a connection between us, dreamlike, but real.

The GPS beeped, signaling that I was approaching my exit. I looked at the miles to destination reading on the monitor, twenty-three miles to go. Within thirty minutes, I pulled into the same Elliott State Park campground as Rich and his friends had in '70.

As I hammered tent stakes into the ground, setting up for the night, I heard a beautiful harmony: Crosby, Stills, Nash and Young sang "Déjà Vu". Was this my mind telling me I was on the right track? I hoped so.

Chapter Nine

When I awoke, sweat was oozing from every pore of my body. I shouldn't have bought that below zero sleeping bag after all. My tent was stifling hot. Hoping for relief, I unzipped my bag, opened the flap of my tent and stepped out in my briefs. No breeze was stirring, just a sticky humid summer day.

I put on shorts and a tee-shirt, ate a cold breakfast of trail mix and drank a warm bottle of OJ. I had forgotten to replenish ice in my cooler. The bottom was filled with six inches of lukewarm water. Bottles of seltzer, beer and OJ were bobbing up and down, like sailboats in a harbor.

I sat in my camp chair beside my tent under an umbrella of tall oaks. *So this was where Rich and his friends camped their first night on the road?* I opened Rich's journal to the first page,

Day #1, June 21, 1970 (Elliott State Park, Pennsylvania)

Our journey's begun! I'm traveling with three friends. If I'm Moses, then my friend Ken is Jesus. He plays guitar and harmonica. We love to sing along.

Ken's girl Sally is a free spirit, connecting us with Mother Earth. She has silver and turquoise rings on every finger, even a few on her toes. Ginny is my college girl. She's out of sight. Always reading something and telling us about it. Rounding out our family is me.

Crosby, Stills and Nash sing the famous song playing in my head—"Woodstock". And that's what I'm seeking-to set my soul free. I didn't get to the concert, but its spirit is with me all the time.

We're heading cross-country and want to experience everything—the great outdoors, National Parks and Native Americans. Oh yeah, sex, drugs, and rock and roll, too. Thank God for my monthly VA check. Its bread we need for our trip.

I'm driving Ginny's VW bus. It has a ragtop sunroof that lets me touch the sky. We customized it with psychedelic peace signs. From the driver's seat I have a far out view of the open road. The rear engine is great on gas, though it doesn't go up hills worth a damn.

Ken's driving with Sally in his VW camper we painted with neon rainbows. He's leading the way to our new home we're renting from his uncle in Corrales, New Mexico. We're forming a commune. Each of us will contribute to our loving and peaceful community.

Simon and Garfunkel's song "America" could have been a splendid soundtrack to the beginning of Rich's journey. As I read on, fragments of a decades-old scene emerged as Rich and his three friends materialized before my eyes.

∞

I saw them drive through the hills of Pennsylvania. They got to their campsite at sunset and parked the vans side-by-side. Sally and Ginny pitched Rich's backpack tent as Ken and Rich piled split logs in a fire ring.

Sally made a garden salad from fresh vegetables while Rich set up a propane camp stove. He put water in a pan and placed it on a burner for fresh corn on the cob. Soon, the four of them sat on both sides of a wooden picnic table to enjoy their first communal meal on-the-road. They held hands as Rich said grace, "Thank you Jesus for watching over us today and for bringing us to this fine camp."

They sat on logs around the fire ring as darkness fell. Ken opened a bottle of Boone's Farm apple wine, took a swig and passed it around. He put on the Doors album, *Strange Days* and turned up the volume to let everyone know he loved, "People are Strange." They sang along and pointed to one another. Rich rolled a huge joint, as thick as a cigar, lit it, took a toke and passed it around. Then, he lit another one and did the same. Ken put a match to the kindling and they watched as their first campfire began to shed light on the darkness around them.

When the flames turned into a bed of red hot coals, so did they. Rich joined Ginny in the tent. Ken and Sally paired up in his camper. It wasn't clear if any of them would get any sleep. No doubt, everyone was smiling as they headed to bed.

The lights went out one-by-one inside the tent and camper. After a time, perhaps an hour a light flashed on in the tent. I saw Ginny's shadow against the wall of the tent kneeling beside Rich shaking him and shouting, "Wake up! Wake up!"

∞

The scene vanished as a park employee shifted a Cushman cart into reverse and backed up on the service road behind me. I thumped Rich's journal shut and stared into nothingness. I shook my head. *What the hell had I witnessed?* It was time to turn in for the night and what a night it had been.

Chapter Ten

With the morning light, I knew I had better get on the road. I had at least six hours of driving ahead of me to get to Rich's next stop—Pokagon State Park in Angola, Indiana. I filled the tank at the interstate and got on the highway by 11:00 am. As I crossed Anderson Creek, I heard, *Morning, Danny.*

"Good Morning? Where the hell did you go yesterday? One minute we're talking about growing up and the next, poof, you're gone."

Just like life, isn't it? Rich snapped his finger. *One minute we're here and the next we're not.*

"Maybe. But I still don't understand, I muttered. The lyrics from Marvin Gaye's "What's Going On?" throbbed through my mind.

I accelerated to 70 mph, set the cruise control and heard, "Do you remember when Mom left Dad?"

"Holy shit, Rich. Why that topic?"

Why not?

"It's painful, that's why! That day was the most traumatic of my childhood."

It was for me too. I'll never forget it.

∞

It was a typical night in the summer of '59. After dinner we were watching *Terrytoon Circus*, a bedtime ritual for us Duffy kids. Rich crawled across the floor to turn the volume down so Mom wouldn't hear Clownie say, "It's time for all good girls and boys to go to bed." What we didn't know was that we wouldn't be *going* to bed that night. In fact, we wouldn't be sleeping in our own beds ever again.

I heard Dad yelling and banging on the front door. "Dad's home," I whispered. *The closet.*

Mom swept Rich, Sue and me from in front of the TV and helped us into the bedroom closet. "Keep quiet." We squeezed in between the clothes and stacks of shoes and boxes. She left four-year old Ray asleep on the bottom bunk and propped baby Eileen on her hip as she went to let Dad in.

My Dad was a decent enough guy when he was sober. His full-time job was driving a bus for the Red and Tan Lines. His part-time gig was superintendent of our apartment building. The main benefit of the job was basement living quarters. Unfortunately, for Mom and us kids, the apartment building was right next to Lucky's Tavern.

Dad's nightly routine was as certain as the bus schedule he followed. After each shift, he gravitated to his favorite stool and bellied up to the bar. He knew his wife and five kids awaited him fifty feet away. But, family be damned; he seldom arrived on time for dinner. Each night he had a more important engagement and after a half-dozen Schafer drafts and a few shots of Seagram's, he morphed into an ornery, belligerent bastard.

The bartender had a lot of practice flagging my father, then telling him to go home and sleep it off. But he couldn't just come home and go to bed, at least not before having his nightly face-off with Mom.

As we huddled inside the closet, this night seemed different from others. Dad got louder and louder. Rich put his ear against the closet door and whispered, "Mom can't get Dad into bed." Then, he turned the knob, slowly creaked open the door and started crawling across the floor to the bedroom door. I followed him, leaving Sue behind, clutching her knees against her chest and whimpering.

We peeked around the door frame and saw Dad's lanky silhouette as he stood in the living room doorway, still dressed in his bus driver uniform and cap. Each time Mom tried to walk through, he stepped in front of her. She looked up at him and said, "Let us by."

"Not 'til you tell me what you did to my car. It won't start," Dad yelled.

Mom scrunched her face at him. "I didn't do nothin'."

"What did ya do to my car, bitch?"

"Nothin'. Besides you're too drunk to drive, Duffy."

"I'll do whatever I damn want to, you bitch!"

Rich and I watched as Dad grabbed Mom, putting one hand around her neck and the other around Eileen's. Mom screamed, "You're choking us, Duffy! Stop!"

Rich reached behind the door to grab his bat. My mouth dropped as I saw him run down the hall, swinging it over his head, shouting, "If you hurt 'em, I'm gonna whack you!"

Dad scowled at Rich and snapped, "Did you say you're gonna whack me?"

"I'll hit you with my bat."

"Hell, you better not if you know what's good for you."

"I will if you hurt 'em. I'm not afraid of you. Let 'em go!"

Dad released his grip on Mom and Eileen and went to grab the bat from Rich's hands. Mom wedged herself between them and hollered, "You're scaring the hell out of the kids! Get out or I'll call the cops!"

"I'll do whatever the hell I want," Dad uttered. He stumbled out the door and banged it shut. Mom ran to the phone as Eileen's screams echoed down the hall.

Mom quickly gathered us up. "We're gettin' outta here." She led us across Teaneck Avenue in our PJs and bare feet, Eileen on her hip. Sue held Ray's hand with Rich and me following behind. She helped us into the car, took something out of her purse, popped the hood and ducked under it. She slammed it, jumped into the driver's seat, and I heard her mumble, "Please, dear Lord, start." She pumped the gas a few times and turned the ignition—vroom!

Rich sat in front; the rest of us were crammed in back, silent. The only sounds we heard were Mom accelerating, braking and an occasional blinker. Sue held my hand, and I squeezed Ray's to stop it from shaking.

"Where're you taking us, Mom?" I managed to ask.

"You'll find out when we get there. We can't live in a place where your father scares us to death. That's the last time he's ever doing that."

∞

My hands were frozen to the steering wheel as I looked over at Rich, sitting next to me. Telephone poles whizzed by behind him, interrupted by a fire engine red Coke logo on the side of an eighteen wheeler.

"I think our childhood ended that night when you stood up to Dad. I only wish I could have done the same."

Rich glanced at me. *I'm sure if you were a few years older, we woulda double-teamed him.*

Chapter Eleven

It wasn't a long trip. Not nearly enough time for an eight-year old kid like me to understand what Mom really meant.

Before we knew it, the six of us were standing in Gram's living room. We had been there before, on Sundays and holidays when our aunts, uncles and cousins would visit. Tonight would be different, though. We were staying overnight—the first of many nights to come.

When we visited in the past, we stayed downstairs. On nice days we sat on the porch wall and picked green shoots off the hedge that separated the neighbor's driveway from Gram's house. A few times we snuck upstairs to see the bedrooms where Mom and her two sisters and four brothers had lived while growing up.

Whenever we passed the attic stairway on the second floor landing, my oldest cousin Robby would remind us that Gram had once sent him to the attic for misbehaving. The thought of him, or any one of us, trapped in the attic frightened me.

Mom must have told Gram we were coming because she greeted us by pointing to pillows and blankets stacked on the sofa. Gram marched over to the stairs, crossed her arms and announced, "The older boys will sleep in the attic."

Rich and I stood holding our breath, not saying a word. Our eyes met in disbelief. *Does Gram hate us? Why is she punishing me and Rich?* I was expecting Mom to ask if we could sleep in a bedroom. She looked down to avoid Gram's eyes and nodded her head. "OK, Mom."

I couldn't believe what I heard. I had never been in the attic. I imagined it full of cobwebs, spiders and bats. Every night Dad came home drunk, the darkened closet called my name. I didn't want to be trapped in another web of darkness.

At the top of a steep set of open stairs was a wooden door, lying flat with hinges mounting it to the ceiling rafters. It dared to be opened. Rich led the way. Both of us clutched our pillows and blankets in our left hand and held onto the thin railing with our right. Each step took us closer and closer to the unknown. I wiped sweat from my forehead with the sleeve of my PJ's. My knees were wobbly, and my feet seemed stuck to the floor. Rich rubbed his brow with the back of his hand, looked at me, and pointed his finger up. "Almost there."

I felt like I was going to throw up, so I swallowed hard. Rich handed me his pillow and blanket, tilted his head, and took a deep breath. Using both hands, he pushed against the door and let out a grunt. "This door's heavy."

Rich's legs did the rest of the work; with each push, the door inched open. At first it creaked, releasing dust and dirt onto our heads. I sneezed twice, almost losing my balance, but held onto the railing. With a final thrust, he shoved the door into an upright position and let out a deep breath. Rich climbed into the stifling attic, peered at me over the opening, and extended his hand. I took it and looked into his eyes as he smirked. "Welcome to Hell."

Chapter Twelve

We crawled across the floor boards and propped our backs against an old wooden steamer trunk. All I could think about was a bat making a nest in my hair. I put my hands over my head, held my breath and whispered, "Please God, no bats." Rich reached above me and pulled on a string; a single bulb emitted its desperate hue. A stained sheet barely covered a double mattress discarded on the floor beside the knee wall below the roof rafters. An orphaned oak dresser stood in the shadows, its back ignoring the makeshift bed.

Gram screamed from the bottom of the stairs. "Shut off the light!"

Rich pulled the string again. He took a small flashlight from the elastic waistband of his PJ's, its beam our only salvation. I followed the glow of Rich's light to bed and crawled over him onto the side protected by the wall. He handed me the flashlight and said, "You can keep this on for as long as you want."

"Thanks." I pulled the blanket up to my eyes. The wind howled and the roof creaked. Just a few feet above my head, a drum roll of raindrops pelted the roof. With each new sound, I gripped the flashlight tighter and tighter, shining it from one roof beam to another. Then came a frightening flash of lightning and deafening salvo of thunder.

I jumped and reached over to Rich's side of the bed, touching only crumpled covers. "Where are you?" I rolled out of bed; the rough floor boards pinched my bare feet. I saw his shadow in front of the side window. He turned, pulled up his underpants, and smiled.

"I had to go real bad and couldn't hold it. I wasn't gonna pee in that ole milk bottle Gram gave us."

Well, now I had to go real bad too. I followed Rich's lead, pulled down my underpants, stood on tiptoes and peed through the screen to the ground three stories below. This became our nightly ritual, a secret we didn't dare share with anyone. A few weeks later, we tried not to squirm in our seats at the dinner table when Gram told Mom that her favorite rose bush had died. Rich and I made eye contact but remained expressionless.

∞

My life changed living in the attic with Rich that summer. When he clutched my hand and helped me into the attic, I knew right then and there that I didn't have to face my fears alone. He was with me. That made all the difference. What once were a few fond childhood memories of my father and me, faded to tainted shades of grey. In my father's absence, I wanted to be just like Rich.

Occasionally, fragments of my childhood memories evoke a sense of panic, fear and helplessness. During those moments, I remind myself that it was all in the past. But, sometimes the past doesn't always stay where it belongs. In fact, too often the past becomes right now.

∞

My cell phone rang, arousing me from my reverie. I let the call go to voicemail. The only reasons I brought it along were to use the GPS app and in case of an emergency. The GPS display read thirty-four miles to my destination, Pokagon State Park, Angola, Indiana.

Chapter Thirteen

I awakened and peered outside when I heard a rustling in the thicket next to my tent. Six wild turkeys scampered from the bushes. It was as good a time as any to get up. Especially, since I hadn't slept much during the night, attempting to find a balance somewhere between my pent up anger about Rich's abandoning me and my interest in sharing experiences with him again.

Maybe a run would clear my mind. I put on shorts, sweatshirt and tied my running shoes. An outdoor display map showed the Old Horse Trail encircled the park. After stretching, I turned on my iPhone, inserted earbuds and selected my 60's mix. I entered the bridle path, following the trail's descent. I crossed the bridge over Stony Run Creek, took short steps as the trail began to rise and then lengthened my stride when the path flattened out.

I began sweating as I absorbed the warmth of the early morning sunshine, refracted by cool mist rising from the hillside. Immersed in the tempo of crossing the countryside, a sense of timelessness enveloped me. My mind transcended the rhythmic motion of my legs in concert with my body.

"Ahhhhh," I said, inhaling moist cool air as I quickened my pace. "Huff, huff, blow! Huff, huff, blow!" My body propelled my consciousness along the intricate pathways of the landscape.

I was calm. No barriers, real or imagined, were between me and my surroundings. My feet were extensions of the ground. The motion of the wind swept me along. The mountain air filled my soul. All these forces united me with nature.

Yet, I knew this gift of inner peace and serenity would slip away if I dared to think about whether my recent encounters with Rich were real and would continue. *Was I really traveling with my missing brother or was I going crazy talking to his voice in my head?*

My run should have relaxed me, but my mind kept revisiting those questions as if I were caught in an infinite loop. As I cooled down, my body mirrored this action. I walked in circles around my tent and camp chair, one rotation after another. Sounds of Steppenwolf's "Magic Carpet Ride" resounded through my earbuds; something about believing is seeing. *Could that be it?* If I believed I was talking to Rich, he must be real.

I grabbed Rich's journal on my third pass around my camp chair and began reading his next entry while continuing my roundabout path.

Day #2, June 22, 1970 (Pokagon State Park, Indiana)

Made it thru Ohio and just over the border into Indiana. What a boring drive. We sucked way too much polluted air and we're all coughing. Can't wait to get out West and breathe fresh air. After dinner, I read the good word from Revelations.

"Blessed is the one who reads aloud the words of this prophecy, and blessed are those who hear it and take to heart what is written in it, because the time is near. Look, he is coming with the clouds, and every eye will see him, even those who pierced him and all peoples on earth will mourn because of him. So shall it be!"

The time is near and he is coming. Will we be ready?

There goes Rich again, predicting the end of the world. A breeze blew through the red maples surrounding my

39

campsite. I inhaled deeply, exhaled and collapsed in my chair. I poured myself some tea with the hope that something hot would help me relax. With each sip, I turned another page of his journal and found myself sitting behind Ginny and Rich in the rear seat of the VW bus.

∞

"Let's hear some Cream." Ginny put the album *Disraeli Gears* into the tape player. "I love 'Strange Brew' and 'Sunshine of Your Love.' Don't you?"

"Yeah." Rich beamed. It wasn't just a polite "thanks for having sex with me last night" kind of grin. It was a radiant smile that communicated they had experienced something unique, an intermingling of souls. "Do you know you make me happy?"

Ginny couldn't take her eyes off Rich. "I hope so. I'm excited about you and me."

"I'm not sure why it took us so long to get together. But, we finally did. The rest will be history."

"I like the idea of making history with you. Making love with you last night was special. One moment you were tender and another intense. I felt things I've never felt before." Ginny cracked a smile.

"You caught my eye the first time I saw you at the park. You looked groovy in that silky flowered dress that shimmered as you walked."

"I needed to clear my mind so I headed to Winding River Park."

Ginny had just dropped out of Montclair State College because she wanted to major in organic gardening, not Algebra and Western Civ.

"You're still my college girl. When we met I thought you had it all and now I know it."

Ginny giggled. "Really? I have it all? Such as...?"

"Well, I love your blue eyes, long blond hair and those little blue beads in your braids. You're such a free spirit."

"OK, my turn. Let me tell you a few things I adore about you. I love the gap between your front teeth; your crazy hair, funky beard and penetrating eyes. You have such a sense of adventure. When you heard Ken's Uncle had a rental home in New Mexico, you said, 'Let's go.' At first, I wasn't sure if you actually meant it or fantasized about living in a commune. But, you followed through. Now I can't wait to live there with you."

"I'm looking forward to making a life there with you, too, maybe build some furniture for us and even try to sell some."

"I can't wait to plant my organic garden and grow our own vegetables. That *Whole Earth Catalog* I brought along should come in handy."

"It'll be a gas." That reminds me. We need to stop for gas, and I have to take a leak. OK?"

"Sure. I gotta pee too."

Rich and Ginny held hands as they entered the gas station. Rich smiled at the man behind the counter. "Peace, brother."

The man wrinkled his brow, pursed his lips and spat, "Peace is the sign of the American chicken."

Rich stepped back and waved his hands. "We don't want trouble. Just some gas and to use your bathrooms."

The man's eyes were riveted on Rich's as he pointed to the door. "We don't serve long-hairs."

Ginny caught his arm and led him to the door. "It's OK. Let's get out of here."

Rich turned and raised his hands, giving the man the two-finger peace sign on both. Then he clenched his fists into two middle-finger salutes, smiled and walked backwards out the door.

"Don't come back, hippie freak!"

"Don't listen to him. He's nobody. Let's go to another station."

"Sure. It just pisses me off knowing that I risked my life in 'Nam for a guy like him." As Rich got back in the van he kicked over a four-foot high display of motor oil cans stacked between two gas pumps. He drove away, looked in his rearview mirror and snickered as dozens of cans rolled along the pavement behind him.

At the next station, the attendant filled their tank. Rich drove around back so they could use the bathrooms. Ginny was first out and waited for him. Rich threw open the door and jumped in front of Ginny. "Boo!" He turned in a circle, shook his head and sprayed a ring of water droplets from his locks.

"You scared me and you're getting me wet, silly."

"I was just trying to have some fun. I thought you needed some too, especially after getting hassled by that redneck."

Ginny wrapped her arms around Rich. "Nothing's better than cool fun. I've already forgotten that nameless hick."

Rich pulled her close and kissed her. "Nothing's better? How about cool sex?"

"Yes. I like that much better." Ginny held Rich's hand as they walked back to the van. "How about me driving? So far, you've been behind the wheel the whole trip."

"You can take over and I'll relax and enjoy the view."

Ginny loved Rich's energetic spirit, always in motion—a bundle of nervous energy—unfocused and undirected. It was good to see him sitting still for once. She leaned over, put her hands on both sides of his face and looked deep into his eyes. She kissed him, threaded her fingers through his messy brown hair and whispered, "I love you."

Rich yanked the curtain across his portion of the windshield and Ginny followed suit with hers. "Instant privacy," she said.

42

He pulled her onto his lap and returned her open-mouthed kiss. His fingers slipped under her blouse and he caressed her breasts. "I want you, right now," Rich whispered. He took off his robe and urged her to straddle his legs. Ginny shimmied off her jeans and squatted on his lap. She took a shallow breath as he entered her, arched her back and held onto his shoulders. She screamed just before they climaxed and collapsed in each other's arms. They dozed, their bodies entwined until Ginny awakened.

"My leg is asleep. I have to get up."

"Huh? What?"

"Nothing. I just have to walk around." Ginny hopped out of the van naked, then snatched her jeans off the floor and pulled them on. As she got back in the driver's seat she leaned over to kiss Rich. "That was very cool sex." She adjusted her seat, mirrors and buckled up. Then, she started the engine, put it in first, and popped the clutch. The van stalled.

"Try again. You just have to get used to the clutch."

Ginny nodded, restarted the engine, eased off the clutch and they were off. After a prolonged period of silence, Ginny said, "Something's bothering me about you Rich. Can I talk to you about it?"

"Sure. I'm an open book. You can ask me anything."

"Well, after we made love last night, we fell asleep in each other's arms. I woke up during the night because I heard you shouting in your sleep. Do you remember dreaming?"

"Nope. Maybe you heard someone in another tent."

"No. It was you. You said, 'We're trapped.'"

Hearing Ginny's words, Rich's focus became transfixed on the distant horizon. Darkness enveloped him, as if day suddenly became night. He was dreaming with his eyes wide open.

∞

He covered his head when he heard an incoming mortar round. Hot shrapnel seared the back of his hands, and some ricocheted off his helmet. He smelled the pungent aroma of gunpowder and tasted the bitter metallic tang of blood. The ground caved in and he was being buried alive. His bloody fingers clawed for a handhold, grabbing for something to lessen his inevitable slide into an abyss.

∞

"Rich, Rich!" Ginny cried as she pulled onto the shoulder of the road. Rich was startled back to consciousness, gasping for air. His surroundings came into focus and he heard Ginny's distant voice. "Relax, Rich. I'm with you." Regaining the natural rhythm of his breathing, he saw Ginny leaning over him.

"What's wrong?" she asked in a whisper.

"I don't know. I was back in 'Nam. One minute, all my buddies and me were in our bunker. In the next, we took two direct hits that blasted us into the air. Then we crashed to the ground. Fire and smoke were everywhere. I heard cries for help, but couldn't move."

Tears came to her eyes. She held him tight, both arms encircled his shoulders. "Don't worry, Rich. It's over. I'm here with you."

"Those episodes aren't going away." Rich hugged her, his face pressed against hers. He tasted a teardrop on Ginny's cheek. It reminded him of the salty taste of the sea when he swam in the Atlantic. He kissed her and whispered in her ear. "Thanks Ginny. I love you."

Cream's "Sunshine of Your Love" resonated from the speakers. They held hands and stared out the window.

∞

The rumble of an outboard motor echoing across a nearby lake brought me back. I turned and saw a lone fisherman sitting astern in his boat, one hand on the tiller and the other clenching a pipe in his mouth.

Chapter Fourteen

Where did the time go? I was off to a late start. I got busy breaking camp and repacking the car. I stopped for gas, picked up snacks, ice and a few bottles of water. I punched my destination into the GPS: Hooppole, Illinois. The route showed over the next five hours that I'd be traveling through cities like South Bend, Gary and Joliet. All I cared about was getting west of those places and putting them behind me.

The trip was uneventful; the dotted white-line was a blur as mile after mile passed behind me. I was hypnotized by the open road; cornfields swayed in the wind as far as I could see. I didn't feel like talking. Maybe, I was trying to process what I had learned about Rich.

It was dusk by the time I arrived in Hooppole, so I stopped for dinner at a bar called Smitty's, just ten miles from my campsite. The sign out front touted that they had the best burgers and coldest beer in the state. I thought I'd find out for myself. When I opened the door, I stepped into a cosmos of stale beer, charred beef and burnt onions. It was dark and quiet with a dozen men sitting around a mahogany bar pocked with cigarette burns. Several others were seated at tables engraved with the initials of those who had once passed through.

I took a seat at the bar between a couple of arm-wrestling type bruisers dressed in jeans, work shirts and boots. Shaving didn't appear to be an option for these guys. The one on my left wore a Kenilworth cap and had a disheveled beard that spread across his face and down his neck. The one on my right wore a MACK hat that covered his bald head. Bushy sideburns extended to form a beard from one ear to the other.

I ordered the burger special which was 100% Angus beef topped with everything you could think. When it arrived it was the biggest burger I'd ever seen. In between bites, I used about six napkins to wipe the juices from my mouth. The Blue Moon draft was all it was advertised to be, super cold served in a frosted mug.

"What brings you to Hooppole?" Mack asked.

"Just staying the night and passing through."

"Aren't we all."

"Guess so."

"Other than fellow truckers, I don't see many people traveling alone on this highway."

"Oh, I'm not alone," I blurted out. "I mean I'm going cross-country."

"It's a great one. That's probably why I'm a trucker. I've seen many beautiful sights within the US of A."

"I can't wait to get out West."

"That's where distances on the map change from twenty miles per inch to thirty—where the country opens real wide and swallows you up," said Mack.

"Sounds good to me."

"So why Interstate 80?"

"I'm retracing my older brother's cross-country trip back in 1970."

"That's cool."

"He and several friends went out West after he got back from Vietnam."

Ken, the trucker on my left, nudged me. "That was a smart idea your brother had. I wish I had thought of it. I just rolled up my sleeves, stepped into the cab of my eighteen-wheeler and got to work."

"Did that help you cope?"

"I don't know about that. It's helped me keep my eyes focused on the road, always looking ahead not daring to look back."

I nodded and Mack did too.

"What branch of the service was your brother in?" asked Ken.

"He was a Marine with the 81mm mortar division."

"I was a grunt, an Army grunt. Foot soldier is what most people think of... That's what I was, a grunt and a foot soldier. There were so many of us in the Army. After the war, I realized that there was a purpose to the numbers." He paused. "We were expendable."

I looked at him, nodded and remained silent.

"So why aren't you reliving this experience with your older brother? I bet he'd like to make the trip, too. Wouldn't he?" Ken asked.

"I'm sure he would, but we haven't seen or heard from him since he went to Albuquerque in '70. "

"You don't know what happened to him?"

"No."

"That sucks," said Mack. "I had polio as a kid so I was classified 4F. But, a lot of my friends went and came back totally whacked out. They never snapped out of it."

"I can believe that."

"So what are you trying to do with this cross-country trip?" Ken asked.

I paused for a moment. "I'm not really sure."

"Well, I hope it brings you peace."

We finished our meals in silence and I paid my tab. As I stood to leave, I glanced in the wall length mirror behind the bottles of spirits standing at attention on each shelf.

There was no one sitting on either side of me.

Chapter Fifteen

The next morning when I crawled out of my tent, a low ceiling of endless grey clouds were visible for as far as I could see. There had been a wild thunderstorm most of the night, and I had slept fitfully. Cracks of lightning followed by booms of thunder reminded me of the mortar attack Rich had endured and was reliving.

Thin nylon fabric was supposed to separate me from the elements, but it hadn't. Rain drops from the roof of my tent had dripped down on me during the night. My clothes, sleeping bag and tent were sopping wet. I wished there were a Laundromat nearby so I could have thrown everything in a dryer, including myself.

I slipped into the back seat of the GOAT, changed into dry clothes and opened Rich's journal,

Day #3, June 23, 1970 (Circle S Camp, Hooppole, Illinois)

The name of this place sounds like a dude ranch. It was a cheap spot for the night. Nothing special about Illinois. Just another stop on our way out West. Can't wait to see open sky, mountains and rivers. God Bless us.

I closed his journal, tossed it on the floor of the passenger side and got out of the car. I surveyed the wet mass of camping gear piled outside my tent. I unfolded a couple of leaf bags from the trunk, stuffed them full of my wet belongings and jammed them in the back seat. I hoped to hell there'd be a dryer at the next campground.

Interstate 80 was an engineering marvel—an almost endless east-west straight line. Go west young man, I thought as I crossed the legendary Mississippi. It would have been remarkable if it had been the halfway point of my journey. But, it wasn't. I still had many more miles to go to reach that milestone.

After several hours of driving, I passed through Des Moines before I stopped for gas and a bathroom break. Had to make this a fast one if I hoped to keep on schedule. Traffic was sure to get heavier with each passing hour.

Chapter Sixteen

As I got back on the highway, I wasn't sure if I'd be ready to talk with Rich today. The more I thought about it, the more I realized this would be a good opportunity.

You're awfully quiet over there. What are you thinking about, Danny?

Rich's voice startled me, returning me to a more alert state of mind. Once again, I became mindful of the sensations of driving—the pressure of my foot on the gas, the sight of cars passing by and the persistent hum of the engine.

"I'm thinking about a lot. After you came home, you never said anything about your year in Vietnam. I had questions but didn't know how to ask you then. Can I ask you one now?"

Rich laughed. *Sure. But remember the VA said I was partially disabled. Seriously, though. It was the most difficult year of my life. I turned twenty living in a mud bunker in Da Nang.*

"I once asked you about the scars on the back of your hands. All you said was, 'It's nothing.'"

Well, shrapnel under my skin was nothing compared to watching two of my buddies get blown apart by a mortar attack. I blacked out from being hit. When I came to, the ringing in my ears was so loud I couldn't hear a thing. It was like watching a silent slow motion movie. I crawled to one of my buddies and looked him in the eyes. I held his head on my lap and kept saying, "Help is on the way. Hang in there, Jonesy." But, help wasn't on the way. He died in my arms. Rich crossed his arms and looked down at his lap.

I gasped. "There wasn't anything you could do to save him?"

Rich's face was ashen when he looked back at me. *Nothing.* He paused. *That's all I can say right now about 'Nam.* He took a deep breath and exhaled a slow rasping sigh like the sound of a death rattle.

"Maybe we can talk some more about this another time?"

As we sped along, he stared out his window at mile markers as they flashed by, one after another, like crosses in Arlington Cemetery.

Chapter Seventeen

I was stunned. This journey with Rich was taking me to places inside myself I didn't want to go. I pressed my foot to the floor and disengaged the cruise control. I watched the speedometer climb...65...70...75...80. I tried to put some distance between me and Rich's memories. Then, I heard, *What's your rush?* I took my foot off the accelerator and moved into the right lane as the car coasted back to 65 mph. I reset the cruise control and my mind wandered back to living at Gram's in the summer of '59.

∞

We never needed an alarm on Sunday mornings. The *Bergen Record* delivery truck woke us up at 5:30 a.m. Rich pulled the string of the light hanging from the roof rafters. He wore jeans and a tee-shirt to bed so he didn't have to get dressed in the morning. I got dressed and followed him down the attic stairs. A half-dozen stacks of two-foot high bundles of newspapers awaited us—scattered all over the sidewalk. We both grabbed an end and carried bundle after bundle to Gram's porch. They were tightly bound with wire, creating our main challenge of the morning—cutting them open.

"Grampa's workbench," Rich said. We slipped through the narrow door in the downstairs bathroom and recoiled from the musty, pungent smell of cat urine. We held our noses and ventured down the even narrower rickety stairway to the darkened basement.

We didn't know about wire cutters. At least their outline wasn't painted on the pegboard above Grampa's workbench. There was an outline of a pair of pliers, though, with the tool itself hanging in its designated spot. Rich took them down, and we went back outside. We took turns gripping the pliers, wiggling them back and forth until finally we heard the long-awaited snap. One down, five more to go.

"Danny. Stack 'em in piles so we can put the paper together."

"OK." I began to put handfuls of papers in rows.

We worked in tandem. I inserted the first few sections together, and Rich completed them. Our last step was to fold the paper in thirds, inserting it into itself, so we could throw it as we rode along. We stuffed dozens of completed papers into our cloth shoulder bags. Once we got the bags on our shoulders, Rich said, "It's all downhill from here. Just stay balanced."

My shoulder was hurting, and I hadn't even thrown the first paper. *How was I going to pedal the bike, go up and down hills, balance my bag, and keep it out of the spokes?*

"Just follow me."

And, I did. The first hill was the hardest, getting off my bike midway, then walking it to the top. Our customers' addresses were on cards, bound together on a two-inch metal ring slipped over the handlebars. Rich worked one side of the street and I the other. I got better as my load got lighter. I don't know when, but, after a while, it became fun riding alongside my brother, especially when we delivered to those big brick-red houses with the muddy Hackensack River flowing behind them.

Chapter Eighteen

I looked over at Rich. "I learned a lot that summer. I remember your advice before we did our collection on Saturday morning. You said, 'Put the newspaper's money in your right pocket and tips in your left.' I thought that was an easy way to organize my money. Yet, I remember at the end of the day, I always had to reach into my tip pocket to pay what we owed the newspaper."

Rich grinned my way and nodded. *That was a bitch. I guess all we needed was to have a few more people home when we collected.*

I laughed. "Now, that was another lesson I learned from you. Try not to play the bank for deadbeat customers."

As simple as this childhood experience may seem, I learned early in my life how to manage money. I've been frugal, but not cheap, OK. So, I'm guilty of knowing how much money I have at any one time in my wallet, and in the bank.

Maybe there's something to be said about kids having responsibility.

"It served me well," I said.

By the way. I don't know why you think I told you about putting your tips in one pocket and the paper's money in another. Because, you started doing it and I followed along.

"I did that?"

Oh, and another thing I almost forgot. Make sure you fill up before you exit the interstate.

"Not many gas stations on the back roads, huh?"

That's for real.

∞

My head jerked when the female voice from my GPS announced, "680 west exit six miles ahead." I cracked the butterfly window to inhale some fresh air and slapped my cheeks. I exhaled and refocused on my driving. "That's better." I glanced at the monitor and saw I had twenty-five miles to go until I arrived at Rich's next stop, Wilson Island State Park in Loveland, Iowa.

I remembered to fill-up the tank when I exited the highway. But, I had forgotten all about the plastic bags in the back seat that held my wet tent, sleeping bag and clothes. I pulled into the campground intent on finding a washer and dryer. "None, here," said the man at the check-in desk. Maybe I'll find them at my next stop.

It was a clear night with a mantle of stars visible from horizon to horizon. I had always wanted to sleep under them; tonight would be as perfect a chance as any. I took the top down, dumped the laundry bags on the ground and got a dry blanket and my day bag out of the trunk. I was tired, and it was too late to even think about making something for dinner. So, fully clothed, I climbed into the back seat. After attempting a few different sleeping positions, I settled on lying on my back with my head propped on my day bag. Not exactly comfy, but it would have to do for the night.

Locating Ursa Major, I followed its arch to the bright red star, Arcturus, then gazed at another called Spica. I fell asleep under star dust from the Milky Way as it stretched from Cassiopeia in the north to Sagittarius in the south.

Chapter Nineteen

I was awakened at dawn, the mighty Missouri River flowed faithfully a mere hundred feet away. My neck had a kink in it from using my day bag as a pillow, and my muscles were sore from sleeping in a fetal position. With the top down, I figured the least strenuous way out of the car was to climb over the side, so, I did.

Breaking camp should have been effortless. After all, the back seat had served as my futon. With no need to roll up my tent, I hobbled around the campsite then decided to stretch my back by sitting on the ground and touching my toes. It loosened my muscles prior to running, so I thought it would work now, too. "Ouch!" I inhaled deeply. Then I took shallower breaths and persevered until the count of ten. I had hoped for natural benefits of an early morning stretch, but found none. I swallowed an Aleve with a gulp of warm bottled water—mere hydration, not refreshment. Hopefully, I'd soon feel relief.

Lying on the ground beside the car were the two plastic garbage bags containing my wet tent and sleeping bag, jammed inside since yesterday. I leaned against the car, grabbed one of the water laden bags, and, when the bag was over the back seat, I let go. It landed on top of my day bag and blanket. I did the same thing with the other bag, but it burst upon impact, spraying water all over the back seat and my bedding. I shook my head and shrugged my shoulders. *Who knows what fungal growth had been multiplying inside those bags?* I had better find a laundromat today or I'd be sleeping in the back seat again. I knew which one of those choices I preferred.

I leaned against the car and opened Rich's journal to his next entry,

Day #4, June 24, 1970 (Wilson Island State Park, Loveland, Iowa)

Today we started in Indiana, crossed Illinois and we're almost out of Iowa. It was a long day's drive. Ken and I drove our slow going VW's in the right lane. Cars with campers, eighteen wheeler trucks and little old ladies in Ramblers passed by—leaving us in their dust!

I can't wait to get to New Mexico, where the air will be clear, dry and fresh. I want to live in a place where we can enjoy peace and harmony. It turned out that Loveland wasn't anything like its name. I'm tired of getting hassled for being me. Finally got to camp before sunset. Now, we're trying to chill after a shitty day.

After dinner, I read from Peter, "Now who is there to harm you if you are zealous for what is good? But even if you should suffer for righteousness' sake, you will be blessed. Have no fear of them, nor be troubled."

As I continued reading, I heard Rich's voice recounting his travels as if I were listening to an audio version of his journal:

"We were on I-80 west again all day. For some reason, Ken and I forgot to stop for gas at the interstate exit in Loveland. By the time we realized it, we were close to empty without a gas station in sight. We saw a sign, 'Wilson Island State Park-20 miles', so we hung a quick left. Fifteen long miles later, we saw another sign pointing toward a marina, a lucky find to get some gas. We parked both vans close to a boat ramp. On a dock about twenty feet away was a DX gas pump. I got out a five-gallon can and walked up to a policeman wannabe ranger, wearing a green uniform. He took his field glasses away from his face and seemed annoyed that I had interrupted his panoramic view of the lake."

Then, Rich's words morphed into three-dimensional shapes and images. I saw him and his friends as they came to life before me. Just believe, I reminded myself. Just believe. I observed with my mind wide opened.

∞

"Good afternoon, sir. I wonder if I could buy five gallons of gas to get back to the highway?"

The ranger looked Rich over from his beard to his sandals and shook his head. "I only sell gas for boats."

"I know this is a marina. But, we only need a few gallons to get to a gas station."

The ranger turned his head, raised his arm and pointed to his left. "Loveland is twenty miles east."

Rich shrugged his shoulders. "We don't have enough gas to get there."

"You shouldn't come into these parts without enough fuel."

"I'm not familiar with these parts or I woulda filled up on the interstate." Then he pleaded, "Sir, can you spare two gallons—one for each of our vans?"

The ranger crossed his arms, looked at Rich with a scowl and nodded in the direction of the two psychedelic vans. "There's a state law prohibitin' the sale of boat gas for car purposes. If I sell it to you, I'll have to go into double bookkeeping. And, you could be a state inspector."

Rich smiled. "Sir, do I look like a state inspector? Both of our vans have Jersey plates, don't they?"

It was a "Catch-22." The ranger's fabricated excuse let Rich know that he didn't have any power over his circumstance. If Rich didn't get it, the ranger was going to shove that fact down his throat.

Their gas gauges read empty when they arrived back at the interchange to fill their tanks. When Rich told Ginny and the others about his conversation with the ranger, Ginny shook her head. "Consider the source, and take it for what it's worth—a straight guy hassling a hippie."

∞

A Forestry truck drove by on a nearby fire trail, and I was brought back to the here and now. I can't believe it happened again. In thinking about Rich's day, it was apparent to me why he drove over nine hours. He wanted to get as far away as he could from his Loveland experience.

Chapter Twenty

It was 10:00 am, and already the air hung sticky and stiff. I was dripping wet, grumpy and needed to get moving. My lower back was tight and throbbed as I slouched against the driver's seat, started the car and punched in the day's destination: The Badlands National Park in South Dakota. My GPS said it would be a ten-hour, 650-mile trip, my longest day yet. I'd first be traveling north on I-29, then west on I-90. Too tired to put up the top, I hoped that the sun would ease my aching muscles.

I put the Hearst four-on-the-floor into first, gave it some gas, released the clutch and was on my way. In a matter of minutes I heard Rich's greeting, coming from the passenger side, *Yo, Bro'*.

I counted to ten. "Please, not yet, Rich."

Bad night, huh?

"Something like that." I fiddled with my sunglasses and Red Sox cap to avoid Rich's attempts to converse.

The whirling of the tires on the roadway comforted me as my body settled into the bucket seat. I drove for miles unsure if my grogginess was due to lack of sleep, the Aleve or the interminable monotony of the road.

I tried to ignore Rich's never-ending rustling beside me. Out of the corner of my eye, I watched him. First, he'd pinch clumps of beard on his chin, as if he were making sure it was still connected. Then, his fingers would scratch up and down both sides of his cheeks. The result was an unruly mass of beard from his cheekbones to his neck.

I know you're pissed. But, that doesn't mean we can't rap.

"I'm not pissed. I'm just tired and sore from sleeping in the back seat last night."

Did you get any action back there?

I rolled my eyes. "Very funny."

What do you think was the best day we ever had living at Gram's?

"I know what day that was for me."

Rich caught my eye and winked. *Our last.*

∞

My mind focused on the last morning we spent living in Gram's attic. It was in early September of '59. I remember sneezing from the pungent scent of Aunt Eleanor's perfume as she shook Rich and me. "Wake up, boys. Today you're moving to the Jersey Shore." I pulled out my handkerchief from under my pillow and blew my nose. I rubbed my eyes, smiled at Aunt Eleanor and leapt into her arms to give her a big hug. I was glad to see her and to hear we were leaving Grams, even though I didn't know where in the world the Jersey Shore was.

I jumped on the mattress. "Yay! No more sleeping in the attic."

Rich clapped his hands. "We're leaving the Wicked Witch of the West."

Gram had never said one kind word to us that whole summer. We swore she hated us.

Aunt Eleanor put her index finger to her lips. "Shhh, don't talk like that boys. Get dressed, and I'll see you two downstairs. Be careful, we don't want you falling down the attic stairs on your last day."

When we got to the bottom of the stairway, we spread apart the curtain and peered into the living room. We saw aunts and uncles helping Mom pack old grocery boxes with clothes, linens and towels. All of our belongings fit into the trunk of Mom's '48 Plymouth and Uncle Ed's '56 Pontiac Catalina. Mom didn't drive on the Garden State Parkway and wasn't comfortable on other highways, either. So, Uncle Billy got behind the wheel. Mom put baby Eileen and Ray in the back seat with her, crammed in between some of the boxes. Rich got in the passenger seat.

Sue and I climbed in the back seat of Uncle Ed's car. I didn't know where we'd be sleeping that night, but I loved the idea of getting there in Uncle Ed's two-door, burgundy and white hardtop convertible. When he drove with all the windows down, a breeze entered from both sides and swirled our hair around.

Aunt Eleanor sank in the passenger seat, spread a New Jersey map on her lap and announced, "Let's go, Ed." I waved out the back window to Rich and Uncle Billy as we drove off into a sun-filled late summer day. When I turned around, I saw Gram peering through the lace curtains of the front window with a smile on her face—an expression I hadn't seen the whole summer we had lived with her.

Two hours later, we arrived at the Jersey Shore. Uncle Ed stopped at a light, and I stuck my head out the window. The wind against my face tasted like briny salt air, and, from that day forward, I referred to it simply as "fresh air." I inhaled deeply, recalling a family outing to the beach in Atlantic City a couple of summers before.

∞

Dad's strong hands under my arms lifted me over wave after wave as they rolled to shore. I laughed and looked up at Dad's smiling face. "One more time?" Dad and I were alone, just like when we would drive in the car together and I stood on the seat beside him, and put my arms around his neck, his whiskers scratching my cheek. Our trip to the ocean in '57 would be the first, and last, family vacation we'd ever share with him.

∞

Uncle Ed veered off Route 37 east and pulled into the gravel lot of Stewart's, parking between two cars. A boy dressed in a black-and-white striped referee shirt ran over to the car, pulled a pad out of his back pocket and took our order. He returned carrying a tray laden with our lunch and clamped it over Uncle Ed's door sill. My eyes opened wide when I saw the pile of foot-long hot dogs, poking out each end of a bun beside three cardboard boxes overflowing with french fries. I licked clumps of ice as they slid down my frosty mug before swallowing a mouthful of creamy root beer.

It seemed like we were on vacation. If this was what moving to the Jersey Shore was all about, I couldn't wait to experience more.

Chapter Twenty-One

"Ahhh!" Just what I needed, something cold to drink. I smacked my lips and realized my mouth was parched from inhaling clouds of hot road dust. Too bad air conditioning wasn't an option Rich could afford in '66. It would've come in handy on a day like today. I lifted a bottle of water from the cooler and drank it in one continuous gulp. I tossed the empty bottle under the seat, glanced over at Rich beside me and saw that his fidgeting continued. His right hand now intermittently smoothed his beard while his left isolated and plucked random hairs from his chin. Rich couldn't sit still if he sat on his hands. I wondered what he might possibly be thinking, but didn't ask.

I turned my head and tried to make eye contact. "What did you like the most about moving to the Jersey Shore Rich?"

He met my gaze and raised his fists with his thumbs up in the air. *Freedom, man, freedom. Mom worked nights, so I got to do anything I wanted. I had a blast hanging out, especially with the girls.*

I shook my head and frowned. This is when Rich's troubles began. The Earth's axis shifted for us when Mom left Dad and we moved to the shore. Somehow her rules, structure and expectations didn't apply to him. Or at least I think that's what he thought. He began doing whatever he could get away with.

∞

My mother must have felt like a deer on ice—struggling not only to stand erect, but to move herself and her five young children forward into an uncertain future. Ocean County attracted my mother because of its low cost of housing—a requirement for supporting a family on waitress tips. She would be eighty miles from her childhood home and family, but was determined to begin life anew.

We moved into a winter-rental in '59 rent being cheaper than in the summer. However, it would be for ten months beginning the day after Labor Day—the unofficial first day of fall at the shore. It was as if on July 4th someone flipped an "on" switch and countless summer visitors flocked to the shore. Then, on Labor Day the switch would be turned "off" and the flow of visitors stopped, leaving only year-round residents and winter renters.

School began within a week of our arrival. Rich, age 12, was in seventh grade, taking the school bus downtown to Toms River Junior High. Sue, Ray and I rode a school bus for the first time to East Dover Elementary. Sue was in sixth grade, I was 8, entering third grade, and Ray, age 5, was in kindergarten.

Sadly, my sister Sue's childhood ended that fall at age 11. Mom expected her to serve as our Nanny. Sue's days began holding Ray's hand on the bus and walking him to his classroom. When she came home from school, her household duties began as Mom left for work. She warmed up dinner Mom had prepared during the day and supervised Eileen, Ray and me until Mom returned home around 9:30 p.m.

We three oldest had chores which included washing, drying and putting away the dishes. Each day our tasks changed. All we had to do was look at the wall calendar to the current date to see our after dinner assignments. Mom didn't leave any room for argument when she printed our first initials neatly within each box. But, there were times when Rich must have been hypercharged from preteen hormones because he'd rather be anywhere else, doing anything other than the dishes. His schemes to avoid washing dishes took more effort than it would have taken him to complete the task in the first place.

One of his first attempts involved putting all the dirty dishes, flatware, pots and pans in the oven. To him, they were invisible, so he no longer had any work to do, and out the door he'd go for the night. Another time he stacked everything in one side of the double sink and slid the enamel drain board over the top. Presto! No more dishes, so Rich was out once again free to join his friends. Sue and I would just shrug our shoulders at one another knowing that Mom would catch up with him when she got home. When she did, Rich would be standing beside the sink, in Mom's purple-flowered apron, not just washing the dishes, but drying and putting them away too. I smiled as I observed the consequences of Rich's antics, but knew that I'd never mimic them and add to Mom's frustration.

∞

My head nodded and I awoke from my daydream with a start. "What the hell?" A shadow was looming up ahead, "Caution Horses" was written across the rear double doors. I hit the brake and jerked the car into the left lane, narrowly avoiding a rear end collision. The driver blasted his horn and gave me the finger when I drove past.

"Whoa!" My body spasmed in sync with the pounding in my chest. "Phew! That was close." *Where the hell have I been?* From now on, I have to concentrate on my driving.

∞

I whizzed past a sign, "Leaving Buffalo Gap National Grassland." I shook my head, removed my glasses and rubbed my eyes. I didn't remember entering it. *Had I really traveled so far today?* I had suspected I was traversing the Great Plains. Now, the sign confirmed it.

My GPS display told me that I had an hour to go before I got to my destination. *But, where was Rich? Wasn't he here a minute ago?* I looked beside me and felt my brother's presence. Maybe it was because, over forty years ago, he too had exited this highway on his way to discover the vast prairie and barren landscape of our mutual destination—the Badlands National Park.

Chapter Twenty-Two

I was lucky to have exited in Wall, South Dakota, saving me an unwanted hour of driving in the dark on the winding Badlands Loop Road. Still, nine hours of high-speed driving and a wasted hour at a no-name laundromat had totally wiped me out. With no energy to set up my tent, I threw my sleeping bag on a picnic table, collapsed on top and didn't move all night.

At sunrise, I sat up and grasped my toes to stretch the muscles in my lower back. I was surrounded by Badlands mountain ridges: natural ruggedness etched in sandstone colors of black, gold and tan. Native Americans named this region because of the difficulty of traveling through its rugged terrain, lack of water and bleak landscape. Two Appaloosa horses were tied up, grazing at nearby campsites; their Western saddles perched atop garbage cans.

I reached inside my sleeping bag, found Rich's journal and began reading his next entry,

Day #5, June 25, 1970 (Sage Creek Campground- Badlands, South Dakota)

So many miles of open road have been getting us down. Today's drive was a bitch from sunrise to sunset. We wanted to get to the Badlands before dark. We made it thanks to a couple tabs of speed for Ken and me. Excited to finally have made it to our first major stop out West.

I put the journal down, reviewed a map of the Badlands Loop Road and decided to run a section of it. It looked like an eight-mile run from the Sage Creek Campground, half-way to Sage Creek Basin Overlook and back. It was chilly, the sun had just crested a nearby ridge, and the air was filled with the scent of pine and wildflowers.

I stretched, then began running along carved steep canyons and high cliffs following the natural contours of the escarpment. The surreal landscape of multi-colored, stratified sandstone altered my state of mind as I observed Rich and his friends from a distance. This time, I was poised behind the van and watched them enter the Badlands. They exited I-90 and stopped for gas in Cactus Flat. As Rich and Ken were filling their gas tanks, Sally handed each a fat joint.

"Hey, guys. All this driving will be worthwhile once you've smoked these. Ginny and I are gonna drive, so you two can relax and enjoy the views."

Rich got back in the passenger seat, lit his joint and leaned out the window. "I can dig it. I'll do the same for you someday."

By the time Ginny got to the Badlands Loop Road, Rich had climbed over the backrest and was lying on the middle bench seat. Through the open sunroof he saw clouds pass on high and imagined himself spirited away, like an eagle flying with the wind.

Ginny put on the Moody Blues tape, *On a Threshold of a Dream*. As an ascending symphony of sound surrounded him, Rich's senses fused with the music.

"Would you look at the mountains, Rich? All those red and orange layers of sand."

Rich sat up and looked out the side windows. "There are spirits here. I can feel them floating all around us."

"Don't freak me out, Rich. All I see is a beautiful landscape of colorful mountains."

"Are we on the Moon?"

"No. You're just tripping it. Try to relax."

After an hour and a half of driving, Ginny pulled into a remote area of the Hay Butte Overlook, and Sally parked beside her. They both held blankets and spread them on the only patch of grass within the rocky overlook.

"This is a cool place." Sally stood on the blankets and took off her sandals. Turning in a circle, she raised her arms and lifted her dress over her head. "Mother Earth," she said, feeling oneness with everything around her. She stood naked, adorned in silver and turquoise bracelets and rings. I saw her figure outlined against the sky, long brown curls flowed across her breasts, almost covering each nipple. The curve of her back and long legs accentuated her natural beauty.

Ginny, Rich and Ken wasted no time pulling off their clothes to join her. They sat side-by-side on the blankets forming a circle with their backs touching one another. "I've never felt so connected to the land, sky and to each other," Sally said. "Let's hold hands." They turned to the person on either side and gave each a hug. Ken lit a joint and passed it to Sally. She took a hit and handed it to Ginny.

Creedence Clearwater Revival's "Bad Moon Rising" let loose from Ken's *Green River* tape coming from the van. "Look over there!" shouted Rich. "Is that a bad moon rising? Will the end be coming soon? Help us, Jesus."

Ginny squeezed Rich's hand. "Relax, everything's fine. You're tripping."

Sally changed tapes. "The Age of Aquarius" resounded from The Fifth Dimension album. "That's better," said Ginny. "This is the dawning of a new day for all of us." She turned to Rich, placed his palms together and cupped her hands on top of his. She looked into his eyes. "Jesus will help you, Rich. May he give you peace and show us the way."

∞

My vision of Rich and his friends disappeared as I came to an abrupt halt in front of a sign, "Welcome to Sage Creek Basin Overlook." I couldn't believe that I had just run eight miles, twice as far as I had hoped to run. Rich's adventures had taken me on a ride through time and space.

Even though I'd never run sixteen miles before, I was sure I'd be able to make it back. I'd just have to go at a slower pace. I took a swig from my water bottle and turned around to retrace my steps back to The Sage Creek Campground.

What could possibly happen to Rich, next? Get caught with his pants down? Sounded about right. I laughed to myself as I turned around and kept running...

Chapter Twenty-Three

"Good Afternoon, everyone!" Ranger White Lance said with a smile. He got out of his car and headed toward them. "You're not having a love-in, are you?"

"Oh, God. No." Sally pulled her dress over her head and stood up. After smoothing it out, she raised her chin and gave him a smile.

"No, we're not. In fact, we were just leaving, right, guys?" Ginny put her dress back on and stood next to Sally.

"We're cool." Ken cupped a roach in his hand and tossed it over the rocks. He gripped a blanket and wrapped it around himself. Ginny pulled Rich's robe over his head.

The ranger looked at the ticket book in his hand and closed the cover. "Well, you're leaving so there's no need to talk about violations of park regulations. Am I right?"

Ginny nodded. "You certainly are. By the way, where's the nearest campground?"

"You're in luck. It's less than ten miles away." At over six feet tall, the ranger towered over them. His black braided hair outlined his face.

"That's cool," replied Ken. "What's it like?"

"Well, horsemen like it. It has beautiful views of surrounding grasslands with the Badlands all around. The best part is it's free."

"Free? Right on, brother."

White Lance smirked. "Though you get what you pay for."

"How's that?"

"No electricity, bathrooms, or water. But, there are a couple of female friendly pit toilets."

Sally grimaced. "No running water or electricity? I can't imagine any pit toilets being female friendly."

Ginny put her arm around Sally's shoulder. "Don't worry, it will only be for a night. We have food in the cooler and water in our jugs,"

The ranger slouched with his thumbs in his pockets. "If you stay the night, I'll most likely see you tomorrow when I begin my shift."

Sally gave him the peace sign. "Thanks, Ranger." Ginny waved as he walked to his car. "We'll check it out. Sure do appreciate your help."

On the road a short time, Ginny smiled when she saw four prairie dogs scurry around, popping their furry faced rodent heads out of a burrow. "I can't believe these fur balls are all over the place." The sign above them read, "Campground, Next Left." She turned onto the entrance road and saw dozens of bison grazing on the grasslands surrounding the campground. "Buffalo, too."

She pulled the van beside a canopied picnic table. Rich opened the door and stepped out landing in a huge pile of buffalo dung. Ginny laughed and leaned out the window pointing and smiling. "Now I have a new nickname for you, Bison." Rich took off his left sandal and scraped it on the dry grass. Hopping on his right foot, he reached inside a nearby garbage can, tore off a piece of cardboard and wiped the bottom of his left foot.

"How about if we start over?" asked Ginny. "Let's move to the other picnic table and try again."

Rich got back in his seat and shook his head.

"You smell, Bison." Ginny started the van and led Sally to another campsite.

Within minutes, they were startled by gunshots. "Jeez, those guns are loud. Do you think they're cowboys?" asked

Sally. Two guys wearing tan Stetson hats were fifty feet away pointing handguns at a makeshift target.

Ken paced with his hands in his pockets. "Looks like it to me. I hope they don't keep it up for long. They'll spook us and the horses."

Chapter Twenty-Four

Bam! Bam! Bam! The gunfire echoed off the blood red speckled mountains. I saw him as clearly as if I was sitting on top of the van looking through the open sunroof. Rich's vision blurred and pulsed as he crossed a threshold from the present to the past.

∞

How many VC had he killed that day? How many innocent men, women and children? He knew he was responsible, even though he hadn't pulled a trigger or thrusted a bayonet. He had just returned from a fast-moving recon mission with his Vietnamese Patrol sighting VC activity and calling in coordinates for mortar shelling. He could smell the fetid trail of blood and gore all the way from the hamlet along the river to his bunker door.

The heat and humidity was oppressive like sandbags collapsing all around, entrapping him in his airless tomb. He gagged, couldn't swallow or take a deep breath. His legs were aching and his feet were swollen and blistered—remnants from his twenty-five mile hump into the jungle. Exhausted, he collapsed in his darkened mud bunker, covered in orange-red dirt of the bush. The enormity of his actions haunted him. So many soulless ghosts, and the devil himself, taunted him to Hell.

"Help me, Jesus," he whispered. He sat up, looked around and lit a few candles to distract him. In the flickering light he saw two unopened letters beside his bedroll. One was from Mom and the other from his wife. He'd been worried about Diane lately wondering what prevented her from writing to him these past few weeks. Maybe she had a good reason, a cold or the flu. She may have had to work nights to finish a big project. Perhaps she went away with a few friends for a weekend to the Poconos or Atlantic City. Maybe, the military mail wasn't getting through. *There was a war going on, right?*

As his fingers slid along the edge of the envelope, he wondered if Diane had forgotten to put her letter inside. It seemed empty, like a spent cartridge from his M16. He swallowed hard and forced a smile as his fingers tore apart the envelope. Reaching inside he took out a single-folded sheet of paper.

Dear Richie,

I've tried dozens of times to explain things to you in a letter. But I just can't. I'm sorry to tell you this way, but I can't keep pretending. It's over between us. I'm in love with another man. I hope you can forgive me.

God Bless, Diane

His hands shook as he stared at the letter and reread it. Tears streamed down his cheeks, splattering the paper with stains, like ordnance falling from the sky. He gasped for air— once, twice, three times. He slapped his face and tore off his shirt, fighting to wake from his terrible nightmare. He grabbed a shovel to steady himself and began digging. First, using it as a sledgehammer, he raised it above his head and smashed it into the cold, hard indifference of the dirt. Then he shoveled mound after mound of soil creating a womb within Mother Earth. It embraced him as he climbed inside and wrapped his arms around his legs, curling into a ball, rocking and praying for dawn.

∞

Ken scrunched his eyebrows together and looked at Sally. "Do you hear banging?"

"It's coming from Ginny's van."

They ran to the van and looked in the side window. Rich was in a fetal position on Ginny's lap. He was rocking back and forth, his feet keeping pace as he hit them against the side door. Ginny was crying. "Wake up Rich. It's just a bad dream. I'm here with you. Rich?"

Rich sat up, shook his head and his eyes focused on Ginny's wet cheeks. "Why are you crying?"

"Because I'm worried about you."

"Ohhh," he whispered and fell asleep in Ginny's arms.

∞

My legs quivered and my breathing became more labored as I approached my campsite. Exhausted and light-headed I slowed down almost to a walk. I reached into the cooler and took out two cold bottles of water, poured one over my head and guzzled the other. *Had I really just run sixteen miles?*

I flopped in my chair even though I knew I should have stretched after such a long run. My leg muscles tightened; I couldn't move from the physical and mental assault on my body. From that day forward, the depth of Rich's heartbreak stalked me. *How'd he find the courage to keep on going after that?*

Chapter Twenty-Five

That night I experienced a sense of twilight—a semi-conscious state somewhere between sleep and wakefulness. Random thoughts and images were just out of reach of my comprehension. An earworm burrowed in my mind, snippets of Creedence Clearwater Revival's "Bad Moon Rising" played over and over. Someone was putting quarters in a jukebox and hitting replay. I hoped that Rich and I weren't in for nasty weather.

At daybreak, I crawled out of my tent and slumped into my camp chair. My head throbbed, my mouth was dry, and my body ached as if I had been drinking pints of Blue Moon beer all night. My head jerked when I heard Rich's voice, "Morning, Danny." I looked around and saw that I had left the passenger door of the GTO open, probably when I had taken the cooler out of the back seat a few minutes before. No one else was in my camp but me. *Could his voice be coming from the car?* This was something new.

Everything is new. It's a new day, right?

"It sure is but I'm feeling a bit down this morning. Is there such a thing as an emotional hangover? Your Vietnam flashbacks are taking a toll on my mind and body. I can't imagine how you dealt with such hellish experiences."

I didn't have a choice and couldn't stop 'em.

I was weary knowing that Rich didn't have control over his thoughts and knew another day in the Badlands would be good for me. Nothing like a little peace and quiet to restore my body and soul.

It's a beautiful spot to be one with nature.

I chuckled. "I'll keep my clothes on if it's alright with you."

Good idea. I don't think you're much of a free spirit.

"Me either."

I opened a bottle of water and took long thirst-quenching gulps. I cracked open a can of V8 juice hoping it would begin to revive me like it did some mornings after drinking too much beer, though, I really wasn't much of a drinker. After a few pints, my nose gets stuffy, and I'm hit with a severe headache. To tell the truth, three beers is my limit.

My head throbbed and surroundings blurred as I reclined in the chair. Thoughts of Rich and me flashed back to the fall of '59. Rich's behavior began to change from being a normal kid to acting out and pulling away from the family.

∞

Mom had Sundays and Mondays off from her waitress job at the Old Time Tavern. On those days we explored our new surroundings. One warm fall day Mom drove us across the Barnegat Bay Bridge to Seaside Park. It was low tide, and the beach was deserted. Rich, Sue and I tore off our shoes and socks and ran as fast as we could from the warm dry sand to the cold wet sand at the water's edge. The ripples of waves danced around our ankles and numbed our feet.

As I looked north and south over the beach, dozens of starfish and clam shells lay glistening in the sun. I picked up a starfish, and its legs wrapped around my palm. "Whoa!" I turned my hand upside down to show Rich and Sue the hanging starfish. They were wearing the same starfish gloves. We jumped up and down and screamed as we ran along the shoreline putting dozens of starfish and clam shells into our metal sand buckets. "Look Mom," we shouted, but our voices were carried over the breakers by the westerly breeze. Mom shielded her eyes with her hand as we approached the blanket, an oasis amid the miles of sand and dunes.

"Can we keep 'em?"

"You'll have to leave 'em outside to dry."

When we got home, we spread our finds over the back yard and hosed the sand off them. Days later, the faint odor of muddy marshland at low tide emanated through our kitchen window. By the weekend, the back yard reeked of rotten sea creatures, seaweed and jelly fish.

We stood on the back porch watching flies buzz all over our starfish and clam shells. "Throw those stinkin' things in the trash!" Mom commanded.

"You mean we can't even keep one?" Rich asked.

"Sure, you can. If you put it in a Miracle Whip jar with the lid on tight."

We held our noses, but still gagged, as we collected those reminders of our first family outing at the beach.

I never again saw starfish lying along the wet sand at low tide.

∞

The sun had crested a distant mountain on the eastern horizon. I opened the car door and sat in the driver's seat, sipping my V8. *Maybe this would be a good time to root through Rich's stuff in the trunk?* By the time I finished counting to ten, I decided this wasn't going to be the day. *Maybe another time?* I looked over and saw Rich squinting.

"You need a Red Sox cap for the glare."

Rich wiggled his eyebrows. *No, I don't. But a Yankees cap will do me just fine.*

I wondered if he was as comforted as I was by the memory of our first trip to the beach.

The beach and boardwalk were new worlds for us to discover.

As we grew, Rich and I would come to love everything about the seashore. I learned to ride waves at low tide on a raft and to body surf. As a teenager Rich would hitchhike to

Seaside Heights at night when the honky-tonk came alive with carnival rides, games of chance, flashing lights and blaring music. He was drawn there by the sun-specked single city girls who strolled beside the sea.

I pushed the driver's seat back as far as possible, peeled open a mozzarella stick and thought of another outing on Mom's day off.

The section of town we lived in was called Money Island. Captain Kid was rumored to have sailed into Barnegat Bay, cruised up the Toms River and buried treasure along its shore. The river was merely the Minor League in every conceivable way to the Major League, the Atlantic Ocean, four miles east. We lived three blocks from the river's beach, a short walk down the street would have gotten us there in a few minutes. But Mom wanted to explore the shoreline by car, so we loaded up the Plymouth. Mom drove toward the river and stopped in front of a white wooden fence. She hesitated for a few minutes and then decided to drive around it. She should have realized there was a good reason for the barrier to be there. It blocked the entrance to a single-lane pathway winding along a dry stream bed beside the woods. The path had two well-worn ruts with weeds sprouting along a middle ridge. It must have been created by people driving Jeeps and other four-wheel drive vehicles in search of an isolated beach.

Mom drove slowly along the first stretch, then just as the path turned into fine sand she hit the gas and shifted into second. We came to an abrupt stop, as if all four tires went flat at once. Sue, Ray and I were thrown to the floor as Rich's head hit the windshield with a bang.

Rich rubbed his forehead. "Mom! What are you doing?"

I got back up on the rear seat and looked out the side window. We had stopped, but the wheels continued to spin, faster and faster, emitting a high-pitched shrill sound as if the fan belt was loosening from its mount.

Rich opened the front door and jumped out. "What the heck? Stop, Mom! You're just digging us in deeper."

Mom took her foot off the gas, cut the ignition and raised her hands. "Jesus! How stupid can I be? Look what I've gotten us into!"

When we all got out of the car our jaws dropped in disbelief. The front tires were encased in sand up to their hubcaps. The rear tires could hardly be seen at all behind an eight-inch sand dune that had formed.

Mom looked around. "What a mess." No one was nearby to help; we were a quarter mile from the street.

Rich kicked at the sand. "What do we do now, Mom?"

"We get to work digging ourselves out."

We walked along the edge of the woods searching for something to use to dig out. Rich found some tree branches, but they kept breaking when he shoved them into the sand. Mom got on her hands and knees and began clawing at the ground with her fingers. Rich, Ray and I joined her, each trying to dig out a tire. Sue held Eileen on her hip and paced nervously from one side of the car to the other. After several minutes of digging, Mom stopped. "This isn't working. We need a shovel."

"I think one's in the basement," Rich said. "I'll go get it."

Mom lit a Kent and rested against the front fender. I got a beach ball out of the back seat, and Ray and I kicked it back and forth. Rich returned pushing a wheelbarrow filled with a shovel and several pieces of wood. He dug out the front tires and then jammed pieces of wood under and behind both rear tires. I joined him in front of the car, rocking it back and forth as Mom put it in reverse and gave it some gas. After every foot or two, we had to reposition the wood so Mom could get traction as she backed up. It was late afternoon by the time the Plymouth touched solid ground. Mom reached into her purse, pulled out two wrinkled dollar bills and handed one to Rich and one to me. "Thanks for rescuing us, boys."

∞

Mom's foray down the sandy path took its place among many other topics never to broach. We implicitly avoided sensitive subjects which were not ever spoken about, even among ourselves.

Chapter Twenty-Six

It was almost noon when I glanced at my iPhone. I had been engrossed in my reflections and hadn't moved from the driver's seat to wash up or change into clean clothes. I knew it was 2015, but my mind kept drawing me back to the fall of '59.

∞

Seasonal change was evident, as the early morning frost of autumn nudged aside Indian summer days. One Saturday morning, Rich and I went down to the river's edge, skimming stones across its smooth surface. Rich pointed to a nearby pram, a two-person dinghy with a slanted bow and stern, turned upside down on the beach

"Help me with this boat. Will ya?"

"We're gonna take it?"

"Nah. We're just gonna borrow it."

Rich turned it over and grasped the stern. I struggled to get a grip on the metal ring at the bow. We walked a few feet, then put it down on the side of the road. I turned my back every time a car passed. I didn't know what I'd do if someone stopped—probably run into the woods. "Lift," Rich said, again and again. I was walking backwards, the sweat running from my forehead and stinging my eyes. Unable to wipe my face, I kept blinking back the tears that trickled down my cheek. I knew what we were doing wasn't right but didn't tell Rich. I was afraid if I did he wouldn't play with me anymore.

"What are we gonna do with it, Rich?"

"I dunno."

We eventually got it around the back of the house and opened the bulkhead door. Rich stood in the stern as it slid down the wooden steps. The angled bow hit the basement floor and it hydroplaned, as if it was in the river being pulled behind a motor boat. Rich fell backwards and clutched the gunnels.

He stumbled out. "That was fun."

That evening a preppy looking guy with his look—alike teenage son knocked on our front door. They both sported madras shirts, khaki shorts and white tennis sneakers. When Rich opened the door, the man frowned and placed his hands firmly on his hips. "We're here to take back our pram."

Rich walked outside, opened the cellar door and shrugged his shoulders. "I dunno how it got down there."

We watched as they loaded the boat into the back of their Ford station wagon. The man turned and glared at Rich. "What made you think you could steal my boat in broad daylight and get away with it?"

Rich hunched his shoulders and I followed him back in the house. Good thing for us Mom wasn't home.

It was early November of that same year when Mom began getting daily phone calls from the junior high school secretary. "Mrs. Du-u-u-ffy. Richard's not in school again today," sang the now familiar voice of Mrs. Krull. I don't think my mother knew what to do about Rich. Her attempts at communication with him always escalated into a shouting match.

"Why aren't you going to school?"

"I don't like it."

"Well, it's too damn bad. You have to go."

"Nobody's gonna make me!"

And nobody could. Rich stopped going to school that year and never returned.

Too young to have a license or job, twelve-year old Rich had idle time on his hands. There were few year-round residents in our neighborhood and little or no organized sports or activities to channel teenagers' energies. Rich befriended other drop-outs and for fun they began breaking into summer homes vacated during the off-season. After a pattern of B&E's were detected, Dover Township police began close surveillance. Several weeks later, cops arrested Rich as he was boosting one of his buddies through a bungalow window.

Within a few months, Rich faced a juvenile court judge. Mom told us he said, "Without a father to take you to the woodshed, I'm sentencing you to thirty days at Jamesburg Reform School for Boys." Jamesburg, as it was dubbed, was run by the State of New Jersey as a correctional facility where juvenile delinquent boys would be exposed to discipline, structure and instruction with the intent of preventing them from escalating their behavior into higher levels of crime.

Later that night, dinnertime was quiet with all of us in attendance except Rich. Mom had tears in her eyes as she told us, "He acted like a big shot in the backseat of the police car. He raised his handcuffed hands over his head and waved to me. I swear. I don't know what I'm going to do with that boy."

I sat in silence and looked at Mom. I didn't know what to say. She was working so hard to keep our family together. All I could think about for several days afterwards was that I was going to do my best never to upset Mom the way Rich had.

The next Saturday morning Mom told us we were taking a ride to visit Rich in Jamesburg. It seemed like we were going on a fun Sunday outing because Mom made us a picnic lunch and we mixed a batch of cherry Kool Aid in our red and white plastic beach jug.

Mom drove for over two hours on back roads from Ocean to Middlesex County. When we stopped at the entrance gate, Mom gave the attendant Rich's name and the man handed Mom a visitor's pass. We drove under a rusted iron arch, "Jamesburg Reform School." We took an access road across grass fields and parked in the visitor's lot beside an array of three-story brown brick buildings. We criss-crossed sidewalks as we followed signs for Cottage #8. When we entered, we were met by a man wearing a blue uniform with a no-nonsense look on his face. Mom handed Mr. No-Nonsense her visitor's pass. He looked at it, picked up the phone and uttered a few words. Rich sauntered into the room, smiling in spite of all of his long-brown hair having been buzzed off.

"What did they do to you?" I asked.

He stroked the stubbles on his head and laughed. "Nothing. Everybody has to look the same here."

Mom gave Rich a hug. "I think you look good. Let's get out of here."

Rich took the blanket from Mom and threw it over his shoulder. We walked until we found a quiet sunny spot on the grass in the middle of the courtyard to spread the blanket. We sat down, Rich poured Kool Aid into our paper cups and Mom handed each of us a ham and cheese sandwich on a hard roll wrapped in wax paper.

I closed my eyes and imagined sitting at the water's edge on the beach in Money Island. A westerly breeze churned up whitecaps as the tide turned from high to low. I felt myself drift along, glide through Barnegat Inlet and stream into the Atlantic before heading out to sea.

After Rich returned home from reform school, Mom tried her best to find a way to keep us occupied afternoons and evenings. We didn't own a TV, so watching kids' programs wasn't an option. Instead, on Mondays Mom would drive us downtown to the Bishop Memorial Library. It was housed in a historic brick building on Washington Street, right next to Town Hall. Mom watched as Rich, Sue and I got our library cards and then we followed her down a long flight of stairs to the children's section. Afternoon light from the high windows illuminated endless rows of bookcases. Mom told us to pick out books while she went upstairs to browse the fiction section. I moved a stool among the stacks, stepped up and stretched to grab Jack London's *The Call of the Wild*. I was spellbound by the cover image of Yukon sled dogs and the vastness of the great outdoors.

What I remembered the most about our library visits was a children's book called *We're Going on a Bear Hunt* that we renewed week after week. Almost every night after dinner, Sue and I, and sometimes Rich, took turns reading it out loud to Ray and Eileen. As one of us read, the others would slap their knees in concert with the chorus: "We're going on a bear hunt. We're going to catch a big one! What a beautiful day! We're not scared."

∞

I found myself in my camp chair slapping my hands against my lap in rhythmic motion to the childhood story. I had to get moving. *Or did I?* Not really. After all, I'd traveled far this past week and deserved a break. A relaxing evening in camp would do me some good. Besides, I was starving. I had been so preoccupied with my thoughts that I had skipped breakfast and lunch—something I never did. I decided to open a cold bottle of Blue Moon and roast a few hot dogs on my tabletop charcoal grille. That should help to make things right, at least for a while.

Chapter Twenty-Seven

The sun had descended below the distant yellow hills, projecting a jagged mountain silhouette against the evening sky. I lay on top of my sleeping bag; no tent obscured my view of the heavens. I followed the pointer stars of Ursa Major to Polaris knowing that it served as a beacon guiding travelers to true north. A chill in the air, mixed with the sooty stench from a nearby campfire, reminded me of fried liver.

∞

All four of us kids were crammed around our metal rectangular kitchen table with Eileen in her high chair. It was one of two nights each week we'd eat with Mom. She stood at the stove with her back to us wearing her faded purple-flowered apron frying liver in bacon grease. Sue was feeding one-year old Eileen cereal and pureed plums. Eileen kicked both feet in the air with every spoonful. Rich had just returned from Jamesburg. His environment and friends hadn't changed and neither had he, except that his hair had grown two inches and he now tucked a Marlboro behind one ear.

"Fried liver, again," groaned Rich.

"Yes. You'll eat it if you know what's good for you."

Rich kneeled, held onto the backrest of his chair and screamed at Mom's back. "I hate liver!"

Mom turned and faced us. "I wouldn't feed you kids something if it wasn't good for you. And, liver's good. You're gonna like it when you grow up." The smell of it cooking turned my stomach. I hated it too as a kid and never ate it again as an adult.

"Can we eat it with rye bread and Parkay?" I asked.

"Sure. You can put as much ketchup as you want on it. But, everyone has to eat it."

I remember spreading gobs of margarine on slice after slice of day-old bakery rye, stacking the pieces beside my plate. I'd take a deep breath and a huge bite of bread. Next, I'd stab a small piece of liver with my fork, drown it in ketchup and pop it in my mouth. Holding my nose while I chewed lessened, but didn't eliminate, the bitter metallic taste on my tongue. When my plate was empty, I asked, "What's for dessert?"

Mom put her elbows on the table, hands under her chin and leaned in. "Close your eyes and what do you see?"

I liked this game. "I see a big piece of strawberry shortcake."

Sue said, "I see a bowl of chocolate ice cream with a cherry on top."

"How's it taste?" Mom asked.

"Sweeeet."

Rich shook his head. "I don't see no dessert. All I can taste is the lousy liver we just ate." He got up from the table, grabbed his jacket and ran out the back door.

Mom whispered. "And, what do you see, Ray?"

On nights Mom worked, Sue, age 11, was in charge or at least Mom said she was. She never played with her friends after school but went immediately home after stepping off the bus. Mom was busy in the bathroom getting ready for work. She took a drag from her Kent and rested it on the corner of the sink. "I'm in here, Honey." Sue peeked in Mom's bedroom, swung Eileen from the crib to her hip and stood outside the bathroom doorway, glimpsing Mom's reflection. Mom's short brown hair was in rollers. She looked in the mirror, her eyes opened wide as her steady fingers applied mascara. Mom white-washed her matching shoes with the applicator—shake, turn upside down and press and put on her white uniform. The only garment distinguishing her from a nurse was the black apron she wore where she put her order pad and tips.

"I've got meatloaf cooking, and it'll be done soon. Just leave it in the oven 'til you're ready to eat. I have to get going."

Sue shouted through the kitchen screen door. "Supper's ready!"

Eileen was in her high chair, and Ray was at the table when I came in to eat.

"Where's Rich?"

"I don't know."

"Mom said put dinner out at six, so we're gonna eat without him." She stepped across the linoleum floor and placed the meatloaf dish on the table. "Don't touch! It's hot."

Rich came through the door, saw the meatloaf and furrowed his brow. "Yuck, meatloaf. Why can't we have pizza?"

"This is what Mom made for us."

He headed toward the door. "I'm not hungry!"

"Mom wants you to help. You're supposed to do dishes tonight," Sue yelled as Rich slammed the screen door behind him.

Ray banged his fork on the table. "I wanna eat."

"Here's your dinner." Sue held two forks to lift the end piece of meatloaf out, and we all watched it crumble onto the table. She shook her head and scooped the pieces back into the dish.

"I don't want that," Ray wailed, kicking his chair.

"Shut up, will you!" Sue screamed at Ray as she stood mixing the rice cereal. "Hurry. Get me a jar of applesauce from the Fridge, Danny."

I opened two, put one on the high chair tray and the other in front of Ray.

"I don't want baby food."

"Eat it. It's like having dessert before supper."

90

"I'm not gonna eat it and you can't make me."

"Yes, I can."

"No, you can't."

"If you two don't stop, I'm gonna call Mom."

I opened the jar, took a spoonful of applesauce and held it by Ray's tightly closed mouth. He stared at me with defiant eyes. I squeezed his nose between my fingers and when he opened his mouth to take a breath, I jammed in the spoon, pulling it out clean. "Are you gonna listen to me now?" I shouted, inches from his nose.

He squished his eyes together and spit the applesauce in my face.

"You brat!" I screamed as I snatched a kitchen towel.

Ray hit his glass on the table. "I wanna drink!"

I poured Ray a glass of the powdered milk Mom would make us. He sipped it, made a sour face and spit it all over the table. "Yuck! I don't want that."

I shouted. "It's milk! Mom wouldn't make us something that wasn't good."

"Stop! Don't make me call Mom. Let's just eat." Sue sat down, held the bottle to Eileen's mouth with her left hand while eating with her right.

After dinner, we pushed our plates aside for Rich to wash later. I said, "Hey everyone. Who wants to go on a bear hunt?" Ray nodded and Eileen patted her tray and smiled. I opened the library book. Sue and Ray began slapping their hands on their laps and sang with me, "We're going on a bear hunt. We're going to catch a big one. What a beautiful day! We're not scared."

∞

Bears brought me back to the present. I looked around and located Big Bear or the Big Dipper in the sky. I traced the stars in its dipper and handle with my finger. I folded my pillow in half and stared at the stars that punctuated the darkness.

Chapter Twenty-Eight

The campground was silent except for the occasional crackle of burning logs from nearby campfires. I gazed at the sparks floating in the air like fireflies as the Big Dipper and Cassiopeia advanced across the sky in their nightly procession to the western horizon. Sleep evaded me so I sat up and put on my Black Diamond Cosmo headlamp to the first position. I looked like a geek sitting in the darkness with my headband casting a beam of light wherever I turned my head. I located Rich's journal and opened it to the page where I had left off.

Day #6, June 26, 1970 (Sage Creek Campground- Badlands, South Dakota)

The Badlands (Far Out, Man!)

We decided to just chill.

No maps. No highways. No driving.

Today was an illusion, dreamt by dreamers.

Rainbows touched the mountaintops.

In shades of black, blue and gold.

Lonely lunar landscapes surrounded us—

Space voyagers landing on a barren planet.

Rich and his friends gathered around their campsite picnic table sharing a breakfast of blueberries and strawberries.

"Hello again, campers," said a familiar voice as he climbed off his black and white Pinto. Ranger White Lance tied his reins to a nearby post.

"Your horse is beautiful," said Sally. His horse was completely white except for a black spot encircling its left eye and a larger one on its hindquarters. The top half of its mane was black and the bottom white. It stood in the grassy field with its head and neck raised, like a warrior's mare from its ancestral past.

"Thanks. It's a fine example of a prairie horse once ridden by my forefathers. When I ride in the outback I feel a strong connection to my heritage. But, enough about me. What are your plans for today?"

"We'd like to visit an Indian reservation. Can you tell us how to get to one?

"I sure can...because I live on one," White Lance remarked, emphasizing his last four words. "I am a proud member of the Oglala Tribe. My family has lived in Pine Ridge since the late 1800's when we were moved there by the US Government. I'll be glad to direct you to my son Maphee's home. He's about your age and would welcome your visit."

Chapter Twenty-Nine

It was fewer than fifty miles from The Badlands to Wounded Knee, South Dakota. In many respects, it was as if I had traversed a great divide separating wealthy America from the poverty—stricken existence of life on the Pine Ridge Indian Rez. It was unsettling to see so many people existing in dire poverty. Throughout this land, alcoholism is as rampant as jobs are nonexistent.

I sat outside my tent awestruck, being on sacred soil and observing the dignity of the Native American elders. I wondered if Rich felt an affinity with these people and their message of universal love, expressed through their sacred ritual. *Did he yearn to experience the same outcomes as they hoped to achieve; a reuniting of the living with the spirits of the dead and peace, prosperity, and unity to all peoples?*

I was filled with excitement holding Rich's journal, anticipating his interactions with the Oglala people of the Lakota Nation. I paged to his next entry,

Day #7, June 27, 1970 (The REZ, Wounded Knee, South Dakota)

Wounded Knee (A Bad Trip!)

Hope of peace and independence

On the wild open plain.

Sacred soil nightmare

Inflicted by the white man.

Butchered brothers and sisters

Lie scattered all around.

Majestic dreams of hope and glory,

Lie shattered on the ground.

I turned a page and was immersed in a scene with Rich, Ginny, Ken and Sally as they met their new friends.

∞

"Hau, Khola, Hello Friends." I am Mahpee. His resemblance to his father was remarkable. He too stood over six feet tall, with thick, dark shoulder length hair. His smile highlighted his high cheeks and wide face.

"I'm Rich. My friends here are Ginny, Ken and Sally."

"Hello everyone. Welcome to our home."

"Yesterday we stayed in the Badlands, where we met your father. We spoke with him about our hope to stay the night on an Indian Rez," said Ken.

"My father said you are adventurous free spirits. You are welcome to stay on our ancient land. But first, meet my wife Macha."

The epitome of a Native American beauty, she greeted them. Her pitch-black hair was parted in the middle and shimmered in the light as it flowed down her back. She embodied dignity and confidence. "We are a proud, trusting and peaceful people. We try to live by these values every day."

"I'm sure you do," replied Ginny. "This land must have many stories to tell about your ancestors."

"Yes, it does. Most of our history is uplifting. But, the past one hundred and fifty years have been very sad for our people." Macha shook her head and tears welled in her dark eyes.

"Don't burden our guests with the sadness of our heritage," said Mahpee. "Let's first offer them something to eat?"

"Certainly," said Macha. I didn't prepare food for six people. But, we can share what we have as a sign of peace."

Rich held up two fingers. "Peace to you, too."

"We Oglala honor one another by sitting in a circle and facing each other. Please join me outside," said Mahpee. Ken and Rich retrieved two blankets, placed them on the ground and sat down. Sally and Ginny joined them.

Macha passed around several bowls. "Please have a piece of my Indian frybread. You can eat it with chicken and wild rice."

"After a meal, our forefathers would smoke a sacred peace pipe to express good will and friendship to strangers and former enemies," said Mahpee.

"Are there any new traditions? Any involving peyote buttons or other psychedelics?" Ken asked.

"Peyote has a long tradition of being used in Native American rituals and medicines. It's even been used to attain sustained levels of pleasure, bordering on ecstasy," said Mahpee. "My people have used it to alter their mental states, arousing intense introspection and self-examination. You see, peyote is the flame that lights the fire we call 'The Sacred Ghost Dance.'"

Macha added. "You're visiting us at a good time. If you decide to stay tomorrow night you will witness our tradition. It begins at midnight on the darkest night of a new moon and continues for four successive nights."

"That sounds bitchin', remarked Rich. "Do we watch or can we participate?"

"Try to become actively involved, yet also watch everything unfold from a distance, like an Eagle soaring upward," suggested Mahpee.

"Far out, dude," exclaimed Ken. "I'm hip to it."

"The dance sounds very mysterious to me," said Ginny.

"Let Mahpee explain our tradition."

"We've had a rich tradition passed down from generation to generation through our rituals, ceremonies and stories. The Sacred Ghost Dance has been passed down to us for over 100 years. A prophet preached that if the five-day dance was properly performed, the living would become reunited with the spirits of the dead. And, peace and prosperity would unite all native peoples."

"Your prophet had a wonderful vision," Ken said. "Who wouldn't want peace?"

"It turned out that Rez officials were worried about the dancing and asked the US Government to intervene and stop it. The US Army was sent to arrest key leaders, Sitting Bull and Big Foot. Sitting Bull was killed after they arrested him. Two weeks later, on December 28, 1890, members of the Seventh Cavalry killed Chief Big Foot and between 150 and 300 of our people, including women and children. That day was and still is painful to us—becoming known as the 'Wounded Knee Massacre.'" Mahpee choked up and wiped a tear from his eye. He nodded to Macha and she continued.

"Ever since, the Sacred Ghost Dance has served as an important focus for us to respect our forefathers, preserve our culture and connect with ancestral spirits."

Each of them looked into the eyes of the person sitting across the circle. They wrapped their arms around each other's shoulders and leaned inward to close the circle tighter. Ginny began and the others joined her. "Yea, though I walk through the valley of the shadow of death, I will fear no evil..."

Chapter Thirty

At dawn the treeless plain was already a hot, smoldering fire. No creatures stirred as the sun blazed over the eastern horizon of the Rez, inflaming the land of the Sioux Nation. Ken muttered to Sally through his wiry beard, "God, it's hot in here." He sat up on a bench seat that formed the middle bed of his VW camper. Sweat flowed from every pore of his body, as if he had just crossed the finish line of a half-marathon. He turned his head; his long brown curly AFRO stood at attention and swayed, like a field of dry hay pitching in the wind. He reached over and opened the side doors letting in stifling prairie air. The van became blistering hot. "Let's see if it's any better outside." Ken clutched Sally's sweaty hand, and they stepped out of the van.

"I guess not," Sally said, looking into Ken's deep brown eyes. Even though she was tall, she still had to stretch her neck to kiss him.

"It smells like someone's cooking breakfast. Let's go see. I'm starved," said Ken.

Sally and Ken approached the campfire. "Good Morning, Macha. Something smells good. What are you cooking?"

"Good Morning to you, too. I'm cooking a traditional Oglala Sioux breakfast. You tasted my Indian frybread last night. I'm cooking smaller pieces of it this morning and will serve it with wild berries and nuts."

"Sounds good to me. I've never had an authentic Native American breakfast," replied Sally.

Ken sat on one of the logs circling the fire pit. "I like the idea of eating a healthy breakfast."

"Can we help with anything?"

"No, but thank you. Just relax."

"Have you seen Rich and Ginny this morning, Macha?"

"Yes, they were up at daybreak so Mahpee could take them to get clothing from our family and friends. He wants each of you to be properly dressed for tonight's Sacred Ghost Dance.

Ken ate a piece of honey-drenched Indian frybread and licked his fingers. "I'm honored that Mahpee wants us to fully participate in your sacred ritual."

"So am I." Sally tilted her head and looked up. She heard a distant soul-haunting howling. "Are those wolves, Macha?"

"No, they're coyotes telling each other that the night is over. You learn to accept them and their howling as part of living in the wilderness."

∞

Rich put his hand inside a fur-lined boot. "This clothing's authentic?"

"Yes, it's genuine. My people were hunters and gatherers. We worshipped the buffalo, especially when we had to sacrifice one for food and clothing. Every part of the animal was used, nothing wasted."

"Your people taught you to respect animals, even though you had to sacrifice them to live."

"My people honor and respect animals because they give us life. We also respect nature—rivers, mountains and plants. To us, everything is connected."

"Tonight, we'll wear your garments and eat peyote to be part of the Sacred Ghost Dance?"

"You and your friends will join me as my brothers and sisters in search for a spiritual connection to your past."

It was early evening and the desert sky sparkled; precious jewels projected light from a distant past. Rich and his friends joined Mahpee and Macha sitting in a circle surrounding a huge mound of timber. The ritual began as Mahpee lit the kindling connecting them to forgotten memories.

Everyone was wearing sacrificial garments and footwear harvested from nature; sewn with sinew and rawhide. Rich opened his mouth so Mahpee could place a peyote button on his tongue. Mahpee moved in front of Rich's friends, placing a button on each person's tongue and then one on his own.

They all held hands and closed their eyes; meditating as they waited for the peyote to light the fires within them. Rich's legs began to cramp, forcing him to stand beside the massive bonfire. His borrowed deerskin pants and vest partially protected him, but heat radiated on his exposed skin.

He got that sour milk sensation in his stomach and swallowed hard, trying to impede the inevitable. But, he couldn't. He turned and ran outside the fire circle, bent over and puked. His head ached and goosebumps erupted from his neck to his shoulders. He raised his head, dizzy and looked back where he had been standing—seeing wavering shadows—framed by flames of red, yellow and gold. So this is the Sacred Ghost Dance?

He remembered Mahpee had told them, "Peyote is a threshold to greater insight" and began dancing to the rhythm of the beating of drums and the cadence of a chant. He didn't know how he knew the words, but he did and began reciting an ancient phrase, "Michi nkshi tahe'na Ku'piye, Michi nkshi tahe'na Ku'piye." Mapee whispered the translation in his ear, "My child, come this way. My child, come this way."

Rich repeated the words until they became his mantra, opening a pathway to the other side. Dancers all around him chanted songs, their voices intermingling and creating a chorus pulsating with energy. Rich watched the smoke and embers rise from the flames, enveloping him in a sea of collective consciousness. A distant memory took shape before his eyes and he crossed a threshold into the surreal.

∞

Rich lay in water with his buddies, his hand and rifle poised above the surface of a rice paddy. A small cluster of thatched roof huts was before them with elephant grass all around. The scene was serene as he watched and waited. Sunset hues of yellow and orange dimmed the hamlet before them. The Lieutenant signaled to move toward the dwellings and pagoda. Rich and his buddy Murph crawled out of the stagnant water through the mud and tall grass to either side of the temple doorway.

Murph assumed a crouching position, his M16 pointed into the darkness. Across from him Rich got into a similar stance. Murph nodded at Rich and advanced across the threshold. Rich provided cover from behind, heard Murph's footsteps and imagined his movements. Murph's back hugged the wall as he tiptoed to the front of the chapel. He headed behind the altar, put his foot down and both he and Rich heard the dreaded "click." Then silence and milliseconds later, a detonation and explosion. Rich watched as Murph's shadow fragmented in front of him, diffusing into a million points of light. One moment he was there; the next he was vapor. The impact threw Rich to the ground; he fought to catch his breath.

He lay flat on his back, the pagoda a flaming pyre of hate and evil before him.

∞

"Can you hear me, Rich?" Ginny whispered in his ear. Her cheeks were flushed by the warmth of the bonfire as it cut through the desert's evening chill. Rich stared into the fire, powerless to escape from his nightmare. Ginny gazed into his eyes and saw the bonfire reflected within. As she looked closer its flames diminished and revealed an infinite universe of heavenly stars. She saw constellations emerge. Most pronounced was the Summer Triangle with its bright blue-white stars Vega, Altair and Deneb—a harbinger of imminent change. The Milky Way was so vivid, tendrils of clouds with millions and millions of stars encircled the sky.

Ginny floated into Rich's eyes; her body and his were intertwined. Rich's thoughts became her thoughts. His vision became her vision. She felt his nausea as her own. She stood close to the flames and felt the vibration of Rich's voice in her throat, "Murph! Murph! Oh God, Murph!"

∞

Ginny's feet were Rich's as they moved as one—chanting, chanting—dancing with the dead while smoke swirled all around them.

∞

Day #8, June 28, 1970 (The REZ, Wounded Knee, South Dakota)
Hope for the Future
I've come in peace to this sacred land
Welcomed by Native Americans

I walked on soil blessed by their ancestors
And spoiled by the white man
I shall dance the Sacred Ghost Dance again in my sleep
tonight
Among proud and glorious spirits

Chapter Thirty-One

"Welcome to Big Wyoming." *Wasn't that what the sign said several hundred miles ago?* The monotony of driving the interstate lulled me into a daze. There was no traffic and for miles and miles in any direction, all I saw was azure sky. Snow-laced peaks of the Rockies dominated the distant horizon with scattered cumulus clouds floating aloft.

Rich and I sat beside each other not saying a word, just passing time. The silence was reminiscent of the past we shared. Nobody dared to ask; nobody dared to tell. We never talked about things like our estranged Dad, absentee single Mom, kids having to supervise kids, teenagers hanging out at the house each night or Mom dating a man we called Bill. Maybe we were afraid to discover how we really felt about being adrift in the absence of adult supervision. We didn't know any other kids who lived without their dad. I, for one, was embarrassed about our circumstances but tried my hardest to portray my home life as being as normal as any of my school friends.

A pattern of denial had become the norm in my family. We were accomplices with Mom in obliterating our past, which started when we left Dad. It was as if he had died of a heart attack or in a car accident. We never discussed any memories of him, good or bad or the black hole his absence created in our lives. When friends asked about Dad, Mom said, "Just tell them he's a salesman traveling in Africa on business." My eight-year old mouth couldn't say those words with any conviction. So, whenever the question was asked, I shrugged and smiled, didn't say anything and hoped it wouldn't be asked again. I smiled a lot in my youth.

Mom was a high-spirited independent woman. Tactfulness wasn't her style. "I raised five kids by myself, Dammit!" she'd often say. It seemed a likely excuse for being abrasive. She called it, "Telling it like she saw it." Some people might have misunderstood my mother, perceiving her as a *floozy*. But, I didn't. I knew that throughout her life, she taught us many things. Under her hard shell, was a woman dedicated to keeping her children together as a family in spite of the obstacles she faced.

My mother's nickname was Penny, given to her by her high school friends due to her copper-colored curls. Little Orphan Annie might have been a more apt description. She took pride in her appearance—always well-manicured, with plucked eyebrows, painted fingernails and red lipstick. Her inexpensive costume jewelry, necklace and matching earrings complemented her white waitress uniform. Five days a week, at four o'clock, she'd be off to work at the Old Time Tavern.

As a divorced woman, she couldn't aspire to home ownership. No bank would ever give her a mortgage she couldn't afford to repay on waitress tips with six mouths to feed. Consequently, in the summer of '63 we moved into our fourth rental house in as many years.

Mom was able to get us a year-round rental in Holly Village, bordered by acres of woodland, the Bay Drive-In and Route 37, the main corridor from the beach to the Garden State Parkway. Three streets of ranch houses comprised the neighborhood. Most of them had either stone or crabgrass front yards. Ours had neither. Roots of trees protruded from the sandy soil, like mangroves growing in a swamp. There were no city services; each home had its own individually pumped well-water and a septic tank out back.

We lived there during my preteen years. Having discovered girls, I became self-conscious about how I looked. I drove Mom crazy every time we went clothes shopping and searched for "His" brand of straight-legged permanent pressed pants. I wondered how others perceived me, my family, even our house. I took it upon myself to do something about the appearance of our house. I don't know what compelled me to do it, but every few weeks of the summer, I'd use a metal rake to make parallel rows of sand in our front yard. I'd start at the street, whack the rake deep in the ground and drag it as I paced backwards. Then, I'd begin a new row and repeat the process, over and over, like a farmer tilling a field. It must have taken me hours.

The back yard was a different story. A twelve-foot zone around the perimeter of our septic was our own no-man's land. It was an overgrown stinking marshland, overflowing soon after being pumped out. Imagine the six of us taking showers and flushing the toilet daily and Mom always doing a load of wash. After each flush we would hear gurgling in the underground pipe and then look out the bathroom window to see water bubbling up from below.

My Mom's boyfriend Bill was a mystery to me. She had met him in the fall of '63 when she worked a wedding he played at the Old Time Tavern. She told us, "I met a nice man who is a banker in North Jersey and plays in a band on weekends." He was tall, stocky and always wore a white shirt and tie. His slicked back brown hair matched his dark suits and polished cordovan wingtips. One of his distinguishing features was a scar running vertically from his eyebrow to where his hairline once was. Another was his signature limp caused by a polio virus he contracted as a child. Every Saturday night Bill played an acoustic bass fiddle in a four-piece band called Johnny Jay's. The instrument was bigger than he was, and he often wrestled with it, laying it from the back seat to the front of his '62 Cadillac DeVille.

Bill began driving down to the shore to have dinner with us on Tuesday evenings. We kids had to be on our best behavior as we crammed around our formica kitchen table. Bill always wore a suit and Mom got dressed up for the occasion. She would remind us each week, "The butter is for Bill and the Parkay is for you kids." Anyway, it didn't matter to me because I'd never tasted butter. One night we had corn on the cob. Bill would first butter two rows of his corn, salt and pepper it and then move the corn from left to right as he ate each row. He looked like a human typewriter. From start to finish, Bill kept a straight face and so did we. I tried not to giggle when Rich caught my eye. After he left, Rich said, "Do you believe how he ate his corn?"

Mom cleared the table. "He eats different from you kids. He's got manners. "Don't forget, Rich. It's your turn to wash tonight."

∞

It was silent. Rich had drifted away to a place I couldn't retrieve him. He was here but not here. Memories of our living in Holly Village continued to flood my mind.

∞

Mom must have switched her work schedule to a Friday lunch shift because Fridays became date night. She'd bring home a pizza or Chinese food for us kids, then get ready to be picked up for dinner at 7:00 p.m.. It was good to see Mom so happy once a week, knowing that she'd be pampered by Bill. She sewed a half-dozen dresses, wearing a different one each week during those special times away from her day-to-day worries. One had an ostrich feather collar.

Around that time, I began working at Cy's Deli, a long walk from home. I didn't apply for a job as much as fall into it. One day after school, I stopped by for candy, saw there were cartons stacked in the aisles and asked, "Can I help, Cy?" He handed me a box cutter. I'd work Friday night, all day Saturday and return early Sunday morning to put the paper together before opening the store at 8:00 a.m. Cy would stumble in around 9:00 a.m. with a hangover from Saturday night at Olsen's Bar.

On Sunday evening Cy would give me a ride home after work and during the trip I'd rehearse my question over and over in my mind. My mouth would be parched when we pulled into my driveway. I'd grab the door handle and look straight ahead. "Cy, can I have my pay?" He'd look at me, pull a wad of bills from his pocket and hand me a ten dollar bill. I'm not sure why Cy made me ask for my pay each week. Perhaps he thought there was a lesson somewhere in that awkward moment.

That September, I announced to Mom, "I'll use my own 35 cents to buy school lunch." I also began buying my own clothes, saving $20.00 for a burgundy v-neck sweater at Wilton and Wolley's and $30.00 for a navy blue London Fog golf jacket at Feldman's.

I remember sitting in social studies class, showing my friend that I had ten, ten-dollar bills in my wallet. My seventh grade teacher, Mr. Connor said, "Where'd you get the money?"

"I have a job."

"Well, you have more money in your pocket, than I do."

With money in the bank, I started to buy my Mom skirts and matching blouses as gifts for her birthday, Mother's Day and Christmas. Rich's girlfriend Diane drove me to Steinbach's and helped me select correct sizes and color combinations. I knew Mom would wear her outfits on Friday date nights. I don't remember her ever returning any of them.

Mom liked to remind us about the first time Bill invited her out on his 28-foot Chris Craft cabin cruiser. "I'd love to go," she said. "Can my five kids come along?"

"Sure."

With that response, Mom knew Bill was the man for her. Soon after, Mom told us we were going out on Bill's boat. I knew it was going to be a special day because Mom went to Shop Rite midweek and bought hard rolls, boiled ham and swiss cheese. On the day of our outing, I jumped out of bed and ran down the hall to the kitchen where Mom was making lunch. She cut the rolls, put generous portions of thin-sliced ham and cheese on each, then smeared mustard on some and Miracle Whip on others before wrapping them in wax paper. When I returned to my bedroom, all I could think about was the aroma of ham, cheese and mustard. I put on my bathing suit, grey sweatshirt and flip flops, took a beach towel from the bathroom closet and was the first one out the door. Opening the front window of our '51 Merc, I shouted to everyone, "Let's go!"

We boarded Bill's boat at a nearby dock along the Toms River, and he took us to a Barnegat Bay cove off the barrier island in Seaside Park. When it was time to drop anchor, I walked to the bow with him. He said, "You know the anchor's doing its job when you look at the Seaside Park water tower and then at the Seaside Heights one and we're not drifting." Rich was the first to jump in, the water up to his waist. He propped Eileen on his shoulders and waded to shore. We ferried our blanket, towels and lunch bags from the boat to the beach careful to avoid growths of seaweed along the bottom where crabs would nip our toes.

Mom and Bill stayed on the boat, retreated to the main berth below deck and closed the cabin door behind them. We lay on the beach, swam, ate our lunch and entertained ourselves until Mom and Bill reappeared, signaling it was time to return to the boat.

The joy I felt for Mom counterbalanced my confusion about Bill's comings and goings into Mom's bedroom at all hours of the night on Friday and Saturday. I wondered why he never slept over and had breakfast with us. Or why he never was there on Sunday mornings to accompany us to church. One weekend Aunt Eleanor and Uncle Ed were visiting and took Mom out to a bar. "We bumped into Bill and his wife at The Beach Club," Aunt Eleanor told me the next morning.

I stood there looking at her, my chin jutted out and eyebrows raised. "Bill's married?"

"Uncle Ed and I think he's a real creep."

I looked down at my feet through watery eyes. "Jeez," was all I could say. *How could my favorite aunt tell me something like that? What did she think I was supposed to do about it?* I certainly wasn't going to ask Mom or Bill for an explanation. Besides, it wasn't any of my business. I was just a kid. All I needed to know was that Bill treated Mom like a princess; and that was all I cared about.

∞

Mom never mentioned the incident, so Bill became another never-discussed topic within our family. Besides what strangers could have observed, his life was unknown to us. All we knew was that he was a banker who played the bass fiddle on weekends and loved to golf. Bill and Mom didn't share anything else about his "other" life. And, we learned not to ask.

Chapter Thirty-Two

I glanced east at the Big Horn Mountains, a backdrop to horses grazing on miles of green pasture with an occasional cluster of trees surrounding ranches and barns. It certainly looked like the state's nickname: "The Cowboy State." My GPS said the exit for Buffalo, Wyoming was just ahead. I figured it would be a good stop to fill up the tank and eat. I wasn't sure where I'd be able to get fuel as I got closer to Yellowstone National Park. After gassing up on Route 16 west, I crossed the street to the Buckaroo Car Wash. I lined up my tires to the wet ramp. "I'll have 'the works.'" A "cowboy" stood beside me cradling a power washer wand like it was a long range rifle. He took my money, nodded and pinched the brim of his grey Stetson before strutting to the front of the car. I wondered how he kept his brown leather cowboy boots dry with all the spraying he did. Another Stetson-toting cowboy dried off my car and I handed him a two-dollar tip. I saw a McDonald's and reluctantly pulled into the Drive Thru and ordered two double-cheeseburgers, large fries and a seltzer water. "What? You don't have seltzer? Give me a large Coke and hold the syrup." The woman behind the window shook her head as she pushed the soda button on the fountain, filling up my drink.

All told, I was back on the road within an hour. Not bad for a pit stop before traversing the Big Horn National Forest: five-thousand feet of incline over a hundred-mile stretch, culminating in an alpine tundra summit—Powder River Pass. I ate my lunch out of a bag on my lap, never getting out of second gear. As I got closer and closer to the mountaintop, my mind wandered until Rich interrupted my thoughts.

The GOAT's looking brand spankin' new.

"There's nothing like a car wash, tire shine and clean windows to give a car new life."

You're looking good, too. What's happening?

"Not much. All I've been doing while driving is thinking about us growing up. It all comes down to understanding you."

There you go again. You're trying way too hard to figure me out. I'm really not that complicated.

"You may not think you are on the surface. But, underneath, that's a different story."

That was all Rich and I had to say because I became preoccupied thinking about more of our shared experiences at the Holly Village house. I recalled Sunday as being special because it was one of Mom's days off consumed with family time for church and weekly food shopping.

∞

I heard Mom shout in her sing song voice, "Wake up! We're all going to church this morning."

Rich was lying in bed face down, covering his head with a pillow. "Jeez, Mom. It's too early."

"The Lord gives us six days. We're gonna give him one. Get outta bed. You're first in the shower."

"Why can't Sue or Danny go first?"

Mom pulled the blanket off Rich. "Because I say so. Besides, you take the longest."

Rich let go of his end of the cover. "All right already. I'm up."

"You got ten minutes."

I knew I had at least twenty minutes before Mom told me I was next. I don't think Rich ever got out of the bathroom in ten. The scent of coffee bubbling in the percolator mingled with the pungent smoke of Mom's first cigarette and wafted down the hall. The smoke greeted me, stinging my eyes. I didn't care for the smell or taste of coffee, either. A bowl of

Frosty Flakes poured from a plastic bag was what I had for breakfast each morning. After finishing my cereal, I'd raise the bowl to my mouth and slurp the remainder of milk. All that remained was a mound of wet sugar on the bottom.

Rich owned one white dress shirt, grey wool pants and a pair of black pointed toe shoes. Every morning he'd polish his shoes and press his shirt and pants. Then, he'd slick back his hair, put on his black leather jacket and admire his city greaser appearance in the bathroom mirror.

On Saturday night I polished my dress shoes and ironed my dress shirt and pants. I don't know if Mom intentionally gave me a second crease on my permanently pressed pants. But, there was no way I was going to wear them like that. Several weeks earlier, I had asked Rich to show me how he used the iron and spray starch to crisp his shirt and press his pants.

"First, add water and plug the iron in. Turn the knob all the way to red. You have to wait. It's got to get hot. When it starts to spit, you're ready."

"Can I try?"

"Not yet. Watch me. Put your pants on the ironing board. Do one leg at a time. Pinch your fingers along the edge and follow behind with the iron. See how I'm doing it?"

"Yeah."

"Hiss! Be careful of the steam when you lift the iron. Sometimes you get burned. Just, don't be a cry baby. Look at the leg to make sure you did it right. Flip 'em over and do it again to the other leg."

"OK. I'll give the other crease a try."

Rich wiggled his eyebrows. "Go ahead. You're gonna like it and so are your seventh grade girlfriends."

Every Sunday after church I looked forward to our weekly shopping trip to Shop Rite. I don't know if Sunday was a convenient day for Mom or if she needed her tips from Friday and Saturday to pay the bill. But, one thing was certain;

she never had a checkbook. She qualified for and used welfare support and Medicaid to keep her family afloat. However, she was either too proud or embarrassed to stand beside the checkout counter, tear off food stamps and hand them to the cashier with others watching. She forfeited this opportunity to stretch her hard-earned dollars by always paying with cash, pulling wrinkled ones, fives, and tens out of the envelope she had marked in big bold letters: FOOD.

We must have been quite a sight. Sue would push the shopping cart with Eileen in the seat and Ray in the basket, both clutching boxes of animal crackers. Mom would walk beside, taking coupons out of the envelope and checking items off the list she had written on the back. Rich and I would be running up and down the aisles getting items that Mom would shout out to us. I'd try to slip a box of Captain Crunch in the cart. But, Mom would shake her head as she took it out and put it on a nearby shelf. Mom would stand beside the cart at the Deli counter and wait her turn to order one-pound portions of domestic ham, salami and bologna, all sliced thin. Then, she'd get a day-old loaf of rye bread sliced in the Bakery Department. She always put the end piece in her mouth before placing the bag in the cart. Our shopping trip wouldn't have been complete without Mom buying a jar of Miracle Whip, a box of powdered milk, Parkay margarine, and a two-pound loaf of Velveeta cheese. We kids would take turns later that afternoon using the hand cheese slicer so Mom could make us grilled cheese and tomato sandwiches. I didn't know cheese came pre-sliced until much later in life.

∞

I pulled over at the summit and it seemed like I was above the clouds. The treacherous road was behind me, an endless pale blue sky lay ahead. I could only hope that would be true for the rest of my travels. I was chilly wearing shorts, tee-shirt and running shoes. I walked about a mile and crossed a bed of granular snow lying on the ground since the last spring snowfall. I took a selfie with my iPhone, smiled as I held a snowball up to my cheek. It was more like a snow cone—a solid ball of ice crystals.

When I got back to the car, grey clouds had drifted in, and I wondered what had happened to the pale blue sky? The road down was steep winding switch backs. After one turn I'd be on the inside track; after another there'd be nothing on my right except a cliff with thousands of feet of air between me and the valley floor. I held my breath and hugged the white line every time my lane switched to the outside. It was like skiing down a black diamond mogul trail at Killington, Vermont. When I got to the bottom of the mountain, the road leveled off for several boring miles. I developed a case of the blahs as I drove through towns with odd names like Ten Sleep, Basin, Greybull and Emblem.

Chapter Thirty-Three

I entered Cody on the Greybull Highway and heard a dreadful sound, "floovb, floovb, floovb," as if an alien creature was fast approaching. Then, it got louder, "vwoomp, vwoomp, vwoomp." I fought with the steering wheel and pulled into the lot of a professional building on Stampede Avenue. My tire was flat, the driver's side front end lower than the passenger side. I got out, looked at the tire and walked halfway to the building before realizing all the windows were dark and the lot was empty. When I turned around, I couldn't help but gaze at the tire, hoping that it had magically re-inflated. But, it hadn't. I pulled my cellphone from my pocket and stared at its display. I didn't know anyone in Wyoming. *What good would a phone call do me?*

I opened the trunk, and the spare tire was lying on its side underneath my sleeping bag and tent. I repositioned my camping gear and loosened the floor bolt mounting the tire, jack and tire iron to the rim of the spare. I lifted the tire and knew something wasn't quite right. "Damn. It's a donut," I yelled and bounced it on the ground. I remembered telling Gus to replace the spare, but couldn't recall whether or not I had asked him for a full-size tire. "Jeez." I hated riding on a donut. Even if it was only for a short distance. I knelt beside the flat and touched around the edge feeling for the source of the puncture. A bolt the size of a walnut was wedged in the edge of the tread. I couldn't believe it. Now I'd need to buy two tires. I took off the flat, put it in the trunk and mounted the donut.

I was tired, my hands were dirty, and I was starving by the time I slammed the trunk and got back on the highway. In a few miles, I pulled into the Cody Cattle Company, an all-you-can-eat chuck wagon restaurant. I washed up and was seated at a table beside a window overlooking US Highway #14. My waitress swaggered to the table, dressed in a straw hat, red plaid blouse, fringed skirt and vest. "It took twelve hours of slow cooking to perfect the brisket you just wolfed down." She bent over, reached inside her cowgirl boot and pulled out a pad and pencil.

"That's quite a trick."

She winked. "I've got other ones, too. What'll you have for dessert, Honey?"

I sat there and stared straight ahead, didn't dare blink. This conversation wasn't exactly going in the direction I had anticipated. I counted to five in my head before replying. "I'll have the fudge brownie."

"That's it?" She pointed to her chest. "All this for dessert and you want something you can eat with a spoon?"

"The brownie will do just fine."

"Suit yourself."

She returned with a brownie and two scoops of vanilla ice cream on top. "The ice cream is on me."

"Thanks."

She continued to stand beside my table, shifting her weight from one leg to the other. "You know this is Buckin' Bronco Country and I'd be happy to introduce you to it."

No question, riding that Buckin' Bronco was on my mind. But, I knew I'd never act on it. "Thanks, I'm just passing through."

She two-stepped backwards and hesitated for a moment. "Maybe another time."

I knew I'd be staying a couple of nights so I could get two new tires but remained silent as she sashayed away. Perhaps I'd take in a Rodeo by myself tomorrow night.

I drove ten miles out of town. It was getting dark when I pulled into my campsite at Buffalo Bill State Park, gateway to Yellowstone forty miles west.

The next morning, I stepped out of my tent and thought I was immersed in a three-dimensional Rocky Mountain landscape painting by Albert Bierstadt. I remembered this was the real thing. A nearby split-rail fence hugged the Shoshone River as it meandered beside my campsite. I was a "stranger in a strange land" in this pristine landscape of sagebrush and lodgepole pine. I turned around, the majestic hills of the Absaroka Mountains dominated my view with snow-clad Rockies framing the horizon.

After a quick cold breakfast, I headed back to town and stopped at Rimrock Tire and Auto. In addition to two new tires, I figured it was time for an oil change, filter and lube. After all, the GTO was almost fifty-years old, and I had traveled over 1,500 miles since leaving New Jersey. I sat in the driver's seat while the GTO was suspended six-feet off the service station floor. I'd convinced the mechanic that I'd stay put and not do anything stupid like turn on the ignition and spin the wheels or step out of the car.

Rich fidgeted in the seat beside me. *We're just gonna hang here for a while?*

"Guess so." I took a sip of tea as I munched on a trail mix bar. "Why don't we pick up where we left off?"

You mean rapping about living in Holly Village? Those years were bitchin'.

"Remember when you used to lie in bed facedown with the pillow over your head and ask me if it was raining or not?"

If it was raining the car wash wouldn't open.

"If I said yes, you'd go back to sleep and if I said no, you'd have to drag your ass out of bed?"

Yep.

"But, if you didn't work, you didn't get paid, right?"

Yep, again.

"How many half ass jobs like that one did you have after dropping out of school?"

Too many. I drifted from one job to another. Let's see. I worked in the cranberry bogs and at the car wash. I was a cook for a year at Burger Chef. In the summer I worked the night shift at a stand on Casino Pier. I put in sixty hours a week from 5:00p.m. 'til 2:00 a.m. I slept on the beach all day.

"That sounds like a lot of hours at minimum wage."

I didn't have a day off from July 4ᵗʰ to Labor Day. After I stopped working on the boards, I got in trouble with the cops.

"You'd have been better off if you had continued working?"

It woulda kept me out of trouble.

I remembered when Rich got arrested that spring. I was thirteen and Rich had turned seventeen. We orbited in two different universes, not sharing a single friend.

You were lucky not to hang with me and my friends. Most of 'em turned out to be JD's. Rich laughed. *Even me.*

"JD's?"

Juvenile Delinquents.

"Oh. Well, I looked up to you when we were growing up. But, during those teenage years your bad choices seemed to outnumber your good ones."

I guess I didn't think much before I did some things. I know I got in fights on the beach with city guys. A lot of them were bigger than me. They were tall like Dad. Every time I threw a punch at one of 'em, I saw Dad's face and remembered how pissed I was at him for not giving a shit about me.

"I was angry too but chose to pick fights with Ray. I resented how much he idolized you." Ray was too young to understand, like I did, that Rich was heading down a dirt road that was sure to dead end at a precipice.

Rich looked at me and frowned. *Did you warn him not to be like me?*

"In my own way, I tried. But, I wasn't equipped for the job."

Hindsight tells me that it would have been more effective to talk as a family about the emptiness and abandonment Rich and I were feeling. But, face-to-face personal communication wasn't something we had learned from Mom or Dad. The ability to enhance my communication with others became a goal I would spend a lifetime trying to achieve.

"Bluutt, Bluutt, Bluutt." The stuttering blast from an air gun reverberated through the garage and the open window on the driver's side of the GTO. I rolled it up, so the noise would become muffled. I gave some more thought to how Rich chose to deal with our circumstance.

"Have you ever wondered whether the future would have been different if you had hesitated for a moment before doing something? Or, maybe even decided to go in another direction?"

Rich looked at me, his eyes almost squinted shut. *Just because I didn't turn out like you don't make my way wrong. I don't judge you, so stop judging me.*

"I didn't mean to judge you. You did give me a lot of material though. Didn't you? You know, dropping out of school in seventh grade, being sent away to Jamesburg, smoking and drinking at such a young age. What was I supposed to do, applaud you for being such an excellent role model?"

I don't know about that. I do know that I'm not gonna argue with you. It really don't matter whether one choice is better than another. Each one will take you to a different place.

"Like?"

Like Mom's decision to leave the ole man. Don't you think our lives woulda been different if she stayed?

121

"Absolutely. Although in Mom's case, it probably wasn't just one decision, but a whole series of tough choices. She must have told herself each morning that we were doing fine without that SOB in our lives."

Rich hunched his shoulders. *We were doing fine without the ole man.*

"Oh, Really? How were you doing?"

Probably not as good as I coulda been. I don't think I woulda dropped out of school if Dad was there to kick my ass.

I thought the same thing but kept my mouth shut.

Chapter Thirty-Four

My cell phone rang; I ignored it. I put it on vibrate so I wouldn't be tempted to answer it. There was a lull in the staccato racket of the air guns from the garage bay. I cracked the window and shouted, "How much longer?"

Someone thumped a rubber mallet against the oil pan. "Twenty minutes."

I was getting restless sitting in an idle car suspended in mid-air in a darkened garage. I arched my back and stretched my arms. My body sank into the contour of the bucket seat and I couldn't help thinking about our conversation and ways I had "judged" Rich in '64.

∞

Back then Rich, Ray and I shared a cramped bedroom. I was lying awake on the upper bunk. Beside me, a slider high on the wall was our only window to the outside world. The curtain rustled on a gentle summer breeze. Twenty feet away the neighbors' sunflower yellow ranch house was aglow from a nearby street light. No stars twinkled. All the constellations were washed out by a bright full moon. Ray's rhythmic breathing in the bunk below me sounded like a train receding into the night. He slept beside the bedroom wall enveloped in darkness—a dreamer's paradise.

I looked down to the empty double bed beside us. *Where was Rich?* The house was silent except for the insistent drone of a dial tone. I got up and walked down the hall, following the sound coming from the kitchen. Rich was passed out on the floor in a pool of vomit. The telephone cord was stretched from the wall to where it lay next to his ear. I looked over his pathetic body from his slicked backed hair to his pointed black shoes. I vowed right then and there that I'd never end up like him. Yet, as Rich continued to make one bad choice after another, I would get dragged into his drama.

I was on my way to Mr. Landis's English class when I heard my name echo from a hall speaker. "Daniel Duffy please report to the principal's office." I had never been summoned there before. I swallowed hard as I entered.

"Have a seat, Daniel. Detective Yetman has a few questions he wants to ask you." Principal Sweeney closed the door behind him.

I sat in a chair across the desk from Detective Yetman. My heart was racing as I wiped my sweaty palms on my pants. He looked at me with pursed lips and began his questioning: "Do you and your friends go to The Bay Drive-In?"

"Yes."

"Were you there with your brother Rich and his friends last week?"

"No."

"Do you like Clark bars?"

"Yes."

I loved them. But that didn't mean I'd steal them. I learned that Rich was under investigation for breaking and entering, stealing cartons of cigarettes and boxes of candy from the drive-in concession stand.

When the questioning was over, I stood up and avoided Detective Yetman's eyes. To him, I was guilty by association and circumstance. I turned for the door, took a deep breath and slowly exhaled as I walked back to my classroom. Detective Yetman didn't say it, but, I'm sure he thought it: How will these boys survive without proper adult supervision? Well, I did. We were brothers scrambling to find our way to the other side of adolescence. Yet, Rich had taken one path, and, from observing the consequences of his choices, I chose to take another.

"Everything OK, Duff?" Mr. Landis asked.

"Yeah." I let out a sigh and looked down at the floor while nodding all the way back to my seat. I don't know why, but I never talked about my meeting with Detective Yetman with any of my friends. I felt humiliated and shamed. I didn't bring up the topic with Rich, or Mom either.

∞

"Going up!" One of the mechanics yelled.

I gazed out the passenger window as a pickup truck rose in the air next to me. A rack from a longhorn steer adorned its grille. *Was everyone in Cody a cowboy or cowgirl?*

Rich interrupted my thoughts. *You never said anything about that incident.*

I looked over at him. "Hell, I never told anybody."

I buried that experience deep in my mind. After that interview, I couldn't look Rich in the eye without my stomach clenching into a knot and thinking, "I hate you."

Whoa! You never told me that, either.

I hesitated, knowing that in order for me to get past this and move on there were things I needed to say to Rich. "But, that was fifty years ago, and I'm no longer your twelve year old little brother." I took a gulp of water. "Let me tell you now, what I should have told you then: During your teenage years, you were a huge disappointment and an embarrassment as a big brother. If the tables had been turned and I was the older one, I would have kicked your ass."

Rich looked down, his shoulders sank as he covered his face.

I took another gulp of water and my eyes flitted from side-to-side. "Instead of rising to the challenge of being the head of the household, you rejected it. Without someone for the family to lean on, I had to step up in your place. Dammit! I didn't want your position." Tears began to well. I blinked my eyes and scanned the wall in front of me.

I never wanted it either," he uttered into his palms. Then he folded his hands on his lap and leaned forward, trying to make eye contact. *"Are you done? Did you get everything off your chest?*

I continued to look straight ahead. "No. Not quite everything. It'll do for now."

I guess that's how you saw it. One good thing was you grew up quick without me or Dad around. Didn't you?

Rich's words echoed through my mind. Something clicked. *Didn't that make me the man I am today?* I knew I was on the right track. Tears flowed down my cheeks.

And guess what, Rich? There are other things I never told you. Maybe later I'll find the courage to tell you about them, too. But not now.

Chapter Thirty-Five

A jumbled mess of regrets flashed in my mind. I had never had the guts to tell Rich about me and Diane. I needed time to sort it out if I hoped to clear the air with him. *But wouldn't Rich be the one judging me?* I wasn't sure I could deal with that right now.

"Coming down!" the mechanic yelled as the GTO with me in it descended on the lift. I cringed when he slammed the hood, pulled an oily rag out of his back pocket and smeared his finger prints on the fender. I gave him a half-smile and shook my head. He shrugged his shoulders. I backed off the ramp and out of the garage.

It was around noon when I pulled away, getting a glimpse of the town of Cody for the first time in daylight. I approached a cluster of shops and pulled over to take a better look at the rooftop of an antique shop. *What the hell?* There was a forty-foot replica of a Winchester rifle mounted on top about four-feet off the flat roof and pointed straight ahead. *Was it some western symbol encouraging patrons to enter, enter at their own risk, or just keep on driving by?* The message was clear to me. I made an abrupt turn and drove away.

In a few blocks I saw a wooden façade reminiscent of an old west saloon from the TV series *Gunsmoke*. There was a sign out front with a picture of a cowboy riding a bucking bronco. Below the graphic was the word, Cassie's, outlined in neon lights. Bright red, white and blue banners adorned the building like bunting on the 4th of July. *Steak House, Buffalo Bar, Live Local Music,* and *Welcome Bikers* were the messages broadcasted to passersby. I didn't know what a Buffalo Bar was but was willing to find out. When I walked through the door, I saw four buffalo heads mounted on the walls, two were side-by-side behind the bar and one at each end. Buffalo was the main item on the menu.

"Howdy, Pardner. What can I get you?"

The waitress looked like Annie Oakley with a red bandana around her neck and a six-shooter in a holster on each hip. *Did all Cody waitresses dress like this?* "I'm thinking of trying the buffalo steak."

"Well, you came to the right place. We have the finest steaks in the West. The smallest is a 16 ounce Porterhouse. You order 'em as big as you want from there. "How big do you want one?"

"I'll have the 16 ounce." I figured it would be both lunch and supper.

"Sure 'nuff. Oh, there's only one way we cook 'em here—rare."

"Rare?" My preference was medium-well. "Sure, rare it is."

She turned and looked at me over her shoulder. "It comes with a side of cactus flower fries."

I shrugged as she sauntered away. I wasn't a food connoisseur with high expectations for my meal. Though, I was surprised when I popped the first piece of buffalo steak in my mouth. *Was it gamey? Chewy? Tough?* None of the above. It tasted like beef but had a coarser texture and sweeter flavor. I was content when I pushed my plate away after a mug of beer and those fries.

"Will you be going to the Ro-de-o tonight?" Annie Oakley asked in a sing-song voice as she added up my bill.

"Yes."

"Then I'll put your ticket on the tab."

I drove to the Cody Stampede Rodeo grounds and passed under a thirty-foot banner spanning the parking lot entrance, "Welcome to the Rodeo Capital of the World." I had never been to a Ro-de-o before and sensed that many locals came to the same conclusion. They tipped their cowboy hats as they looked me over, from my Red Sox cap to my Khaki shorts. I smiled and tipped my cap in kind as I followed along to the grand stand entrance. Fans were excited as if they were attending a high school pep rally or football game.

I felt like a cow going through a gauntlet as a corral fence on either side of me got narrower and narrower. I handed my ticket to a guy wearing a name tag: Tex. He pointed to the bleachers. "First ones there get the best seats." A man ahead of me began running, kicking up dust in my face. I followed him and bumped into several people wearing tee-shirts, cowboy hats and bandanas lettered with the names of tonight's headliners: Jill Welsh, Barrel Racing; Chuck Schmidt, Saddle Bronc Riding; Brett Stall, Bull Riding and Clayton Moore, Steer Wrestling. *Steer Wrestling?* Now that was something I had never heard of.

"Where are you, Bub?" a teenager yelled from a section of the bleachers behind me. A child dressed as a cowboy sat a few seats away and shouted to his father, "I want Bar-B-Q." Another asked, "Can I get Nachos, Dad?" It seemed everywhere Americans went: a sporting event, the mall, a concert, the circus, the boardwalk, even the great outdoors, food and drink were the centerpiece of their experience. I guess a Ro-de-o was no exception. I got myself a cold draft beer and a Bar-B-Q sandwich. When I sat back down I scanned several of the signs that decked the infield fence: *Buffalo Bill Cody Beer*, *Wrangler Jeans* and *Ram Trucks* dominated the display. The two-hour show fulfilled its promise of being a high-energy Ro-de-o with bulls, broncos, cowboys and cowgirls. On the drive back to my campsite, one cheer from the PA echoed in my head, "Cody is Ro-de-o, Cody is Ro-de-o."

Chapter Thirty-Six

It was too beautiful a night to set up my tent, so I spread my sleeping bag on top of a nearby picnic table. Millions of stars sparkled above the mountains in the pristine, high desert air. I lay back and thought about Rich. We hadn't spoken since I left the service station and I wondered why until he said, *So you've been out partying, huh?*

"Just relaxing after dealing with those two tires."

But we left off rapping about an important time in my life.

"Really?"

I had just met Diane, and the court date was coming up about my B&E.

Meeting Diane was the best thing that ever happened to Rich. She talked him into changing his hair style from a pompadour to a Princeton and influenced him to change his clothing from "city-greaser" to "collegiate." After a while, she started working on me, too. In no time, I was sporting the same haircut and wearing khakis with penny loafers.

Absolutely. I loved everything about Diane. Her good looks for sure. We made a great couple, especially out on the dance floor.

"What happened with your court case?"

Diane went with me so I could tell the judge she was helping me turn my life around. But, he didn't let me off the hook. That was when he gave me a choice: Go to jail or enlist in the service. I chose the Marines and from that moment on everything started to fall into place for me.

Chapter Thirty-Seven

Within sixty days of Rich's enlistment, he would be on a bus for boot camp in Parris Island, North Carolina. As the day drew closer we decided to throw a farewell party for him on Labor Day weekend. That Saturday morning, I dragged a metal rake, back and forth across sand in the front yard, smoothing it into fragile furrowed rows. However, I knew the back yard would be a challenge.

Mom must have pleaded with the landlord because after breakfast a tanker from Olsen's Septic Service backed down the gravel driveway. Mom looked out the window when she heard the diesel engine of the pumper. "Finally! Let's hope we don't see any bubbles over the septic this weekend.

I ran to greet Aunt Eleanor and Uncle Ed when they pulled into the driveway. "I want to cut the grass over the septic," I announced. "Our neighbor Mr. Tucker let me borrow his lawn mower but Mom said to wait until you got here."

Uncle Ed placed his suitcase on the ground. "I'll help you. First, we'll have to check the gas and oil. We can start right after the truck's gone." Soon, he and I were standing outside the twelve-foot span of tall weeds growing over the septic. I sniffed and gagged, overcome with the offensive reek of what smelled like rotten eggs.

Uncle Ed sniffed. "Still pretty ripe. That guy sure stirred things up. Didn't he?"

I blinked my eyes, pulled a handkerchief from my pocket, covered my nose and looked at Uncle Ed for guidance.

"It'll be OK. We'll just have to hold our breath while we're cutting." He leaned over and grabbed the starter cord, pulled once—nothing, twice—nothing. When he pulled a third time, he stumbled backwards, almost falling. The handle and three-foot piece of rope dangled from his hand.

My eyes widened as I shouted, "Are you OK Uncle Ed?"

"I'm fine. But, this is what happens when you borrow someone else's stuff."

I shrugged my shoulders. "I guess I'll bring it back to Mr. Tucker."

"Tell him what happened."

My friend George was standing behind us. "My Dad's got something that'll help and it doesn't have a cord." He went home and returned in a few minutes with a long-handled brush cutter.

"Thanks George. I guess we'll be practicing our golf swing today. Won't we, Danny?"

Rich's friend Larry pulled into our driveway in his dad's Ford pickup. All morning they shuttled picnic tables and lawn chairs from our neighbor's yards to the shaded corner of our yard. By early afternoon they backed up one last time. They dropped the tailgate, pushed a galvanized tub of ice and a keg of Schaefer beer to the edge and lifted it to the ground.

Soon after 5:00 p.m. aunts, uncles, cousins, and friends began flowing out of cars parked in our driveway and up and down Alfred Lane. Everyone wanted to shake Rich's hand and talk with him and Diane. He looked good standing next to her wearing his yellow oxford shirt, narrow navy blue tie and khaki pants.

Mom's boyfriend Bill got his Polaroid camera out of the trunk of his Cadillac. "Let's take a Duffy family photo." He positioned us in a line beside Uncle Ed's red Pontiac Catalina. Gram was at one end, smiling for the first time ever in the presence of the Duffy's. Next was Eileen, Ray and me, followed by Sue, Rich and Diane. Mom was at the other end, smiling at Rich, oblivious to the camera. She seemed happy, perhaps even relieved that Rich had found a new direction in his young life.

Now, whenever I look at that photo I still wonder why skinny me was shirtless and barefoot. Everyone else was dressed for the occasion. Maybe I was in the middle of washing up after cutting the grass over the septic and didn't want to miss out on being in the family photo. Other than at the beach, I couldn't remember any other time I was bare-chested in public, let alone, posing for the camera. Once I became a teenager, I learned to keep my shirt on for fear that I'd scare girls away.

That afternoon, I followed Rich around as he walked and talked with guests. "Hey little brother. Will you do me a favor? Keep an eye on Diane for me? I'll be at boot camp for two months."

I smiled at Rich, then looked over to Diane sitting on a yellow and white webbed folding chair. "Of course." I put my arm around his shoulder and squeezed. "I'll miss you."

He grinned and winked.

Chapter Thirty-Eight

Two months later Mom and I sat on a wooden bench in the lobby of the Lakewood Bus Station waiting for Rich's return. I popped a Sen-Sen in my mouth; tingling bursts of licorice exploded on my tongue. "How'd he look when you saw him at graduation?"

"He seemed the best I've ever seen him. So handsome in his dress greens." Mom opened her purse and handed me a photo. "Having our mother and son photo taken together was the proudest moment I ever had with Rich."

"Looks like boot camp did him some good."

"All I can say is he's a different son than the one who stood before the judge four months ago."

I couldn't wait to see him for myself. Rich told me how hard boot camp was in his letters. I wrote back to tell him how proud I was of him.

"Hey Rich!" I waved as he walked through the doorway, a huge brown canvas duffle bag draped over his shoulder. As he walked toward us I saw there was something about him I had never imagined would be possible. He stood tall in his uniform and cap. He looked so serious. "No nonsense" came to mind when I looked at his face, especially his eyes. He moved slower, more deliberately. He carried himself with a lot of self-respect and confidence, traits he hadn't demonstrated before. I was proud of the person Rich had become. Someone I was now thrilled to call my big brother.

I ran to Rich to give him a hug. He put down his bag and motioned for me to stop. I looked at him and frowned. "Hey little brother. Let me show you how men say hello to each other." He stuck out his right hand and nodded. I did the same, and our hands met.

"Always give someone a firm hand shake and look 'em in the eyes. Nobody wants to shake hands with a dead fish."

I shook Rich's hand and looked him straight in the eyes, something I hadn't done for a long time. "I'm glad you're home." Rich's hand-shaking lesson became an important skill I'd use throughout my life. I often grinned when I shook hands with someone. One part of my smile was for my friend and the other was for my brother.

Mom pushed between us, her arms wrapped around Rich's neck. "I don't care what you say. I'm still your mother, and I'm gonna kiss and hug you all I want!"

Rich nodded that it was time to go. "It's pouring out!" Mom said.

"I'll get the car." Mom handed Rich the keys, and he paced out of the bus station as if it were merely a cloudy day. He pulled Mom's '51 Merc up to the door and honked. I fought his duffle bag with both hands and dragged it across the floor. When Rich met us at the door, his broad smile reminded me that my brother was somewhere underneath those dress greens. The smell of diesel fumes and dust lingered in the air as Mom, and I ran to the car, splashing through puddles. Rich opened the passenger door for Mom, and I climbed in back.

The sun broke through the clouds. Mom pointed, "There's a rainbow!"

Chapter Thirty-Nine

Later that afternoon Rich and I were sitting at the dining room table. I was eager to hear more about boot camp. "You look great. Did you put on weight?"

"I sure did. For two months straight, we were up at 5:00 a.m. We had to shit, shower and shave before 5:30 a.m. roll call. Then, I had a few minutes for chow in the mess before morning P.T."

"P.T.?"

"Physical Training, and we had a helluva lot. Not only did I put on a few pounds, I added muscle too." Rich looked at me, raised his arms and bent his elbow to flex his biceps, just like Popeye. "Feel this."

I squeezed his muscle. "Wow! You Marines are tough."

"We have to be. We're the first ones they send into battle. I learned how to fight and to count on my buddies, and they have to count on me. Marines don't ever leave anyone behind." Rich's last few words seemed to catch in his throat.

"Did you make any friends?"

"Sure did. My best buddy is a black guy whose last name was right before mine—Daughtry. I stood at attention, staring at the back of his head for more hours than I care to remember. His bunk was next to mine. He taught me how to speak jive talk. He called it 'rap.' Can you dig it, man?"

"I sure can."

"Well, dig this: after the first month of boot camp, it started to get cold in the morning, so me and Daughtry had a brainstorm. Our uniforms would get cleaned and returned covered in plastic. We decided to wrap it around our legs before putting on our socks and fatigues."

"Did it help?"

"We were warm for the first few minutes of P.T. but when we started sweating the plastic stuck to our legs and we froze. There was no way we were going to ask our drill instructor if we could stop to take off the plastic. If he ever found out about our sissy scheme we'd still be running laps around that P.T. field." Rich slapped me on the back and arched his eyebrows.

"Where does your friend live?"

"Philly. He and his girlfriend are going to visit us in a few weeks. You'll get a chance to meet them."

"Cool."

Chapter Forty

I was dizzy as I sat in my car outside the Cody Diner. Secondhand smoke from two guys who were at a table next to me infiltrated every pore of my mucus membranes. I gulped a mouthful of water, swished it around and spit it out the window. No relief. I reached for a stick of Trident to rid my mouth of the tinny taste of nicotine. I couldn't help but rub my eyes. I knew better, but did it anyway and the stinging got worse. What I really needed were eye drops I didn't have. I pulled out my handkerchief and poured water on it before dabbing one eye and then the other. Finally, some relief.

Inhaling someone else's cigarette smoke reminded me that Rich began smoking at age twelve. Mom condoned it because she had set the example. It would be years before I realized that my sinuses and lungs couldn't tolerate any airborne assaults which would trigger an allergic reaction. My thoughts focused on Rich's return after graduating from boot camp. He had a few weeks leave before having to report to Camp Lejeune. He and Diane seemed so happy. They were inseparable.

His first Saturday home we were at the kitchen table having breakfast. Rich declared, "Me and Diane got engaged!"

I looked him in the eyes and gave him a firm hand shake. "Good for you."

"Do you have a minute?" Rich put his arm around my shoulder as he led me to the sofa. With a cup of coffee in one hand and a Marlboro in the other, he explained, "Next Sunday, I'll be leaving for North Carolina. I hope to be home every other weekend."

"That sounds good."

"Well, I'll be home if I'm able to buy that new car I've been looking at."

"Cool. What kind?"

"I've got my heart set on a candy apple red GTO convertible."

"Really? That's the coolest car ever. Does it have bucket seats?"

"Sure does. And a Hurst four on the floor." He looked at me and nodded. "Pretty soon you'll be getting your license, right?"

"Yes. I can't wait."

"When you do, I'll let you drive it."

I jumped up from the sofa. "You will? You'll let me drive your GTO?"

Rich caught my arm and pulled me back down next to him. "Sure, but there's one thing I've got to work on—the down payment."

I slumped against the cushion. "Ohhh. The down payment."

"I have enough cash for the registration, plates and insurance. I only need $250.00 more."

"$250.00?" I had been saving money for two years so I could buy my own car. I was attempting to subtract $250.00 from my $1,200.00 savings account balance when I heard myself blurt out, "I'll loan you the money."

"Really? You won't regret it." Rich stood and shook my hand again. "I've got to call Diane and tell her the good news. Don't worry, we'll start repaying you as soon as we get our feet on the ground."

"When will you need the money?"

"We'll go to Trenery Pontiac on Monday after Diane gets off work. Can you have it by then?"

I forced a grin and swallowed hard, calculating how many hours I'd have to work to replenish the money. "Sure, Rich. I'll go to the bank after school."

Chapter Forty-One

One Sunday, Rich and Diane were going to join us at church. I was putting on my white dress shirt. Rich asked, "Why are you still wearing those clip-on ties?"

I buttoned my collar. "They're quick and easy." I had never questioned the black satin clip-on tie Mom handed me years ago for Sunday services.

"It's about time you learned how to tie a Windsor knot."

"A what?"

"The kind of knot we Marines tie when we wear our dress greens."

Rich held out a charcoal tie and motioned for me to follow him to the bathroom. He stood behind me, took a long drag from his Marlboro, placed it on the edge of the sink and exhaled over my shoulder. The smoke bounced off the mirror, dissipating in every direction. It stung my eyes, but I could still see our reflection.

His arms surrounded my shoulders and his muscle tee-shirt exposed tattooed biceps. "Mom" was etched on his left and "Diane" on his right. He held both ends of the tie in front of us, then draped it around my neck. His hands smelled like tobacco from a musty field. I was mesmerized, watching his fingers move in concert with his words. His movements were as graceful as a weaver's: around once, around twice, then, under, up, over and down. Rich's fingers pulled and tightened the knot at my collar. "There. A perfect Windsor."

"How about if I just loosen it and slip it over my head each week after church?"

Rich looked at me in the mirror and chuckled. "No. You have to do it yourself. What are you going to do when you want to wear a different color tie?" He took another drag from his cigarette and exhaled. "OK, now you try and I'll watch."

I must have made a half-dozen attempts to mimic the motion of Rich's fingers, guiding the tie along its journey until I finally heard, "That's it, Danny!"

The ability to tie a Windsor knot would eventually become an important ritual in my life. I must have tied that perfect Windsor knot every morning for thirty-five years of my career. I swear, on some days while I was tying that knot, my eyes stung from Rich's cigarette smoke, and I saw his reflection smiling at me in the mirror.

Chapter Forty-Two

Rich was a good looking guy who made a great first impression, especially in his Marine Corps uniform. His thick chocolate brown hair framed his chiseled jaw and broad cheekbones. His pug nose and dimpled chin accentuated his winning gap-toothed smile. People were drawn to him, especially the girls.

But, his second and third impressions weren't as endearing. The more you got to know him, the more likely you were to see some flaws, namely, his self-centeredness. He focused on satisfying his own needs and desires, often at the expense of others. He was a master at manipulating people to get what he wanted.

For example, after getting the GTO, Rich established a bi-weekly routine of driving from North Carolina to New Jersey and back. He always had a carload of guys with him who'd pay him gas money to take them to and from their hometowns along the I-95 corridor and the New Jersey Turnpike. He'd drop them off on Friday night and pick them up again on Sunday afternoon at designated rest stops along the way. Once home he had all day Saturday and most of Sunday to visit with Diane and friends.

I don't remember Rich spending much time with me and the family. I guess he and Diane were busy planning their wedding with full military regalia. Rich was also meeting with a priest because he was converting to Catholicism—Diane's religion. Rich seemed so busy I didn't bother asking him if I could drive the GTO or when he would start repaying me the money I loaned him. I thought I'd wait until he and Diane had their feet on the ground, just like Rich had suggested. I'd ask him after his wedding.

On weekends Rich was home my things started to go missing.

"Have you seen my navy blue sweater, Mom?"

"No. Did you look in your closet?"

"Yes. I looked in my dresser too. There's no sign of it."

"It'll turn up."

Well, it didn't appear and neither did my London Fog jacket which I couldn't find a few weeks later. One Monday following Rich's weekend visit, I was getting dressed for school and my desert boots weren't in my closet. I looked under the bed and in the living room by the sofa. They were nowhere to be found. My desert boots? I remembered taking the bus to New York City with my friend Tony, then walking from Port Authority to the Village to buy my first pair of desert boots. They were my favorite shoes and now they too were among the missing.

Could Rich have worn them back to North Carolina? If he did, he should have asked me first. *Wouldn't that have been the right thing to do?* If they didn't show up soon, I'd have to ask Rich when he got home.

Two weeks later I was tight-jawed as Rich sat at the dining room table eating Mom's warmed up stuffed green peppers. "Hey, Rich. Can you help me with something?"

"Sure. What do you need?"

"I haven't seen my desert boots in two weeks. Have you seen them?"

Rich shook his head. "Nope. Haven't seen them."

I looked at Rich and swallowed hard. "You haven't seen them? They just walked away?"

His eyes averted mine. "Guess so."

By Rich's next visit home, I had installed a hasp and padlock on my closet door and put all my shoes and clothes inside.

144

"You got everything under lock and key now?"

"I don't want any more of my clothes disappearing." Rich looked at me and nodded his head as he walked away.

As a kid I learned early on to solve problems. My mother couldn't afford to buy things she considered luxuries, so I had to work to get them. Keeping track and taking care of my personal belongings became a necessary habit. I had to establish some sense of order in my otherwise chaotic environment. I've always prided myself in my ability to overcome obstacles. It has contributed to my belief that I'm "in control."

Chapter Forty-Three

My initial impression that Rich had dramatically transformed himself during boot camp faded to a more realistic understanding that his polished façade only masked his unresolved impulsivity and selfishness.

One Saturday, Mom was vacuuming the living room carpet, and I was in my bedroom. She was propelling the vacuum with a vengeance, thrusting one-way, then backing up and thrusting again and again.

"He does whatever the hell he pleases. All he cares about is himself. He takes, takes, takes. If he could, he'd take the eyes right out of my head."

After parrying with the vacuum, I heard her grab the cord, pull the plug from the wall and crumple onto the sofa with a hopeless cry. I got up from my desk and walked into the living room. Her body was pressed into the cushions as she held her knees close to her chest. She began rocking back and forth as if wrapped in a cocoon.

I sat beside her, my arm around her shoulder. "What's wrong Mom?" I whispered.

Her eyes, filled with tears, gazed vacantly at the wall. "Nothing."

I saw Mom's handwriting on the front of three envelopes beside her and picked them up. Every one of us kids knew how Mom budgeted her money and how important it was for her to pay bills on time. She had a half-dozen envelopes in her top dresser drawer marked Rent, Food, Electric, Gas, Phone and Christmas Club. Throughout the month she'd deposit crumpled five-, ten- and twenty-dollar bills into each one. I looked inside them and they were empty.

I hugged her as she wept on my shoulder. "How could he do this to you, Mom? How could he be so selfish?"

∞

Beep! Beep! Beep! I was awakened from my daydream as an F250 backed beside me in the lot of the Cody Diner. Doubled up with stomach cramps I thought, "Damn you Rich." There you go again, not caring who you hurt. *For what? To make your car payment and to buy a carton of cigarettes?* I hoped to hell that I wouldn't be talking with him again today.

Chapter Forty-Four

I held onto each side of the steering wheel and shook it. "Damn you, Rich. You hurt Mom." Then I counted to ten. Wait! *Wasn't that incident over forty-five years ago?* I knew it was, but that didn't make it any less painful to remember. I tried to give myself an attitude adjustment. Just think positive thoughts. After all, it was another beautiful summer day and I was enjoying being on the open road.

What else could I think of? I've had phenomenal experiences the past few days and nights in the Badlands, Pine Ridge Indian Rez and even in Cody, Wyoming. I smiled. Now, that was better. Besides, it's taken me over 1,800 miles to get where I was, and it has been worth it. Today's destination was bound to be one of the highlights of my trip, Wyoming's Yellowstone National Park. I was psyched to be at the gateway of my outdoor adventure. In reading Rich's National Park Guide, I was amazed at all the natural wonders within Yellowstone. The park encompassed over two million acres, larger than the states of Delaware and Rhode Island combined. It would be a short drive of forty miles until I was in the midst of a wilderness wonderland.

I let out a sigh, turned the ignition and pulled out of the Cody Diner onto Route 16 west. After a few miles, I heard, *What's up, bro?*

I vacantly gazed ahead. *Just breathe,* I reminded myself.

You're a real downer today.

I clenched my teeth. "I am. My mood changes as often as the elevation does on our trip. One day everything seems fine. We're experiencing life on the road together as brothers. The next, I really don't know who the hell you are." Then, I took a deep breath and burst out, "I've been thinking about your lying and stealing. Pure bullshit."

Chill. I'm not the same person I was when we were growing up.

"You're not?"

Hell, no. Are you?

"I don't think so. Well, maybe..." I knew that I've learned from many of my life experiences. Even some of the negative ones have shaped me to become a better person.

Of course they have. They're life's lessons. I've had a lot of them, too.

"I guess you're right. Maybe talking is a good idea. But it's hard for me to remember Mom being so upset and not being able to undo anything that you caused."

Control is an illusion.

"What do you mean? Haven't I had control during this trip? I've decided where to stop and what to do."

You might think so. How do you know it wasn't just the unfolding of your karma?

"My karma? What the hell's that?"

It's your destiny. Some people call it fate. My friends like to say it's a lot like '69', you receive what you give. Rich smirked. *And the better you are at giving, the more you will receive.*

I shook my head and laughed. "I've known that as reciprocity. What you give out, you get back."

Rich rolled his eyes and shook his head. *There you go again, complicating the hell out of something. This time it's an ancient spiritual principle.*

"How does karma relate to us and our trip?"

Your idea to fix my GTO and travel cross-country started everything rolling. Look what's come your way.

You're driving my classic muscle car cross-country, something not many people get to do in a lifetime. What you and me have been experiencing is priceless. Aren't you glad I came along for the ride?

"I guess so. No, that's not right. I'm really glad we've spent time together. In fact, there are no two ways about it. I've really enjoyed my trip or I should say your trip."

My trip was bitchin'. It blew my mind in '70. Now this summer it's our trip.

I turned the table on Rich. "But, what about your karma?"

What about it?

"Well, your decision to drive cross-country was part of it, right?"

Absolutely.

"Was driving cross-country a good way to clear your mind of bad karma from Vietnam?"

Not quite. But, it sure helped. You know what they say, "Wherever you go, there you are."

"Even though the scenery changed, you couldn't escape?"

Something like that. I really don't know for sure.

"What was your most difficult challenge in Vietnam?"

Rich glanced out his side window as a Home Depot eighteen wheeler passed by. He let out a sigh and focused on the distant horizon.

I spit in the face of fear each day. Some evenings, Command said it was going to be a rough one. We would be air lifted off our desolate hill and brought to an aircraft carrier until daybreak. Most nights we were left on the hill to fend for ourselves. I prayed that Command made the right decision to keep us there because all Charlie had to do was zero their mortars in on us and we were as good as gone."

150

"Do you think they left you there as a decoy?"

I don't know why some nights we were evacuated and others we weren't. But, one night Command wasn't right, Charlie let us have it, and our asses were handed to us. All we could do was lay in our bunkers and put our hands over our helmets. I got religion fast, praying to Jesus that I'd get to see dawn. Two of my buddies didn't make it through the night. I think of my friends Jonesy and Scotty every day. They were cut down in the prime of their lives. For what?

"Jeez, Rich. I'm so sorry."

Tears came to his eyes. *Me too. Sometimes the same bloody scene plays over and over in my head. I'm not always asleep when it happens. Maybe I'm going nuts.*

You're not going insane. That was a bitch of a situation for anyone to have to deal with."

It was. I thought of contacting Jonesy and Scotty's wives after I got back to the states. But, I lost the will. I couldn't think of anything I'd be able to say or do to make them feel any better. What do you say to your buddy's wife and kids? 'Your dad was a hero' or 'Your dad died for our freedom?' I just didn't believe all that shit anymore to say it to someone's loved ones. I saw too much in 'Nam, and it made me sick. So, I didn't say nothing.

Rich turned away and looked out his side window. I heard his muffled sobs and didn't know what to say or do. Then, I whispered, "I understand... You were fighting a war you didn't believe in..."

Jim Morrison wailed "Break On Through" from the *Jensen* speakers. As if on cue, both of us reached for the volume knob of the tape deck. My palm covered the back of Rich's scarred hand. His embedded particles of shrapnel became braille as our fingers intertwined. I paused, filled with a sense of oneness. Maybe I had to break on through and get free from something. Perhaps I had to let go of my view of Rich from the past. *What good had that image of him ever done for me anyway?*

My attention returned to the road. Sobs surfaced as a fireball first centered in my stomach, then burned through to my soul. I looked at him and thought rather than said, *You're not alone. I'm here for you.*

Rich pursed his lips as tears fell from his eyes, too. *I've known that for a long time.*

Chapter Forty-Five

It started to drizzle, and the temperature had plummeted. I pulled over to put the top up. I fumbled through the trunk to find a pair of jeans and my New England Patriot's fleece. I got back in the driver's seat and put them on directly over my shorts and tee-shirt. Then, I idled the car, turned the heat to high and thought about what Rich just told me. How could such a disturbing experience like that not dominate his thoughts? Hell, just hearing about it disturbed me.

I put the car in gear, stepped on the gas and released the clutch. In a few minutes a sign read, "Welcome to Yellowstone's Eastern Gateway." I took a deep breath and slowly exhaled. I reminded myself to just let my depressing thoughts drift away. I opened the window and inhaled fresh ion charged mountain air. I was beginning to feel rejuvenated until I saw dozens of cars with pop-up campers all around me, each one jockeying for position. Kids were screaming in the back seat of the Camry next to me. A Golden Lab stuck his tongue against the window and panted in my direction.

As I inched my way to the gatehouse, I was amazed at the paradox before me. On one hand, I was at the threshold of one of the world's most pristine wilderness preserves. Yet, on the other, I was immersed in bumper-to-bumper traffic spewing fossil fuel emissions into the natural environment. I showed the park ranger my driver's license, qualifying me for a National Parks Senior Pass and paid my ten dollar lifetime fee. What a bargain!

I weaved my way through a series of switchbacks, remaining in second gear as I ascended Sylvan Pass. I put Grand Funk Railroad's "Closer To Home" into the tape deck and hummed along, hoping that I was getting closer and closer to the home Rich had been seeking. The louder I hummed the clearer the image became of Rich and his friends as they traveled this same roadway.

Chapter Forty-Six

Rich lifted his hand from the steering wheel and pointed. "Wow. Check out the sign, 'Sylvan Pass Lookout, Elevation 8,541 feet.'"

Ginny closed the map and tossed it on the floor. "We're finally here."

Rich pulled into an end parking space. Ken parked beside him. "I hope our long slow drive up this mountain is going to be worth the view."

Ken hurried to the rustic rail fence overlooking the vista. They all joined him, resting their arms along the top rail. Their eyes and mouths opened wide as they scanned the horizon from one mountaintop to another. Silence enveloped them.

Ken lit a doobie, took a hit and passed it to Rich. "This will help those mountains come alive." Rich took a drag, held his breath and handed it to Ginny.

Sally took out a bottle of bubbles and started blowing them. Iridescent globes shimmered in the wind, a veritable universe spinning before their eyes.

"Wouldn't it be cool to be inside one of those bubbles and float over the countryside, Ginny?"

"It sure would. I'd love to go higher and higher with you."

"Let's take another toke of that joint and see how high we can get."

Ken got two blankets from the van. Rich helped Ginny and Sally over the fence, and they sat in a row, cross-legged, gazing in reverence at the landscape below.

Ken put Sly and the Family Stone's "I Want To Take You Higher" tape on, and they all began singing along.

Rich stomped his feet. "This view sure will take me higher."

"It's a nature movie I'd never get tired of seeing." Sally raised her arms over her head as Ken helped remove her dress.

Ken lit two more joints, passed one to Sally and the other to Ginny.

Sally fought to hold the smoke within her lungs "Now, I can truly connect with Mother Earth," she said in a high pitched voice. She handed the joint back to Ken and exhaled slowly, placing her hands together in a prayer position. "Aum. Aum," she chanted.

The others wasted no time joining Sally in her nakedness and mimicking her pose. They echoed her mantra— chanting, chanting—evoking metaphysical forces from an unknown universe.

∞

I hit the brakes hard when I saw red lights flickering up ahead. *A traffic jam in Yellowstone?* The sign read, "Fishing Bridge Campground, Next Right." There was a long line of vehicles ahead of me, cars with campers and motor homes, all with their blinkers on. Guess these folks had the same idea as me. I turned and crept along a narrow road leading to my campsite. I played Norman Greenbaum's "Spirit in the Sky" album. As the title cut began campers walked beside me singing the familiar lyrics and clapping along to the beat: Boom, Bup, Ba, Boom, Boom, Boom... Boom, Bup, Ba, Boom, Boom, Boom...

∞

I set my tent beside the fire pit, which consisted of four pieces of rebar, bent and welded together for a cooking surface. I placed my frying pan on top and swore I smelled fried eggs and bacon sizzling in the open air. Maybe tomorrow morning I'd be able to taste it, too. The sun was setting over

Yellowstone Lake, and a chilly breeze churned up white crested waves of foam.

It had been three weeks since I began my journey and I again debated whether or not I felt like rummaging through Rich's stuff in the trunk. It seemed like it would be an emotionally exhausting task. Maybe I'll attempt it when I have more energy. I reached for Rich's journal wondering when I had last read it. I opened it to the bookmark I had placed at his previous entry. It was dated June 28th, Pine Ridge Indian Rez. *How could it have been two weeks ago?* This trip was flying by... I turned to his next entry,

Day #22, July 12, 1970 (Yellowstone National Park, Fishing Bridge Campground)

All I can say is Wow! Far Out, Man! This land is a sanctuary—the air is fresh and the lake is pure. I want all my senses to be aroused by nature, music and drugs.

As I continued reading, Rich and I began to envision his first day at Yellowstone. The first thing he did was drop a tab of acid. He was peaking by the time he arrived at his campsite. He witnessed a kaleidoscope of images, sun-burnt radiant sky and spirited waters fused together. He jumped into the sacred lake to purify his soul. Then, he lay on the sand beside the wind-blown snow melt and found God in this cathedral called Yellowstone.

The scene was so vivid. The sky and water were swirling blends of purple and blue. He saw an eagle soar, riding the wind, round and round, turning clockwise at least a dozen times. He could see the subtle adjustments of its wing and tail feathers as it floated above him, suspended in space. The eagle looked down, its eyes focusing on his, welcoming him to the spiritual wilderness it inhabited. Rich's soul merged with the eagle, and he floated on an updraft, ascending higher and higher toward the heavens. His eyes pierced the surface of the water, revealing cutthroat trout swimming dozens of feet below.

The wind emitted a symphony of music with hardwoods playing percussion and evergreens adding harmonious ephemeral notes. There was a kaleidoscope of fragrance, mountain wildflowers blossoming with brilliance and the earthy muskiness of the timberline forest. Rich felt himself gliding effortlessly in the air toward an outcrop of granite and slowly descended circling once, twice, before gently settling on the highest ledge. He folded his wings against his body and tucked his head against his breast feathers, safe in the warmth and comfort of his lair.

Chapter Forty-Seven

What a scene! Rich flying over Yellowstone as an eagle. Simply beyond belief. I shook my head and leaned back in my camp chair sipping tea poured from my brother's red and white enamel coffee pot. *How many cups of coffee had he brewed in the carbon charred container?* It sat in the middle of a metal-framed cook stove directly over my campfire. *How many tales could it tell?*

I stood and unfolded my map of Yellowstone, amazed at both its enormity and diversity. It showed that the distance from my campsite at Fishing Bridge to the Canyon area would be twenty miles, a mere fraction of the roadway circumnavigating the park. I refolded the map and slipped it in my back pocket.

I opened Rich's journal and read his next entry,

Day #23, July 13, 1970 (Yellowstone National Park, Fishing Bridge Campground)
Yellowstone is God's great creation—
A natural cathedral!
The river canyons and waterfalls are bitchin'
I'm one with nature!

After breakfast of bacon and eggs, I doused the campfire and watched the embers shimmer from red to orange, then to black. I palmed two bottles of chilled water from my cooler and stuffed them into my day bag, along with two granola bars and a small bag of trail mix. Not only did I love to snack, but also knew these nuts and raisins would give me energy for the day's explorations.

It was a beautiful summer day, so I climbed into the driver's seat and took the top down. Puffy white clouds dotted the sky over a crystalline Yellowstone Lake. I crossed Fishing Bridge and headed north with the sun's rays warming my face and the scent of evergreen floating in the air. The title track of Al Kooper's album, *I Stand Alone* began to play. I envisioned Rich grooving to this psychedelic mix of pop, R&B, jazzy rock and blues. The lyrics must have hit a responsive chord with him as Koop sang that no one was going to tell him how to live his life.

∞

As I listened to the song, I saw Rich and his friends just ahead of me, driving in Ginny's van. I recognized the 60's era VW bus by its New Jersey plate. It was covered in mind-blowing peace signs. I knew it had to be them. *But, how could that be possible? Who knew?* I sure didn't. I told myself to "Just Believe."

I followed them in another dimension of time, watching a cloud of smoke billow out the open sunroof.

Sally held her breath and passed a joint to Ken. "Hey Rich, where're we going?"

"We're going to see more wilderness, Sally. Try to keep your dress on. OK?"

"I'll try. Though, we're already deep in the bosom of Mother Nature. You know what urge I get when I'm around her."

Ken nudged Sally with his elbow. "We all know about your urge to get naked. This pot is an awesome way to connect with her, too. It's made with natural ingredients, ain't it?"

Rich wiggled his eyebrows. "It sure is. Give me that joint before it's gone."

Ginny pointed out her window. "Take the next turn for Le Hardy Rapids."

"Sounds like a great first stop. Thank you, my adorable co-pilot."

I followed the psychedelic van down a narrow gravel road. I stopped at the entry to a small dirt lot and watched as Rich parked on the far side. I pulled in beside them, stooping over as if I was rummaging in my glove box. Sally opened the side doors and walked about fifty-feet to a sign beside a foot worn path.

"Hey guys. It says the rapids are a half-mile away. Follow me!"

Ken headed toward Sally in his cut-off jeans, blue tie-dyed tee-shirt, and brown fringe suede ankle boots. "Wait up a sec." Rich and Ginny joined them at the trailhead.

Sally turned and grabbed Ken's hands, walking backwards. "Follow us."

"How can we follow you, if we're all walking backwards?"

"Real funny, Ginny." Sally turned around and put her arm through Ken's walking forward. "How's this?"

"Just fine."

"Did you guys know that these tall trees are called lodgepole pine?" asked Ginny.

"Now, I do," replied Ken. "I remember Mahpee telling us that his Oglala ancestors used them to make teepees."

"Those Native Americans were the best at living off the land. Weren't they?"

"They were far out! I miss Mahpee and Macha. I want to live off the land too," said Rich.

I tracked them from a distance swallowed up within the lodgepole pine forest. My footfalls were silenced by the natural soft cushion beneath me. I crouched down and picked up a needle, examining it. Not one, but two blades connected at a base. I gathered a handful of others and in each case they were the same, as if nature was saying: "I am simple and complex. Observe me and discover you."

161

I was startled when I heard something. I looked up and saw Rich running directly at me. With no time to stand or get out of the way, I arched my back and squeezed my knees together, waiting for the impact. But, it didn't come. Instead, a breeze wrapped around me as he passed. I turned and saw Rich, running away from me. *Whoa! What the hell had I just experienced?* It was so real being there—the smells, sounds, and sights. Yet, somehow I wasn't there. I shook my head and stood in disbelief, facing in the direction Rich just ran. I reached in my pocket and looked at my iPhone. No cell phone bars were displayed. But, today's date read: July 13, 2015. *What the hell was going on? Was one foot in 1970 and the other in 2015?*

Within moments I saw Rich running back toward me. This time, I spread my legs, folded my arms and waited in the middle of the path. Just like before, he kept coming, oblivious to my presence. When he was a few feet in front of me, I shouted, "Stop, Rich!" and extended my hands toward him. He collided into me and this time a faint breeze passed through me.

My perspective changed as I merged with Rich. He turned in a circle, making me dizzy. I saw through his eyes, raised my hand and looked at the ounce of pot I had just got out of the van. I put the plastic bag in my front pocket and continued running. I hurried along the path and caught up with everyone as they stood beside the rapids. They watched as fish swam upstream jumping in the air, landing in an eddy, then, jumping again and again to their unseen destination.

"Hey guys. Look at the black bear and her cub fishing on the other side," said Ken. Fifty feet away a mother bear squatted on a rock, its huge head and paw suspended over the flowing water. A fish jumped and the paw swung, pitching the stunned fish to the ground. The cub pounced and seized the fish in its teeth. When the fish stopped moving, the cub spit it on the ground. Holding it down with its paw, the cub bit it in two. As it raised its head to swallow, the mother bear tossed another dazed fish at the cub's feet.

I heard myself speak in Rich's voice. "I'm going to give it a try, too." The mother bear raised her head, nuzzled her cub and urged it into the woods. I propped myself between two boulders by the water's edge, squinted and gazed below the surface. Balancing on the rocks, I reached an arm into the icy water and pulled out a slimy wiggling fish, waving it in the air. "Damn, I'm good!" I tossed the fish over my head to Ken and reached back into the water. Sally picked up a stone and ran to help Ken who was trying to get a grip on the fish. Within minutes, I threw five more thrashing fish to Ken and Sally.

"Hey guys, Stop!" shouted Ginny. "You have enough. Don't you know they have eggs inside?"

Ken looked at the dead fish. "Bummer. I forgot why fish swim upstream."

I lost my balance when I turned my head and shifted my weight to see the fish sprawled on the ground. I plunged into the frigid water, caught as if in a swirling Jersey Shore riptide. Don't panic, I thought. Just hold your breath and go with the flow. Relax and let the current take you. "Help me Jesus," I whispered.

"Rich! Rich!" Ken screamed, as he ran along the river's edge. He caught up with me and shouted, "Can you swim to shore?"

My head surfaced, I coughed and gasped for breath. I kicked my feet and my sandals slipped off. I doggy paddled with my head barely above the surface. My body was numb and my Moses robe was as heavy as a bag of bricks. I struggled to stay afloat. Ken and Ginny jumped in feet first. Each put an arm around my waist and stroked the water to keep their balance. I tried to stand on the rocky bottom, slipped and wrenched my ankle. It burned like hell. We reached shore collapsing to the ground, shivering and fighting to regain our breath.

When I rolled on my side I saw Rich, Ken and Ginny lying on the ground next to me, like three beached cutthroat trout. I sat up dazed as Sally ran to them. I took a deep breath and exhaled; the fresh mountain air stimulated my mind. I slipped my fingers through my hair and it was dry. *What's going on? Wasn't I just in the river?*

Ginny put her arms around Rich. "Are you OK?"

He rested his head against Ginny and hugged her. "I'm fine."

Ken helped Rich remove his drenched robe. "You're lucky we were here for you."

"Thanks for saving my life."

"We love you man."

Ginny wrapped her arms around Rich's shoulders and pulled him close. "Hey, guys, let's try to remember to be more careful. Rules are much different in the wilderness."

"Right on," said Ken. "Thank you, Jesus. We are grateful for our lives and fresh food. All reminders of your immense generosity."

"Amen," they all said in unison.

Chapter Forty-Eight

The next morning I lay in my sleeping bag and unzipped the front flap of my tent. I saw Rich and his friends sitting on tree-trunk logs around the campfire.

Ginny handed Rich a plate. "Here's your breakfast. Nothing like the smell and taste of bacon and eggs fried in the great outdoors."

"Don't forget fresh brewed coffee."

"I love it all."

"What are we going to do today?" asked Sally. "We could spend a month here and still not see all that Mother Nature has to offer."

Ken spread a map on the ground. "How about if we drive through the canyon to Mammoth Springs? It's about fifty miles."

"By Jersey distances, that's like driving from the shore to Philadelphia. Though I'm cool with it," said Rich.

I shimmied out of my sleeping bag and put on my jeans, tee-shirt and Teva's. I shook my head in amazement that my ankle wasn't injured. I opened my day bag, munched on a granola bar and headed for Ginny's VW bus. Stepping through the side doors, I straddled the middle bench and positioned myself by the window on the rear seat. It seemed surreal to be there with Rich. *Was I a dreamer in Rich's dreamscape? I* shrugged my shoulders and raised my knees against the back of the middle seat. Then, crouched down hoping that they wouldn't sense my presence.

Rich climbed into the driver's seat and turned his head to the open passenger window. "Hop in everyone. It looks like we're going to have another beautiful day in the wilderness."

"Right on, Rich." Ken threw his backpack onto the rear seat beside me. He took Sally's hand and helped her through the doors.

Ginny sat in front with the map and guidebook on her lap. "We're off."

Sally giggled. "No fishing today, Rich."

Ken tapped Rich on the shoulder. "You were lucky that Ginny and I saved you."

Rich looked in the rear view mirror at Ken. "We all were lucky. Weren't we? I loved our trout dinner. But, I'm not going fishing again today."

Ken nodded as he lit a joint and inhaled deeply. He held his breath before exhaling and passing it to Sally.

"The road to the rapids is just ahead," said Ginny. "Don't turn there again, OK?"

Rich continued to drive north on the Loop Road. "Don't worry. I'm not going back there ever again."

"Our map says we're driving through Hayden Valley. Do you see those dark mounds close to the river?" Ginny asked.

"I see them," said Sally. "What are they?"

"The guidebook says they're buffalo, or rather bison. Hundreds of them have been here in the valley since Mahpee's ancestors lived on the plains."

"That's cool," said Rich. "Why are we slowing down? I see a lot of brake lights up ahead."

"I don't know. I guess we'll have to wait and see. Maybe there's an accident."

As we edged forward, I saw a large dark-haired creature standing in the road. Its huge body was covered in matted fur, and it was taller than the cars that surrounded it. Its massive head was shaped like a bull's with curved horns, piercing black eyes and dark nostrils.

"That animal looks angry," said Rich. "I guess it's telling us who's in charge." He followed the line of cars, snaking around the bison, before accelerating. Rich turned down a narrow, winding road after the sign, "Parking for Artist Point Trail." He drove several miles through the forest before parking in a gravel lot. Ken reached over the seat to grab his backpack, opened a side door and followed Sally to the beginning of the trail.

Sally scanned the trail map mounted under the glass of a rustic wooden kiosk. "Hurry up guys. It says this view overlooks the Grand Canyon of the Yellowstone River. It's a short hike to the viewpoint."

Rich held Ginny's hand as they walked to the trailhead under a canopy of lodgepole pine. "We're right behind you."

I followed a short distance from Rich, shadowing him. I approached him from behind matching his footsteps, one for one. I quickened my pace, and when I blended with him, his stream of consciousness enveloped me.

I turned my head, saw Ginny and smiled, squeezing her hand. She smiled back. The wool fibers from Rich's robe scratched my skin. *Just believe,* I reminded myself. I poked Ginny and quickened my steps. "Let's catch up with them." Ginny jogged beside me, pacing my stride until we meet Ken and Sally at trail's end. I stepped onto the promontory awestruck at the magnificence called Yellowstone. I looked up the canyon as if we were suspended in space, absorbed in the sacred silence of my surroundings. A brilliant blue sky touched the horizon, and steep orange rocks framed the vertical landscape. In the distance, the majestic Lower Falls cascaded into the turbulent Yellowstone River.

I looked into Ginny's eyes. "This place is a holy sanctuary and natural cathedral. If this is anything like heaven, I can't wait to get there."

Ginny wrapped her arms around me in a warm embrace. "It sure is beautiful."

Sally and Ken returned to the trail. "Hey, you two! Come on! Next stop is the Boiling River!"

Rich put his arm around Ginny's waist as they headed back to the van.

∞

I continued to gaze in wonder at the natural beauty all around me. After a few moments, two bearded guys with backpacks approached the viewpoint and startled me from my reverie.

I turned and ran for the path. I didn't pass Rich or his friends on my way back to the van. I hope they didn't leave without me.

Chapter Forty-Nine

"Honk! Honk!" Rich blasted the horn and shouted from the driver's seat, "Hurry up you two, or we men will have to leave without you!"

Ginny laughed as she stood by the door and held Sally's arm. "What men? All I see are two boys." I stepped in and climbed over the middle seat just before she closed the door.

"Very funny. We're right here, aren't we Ken?"

Ken looked at Rich, rolled his eyes and shook his head.

Yellowstone's mid-morning weather was still damp and a chilly 40 degrees. It was a good day to soak in nature's hot tub, the Boiling River. Most of Yellowstone's visitors didn't even know it existed, let alone going swimming in it. Well, it wasn't exactly swimming, more like dipping. You know, immersing your body up to your chin and scurrying around on the rocky bottom like a crab dropped into a steaming pot of water. *Sounds like a good time, doesn't it?*

Ginny balanced the guidebook on her seatback. "It says that the Boiling River is actually the Gardner River. It's not really boiling."

Ken shrugged his shoulders. "Why don't they call it the very hot Gardner River?"

Ginny ignored Ken and turned to Rich. "Just follow the sign, 'Mammoth Springs, 25 miles.'"

"The distances in this park are amazing." Rich put Canned Heat's *Living the Blues* album into the tape deck. The rural hippie anthem, "Going Up the Country" played. Rich fantasized about water tasting like wine. Ken took a swig from his bota bag wineskin and passed it around. He lit a joint, took a hit and handed it to Sally.

Ginny tapped Rich's arm. "Pull over by that sign up ahead."

Rich pulled off the road onto the gravel shoulder and stopped adjacent to the sign. "What's so special about this place?"

"It says we're at the '45th Parallel of Latitude.' In other words, we're halfway between the Equator and the North Pole."

"Anyone interested in heading to either of those places?"

"Not me," Ginny replied. "I like where we're heading, the great Southwest. Besides, from here it's only a short distance to the Boiling River."

I followed close behind as they walked along the trail, heading upstream beside the river. We passed through Rocky Mountain juniper and cottonwood before seeing clouds of steam rise above the tall Douglas fir. I was directly behind Rich when he stopped to gaze into the treetops at the swirling puffs of vapor. I collided into him and once again we were as one body enveloped in a sense of peace and tranquility. Damn, I couldn't believe this was happening again.

"Those clouds of steam are far out!" I said. "We must be getting close to the hot springs." I caught Ginny's hand as the trail descended to the water's edge. Only the four of us were there. The cold temperature must have kept everyone else away. This section of the river was narrow: the side closest to us was tranquil with steam rising along the rocky shore. Rocks were piled parallel to the bank, forming a steaming pool that was just right for soaking. Ken held the bota bag over my head and squirted wine into my mouth. Sally opened her mouth for wine, then tiptoed onto the pebbled shore. She raised her dress over her head and placed it on an outcrop of rock. We followed in her footsteps and shed our clothes, too.

Water and steam cascaded over a rocky ledge as I stood naked with my friends on the river's bank. Maybe there was something to be said about shedding my inhibitions along with my clothes. My skin tingled from my toes to my testicles. I crossed my hands in front of my crotch and glanced at Ginny. She was as pure and carefree as Lady Godiva. She took my hand, and we immersed ourselves in the hot spring. We crab crawled along the bottom, searching for warm swirls and hot currents. We ducked under a granite overhang. Streams of water fell on us and we were absorbed in a rainforest.

I reached my arms out, trying to separate the water and found myself aiming Rich's M16. The steady rain permeated every fiber of my being. My salvation; dry feet, deep inside my boots. It was nightfall and I sat rigid in a tree, high above the jungle vegetation. I swallowed hard reminding myself, "Just breathe." I slowly inhaled, held it, and then exhaled, concentrating on each breath. My only other movement, my eyes as they looked down probing from left to right. Two other buddies were with me in the treetops, a short distance away. The rest of our platoon was hidden in the bush. All of our ears and eyes were focused on the trail crossing. We waited in silence. The only motion, water as it dripped from my helmet and trickled down my neck. One droplet, after another, followed the curve of my spine.

I sensed movement coming toward us. Several silhouettes pointed their rifles, swinging them from side to side as they approached the crossroad. Our platoon leader took the first shot. There was an odd sense of quiet in my head. Then I heard Mom, "Close your eyes and what do you see?" A deer? I held my breath and pulled the trigger. One of the shadows dropped to the ground. I took a bead on another shadow close to a flash of light erupting from the side of the trail but couldn't pull the trigger. Within minutes the skirmish was over.

I joined the others to ensure we offed all the enemy. Walking along the trail, I approached my target and its shadow transformed into a slender young man. He had coal black hair shaped in a bowl cut. He was wearing sandals, the soles carved from discarded tire treads. He was dressed in a dark jacket and pajama style pants. The only characteristic distinguishing him from a civilian was his weapon lying beside him. I crouched down and felt his neck for a pulse—nothing. My buddy Rogers stood next to me. "It's a good kill. He had a weapon and was prepared to use it. It was either you or him, Duff."

I looked at Rogers and nodded. I turned the young man face up, his dark eyes stared into nothingness. He looked more like a boy than a man. No facial hair. Just soft, smooth unblemished skin. The only thing unusual about him was a bullet hole in the middle of his chest with an ever-widening blotch of blood surrounding it.

I reached into his jacket pocket and pulled out a small photo. It was of him and a woman, standing side-by-side, smartly dressed and smiling for the camera. Examining the photo more closely I gasped and fell back on my ass. My God. It looked just like a photo I had of me and my wife and on our wedding day. Tears filled my eyes and tremendous pressure bore down on my chest. I took shallow breaths as I got down on my hands and knees beside him. I whispered, "I'm so sorry. Please forgive me."

∞

Ginny pulled Rich from under the cascading water into the sun-drenched hot spring. "Rich! Rich!" she screamed. "Are you alright?"

"No. I'm not. I need to stay here and soak."

I too crawled out from under the protected overhang, my body numb from the pounding of the water and the knowledge of my brother's unceasing nightmare. I lifted a towel from the rocks, wrapped it around my naked body and squinted at the rays of sunlight reflecting off clouds of steam rising into the air. I flinched when the shot from Rich's M16 recoiled in my mind. I too was caught in Rich's horror and was beginning to understand the significance of his burden. Its weight was choking the life out of him. And me, too.

Chapter Fifty

What a difference a good night's sleep could make. I was refreshed after finding a safe place in my mind to bury Rich's Vietnam experience. I turned on the radio, first heard bells, then bongos and couldn't help but sing along with The Rascals about their optimistic sun-filled tune, "It's a Beautiful Morning." As I sang each verse a cloud of despair lifted and my spirits soared into the crisp clear mountain air.

I had been traveling since dawn from Yellowstone to the Grand Tetons National Park. Because of the mountainous terrain, the 120-mile trip took me almost three hours. I was excited knowing that Rich chose this spectacular wilderness region as an important segment of his cross-country trip.

My stomach growled because I hadn't eaten since I broke camp. I took the turn for Jackson Lake Junction and followed my GPS route to The Buffalo Valley Ranch and Café, five miles east of Moran Junction. When I got to Buffalo Valley Road, I ran into a six car traffic jam. Tourists were rubbernecking to take photos of a black bear and cub as they sauntered beside the road, stopping every few yards to eat berries.

I almost missed the rustic sign built from split rail fencing and crowned with a set of Moose antlers. Hanging below it were a chain of hand-painted weathered wood placards: Café, Cabins, Horseback Rides, Gift and Fly Shop, Float Trips and Fishing Trips.

I pulled into the dusty lot of the roadside log cabin. *Nothing for me.*

"I didn't think you needed anything." I opened the door and stepped out.

∞

How was your lunch? Rich asked as I got back in the driver's seat and started the engine.

"Not as good or as much fun as Chili's. But, there isn't one for miles. Besides, I don't think anyone wants a franchise in this small town. Though, I passed for a local in that family-owned eatery."

Rich shook his head. *Sure. Everyone thought you were a townie.*

I adjusted the rear view mirror. "Maybe I didn't exactly blend in wearing my khakis, white golf shirt and Merrell sandals."

No kidding. For once you're being honest with yourself.

I turned and raised my hands palms up. "What do you mean? I'm always honest with myself. Why are you being like this?"

I'm only messing with you.

I ran my hands through my hair. "Can't we just change the subject?"

Sure. How about this one; think back to our first trip in this car. Remember when I found Dad?

I shut off the ignition, threw the keys on the dash and glared at Rich. "Holy shit. Do you think that topic will chill you out? Because it chills me right to the friggin' bone."

What's the matter? Are you afraid to talk about it?

"I don't know. I haven't thought about it for a long time."

Maybe talking about it will do us both some good. You know, we've come full circle—you and me. Here we are again, side-by-side in my GTO.

I lifted my eyebrows and tightened my lips. "Here we are—you and me. Amazing."

It is amazing, bro. Think of it as a do-over. You know. A second chance to do something.

"A second chance?"

Maybe by talking about it we'll see things differently.

"I don't think my opinion of Dad will ever change."

Who knows? Let's give it a try. I know it was a long time ago.

I swallowed hard. "Well, I'm not sure I'm ready, but here goes... When you found Dad, we hadn't seen or heard from him in ten years." I paused. "Ten friggin' years!"

Rich reminisced. *Remember crossing the Pine Barrens on that lonely stretch of single lane highway? Bouncing along and hearing every seam of those fifty miles to nowhere.*

"Yes, I do. That clunk, clunk, clunk joint slap of the old Route 70 concrete highway almost lulled me to sleep. We couldn't find any FM stations." I gave a thumbs up. "Joplin was our salvation."

You're right, man. Put on Joplin. Don't you just love "Piece of My Heart?"

"I love her bluesy voice." I reached down and put Janis Joplin's *Cheap Thrills* album into the tape deck.

Chapter Fifty-One

The music transported me back in time to a place I wasn't sure I wanted to go. Rich was home for a thirty-day leave prior to his one-year deployment to Da Nang, Vietnam. It was great having him around. At times it seemed like he'd never have to leave. But, I knew each day brought him closer and closer to the unknown.

It was the spring of '68 and Rich and I were driving across the state to meet Dad. We were heading west, crossing the Pine Barrens and bumping along the old Route 70 highway. Limbs of scrub pine trees were encroached along the shoulder of both lanes. No one was in front of us and the road was a straight line to the horizon.

I was a high school junior, and at the age of sixteen fantasized about getting my license and buying my own car. Oh yeah, and I dreamed about getting laid for the first time, maybe even in the back seat of it. I yearned to get behind the wheel and drive—nowhere special—just drive. I dreamed of having an intimate girlfriend in the front seat snuggled beside me. I wanted her to care about me as much as I would care about her.

Rich reached into his pocket, threw a book of matches to me and they landed on my lap. "So guess where we're planning to meet him?"

I was annoyed that he interrupted my thoughts. "I don't know, where?" I picked up the matches and fiddled with them.

"We're going to the same place I found him, in a good ole Irish bar."

"Really? You found him in a bar?"

"I wanted to see him before I left for 'Nam. Because I wasn't sure if I'd be coming back in a body bag or not."

"Hell, Rich. I would have been scared stiff if I was going to war. You know I was afraid for you, right?"

"I knew everyone was."

"How did you find him?"

"Last week I drove across Jersey and walked into one Haddonfield bar after another. Wouldn't you know it, I found him sitting on a stool at a place called O'Malley's."

I did a double take of the name on the cover of the matches, O'Malley's. I dropped them on the floor.

Dad's back was to me so I tapped him on the shoulder.

He turned, shrugged his shoulders and said, "Can I help ya?"

"I looked him directly in the eyes and said, 'Do you know who I am?'"

"He shrugged his shoulders. 'No. Should I?'"

"I stood tall in my Marine Corps uniform. 'I'm your son, Rich.'"

"Wasn't that a hell of a shock for him?"

"I wasn't sure if his surprised look was from recognizing me or shitting in his pants."

I chuckled. "Maybe it was a little of both."

"At that moment, I realized that the only person Dad ever cared about was himself." Rich shrugged. "If his life was this car, he would have put gas in it and run it into the ground." He shook his head.

I nodded and bit my cheek. "So, here you are again. Going back to O'Malley's. Sounds like a great place for a family reunion?"

"Our ole man didn't have a clue what a real family was all about. To him, 'home' was between two other guys at the bar."

"Jeez, Rich. What kind of father abandons his five kids? He just vanished from our lives as if he were sucked into a bottle and couldn't get out."

Rich chuckled. "He probably was and he liked it there."

Just thinking of seeing him again made my stomach tighten. It had been ten years without any phone calls, Christmas gifts or birthday cards, let alone any hugs of affection. What would I say after all this time? What would he say to me? I was glad Rich was with me. He'd know what to do.

I followed Rich through the back door of the tavern, overcome with the smell of cigarette smoke and stale beer. I recognized Dad sitting on a barstool, his beer in one hand and a Lucky Strike in the other. A fringe of curly brown hair wreathed his shiny bald head as if it were demarcating the boundary between youth and old age. I didn't know then that this would be the first of three times I'd see Dad over a forty-year period. Each time I saw him he would succeed in disappointing me more and more.

Dad put his beer and cigarette on the bar beside an empty shot glass. "Hey boys. Whatya drinkin'?"

Rich pulled out a pack of Marlboros and sat on a stool beside Dad. "I'll have a draft. No shots for me tonight."

I stood next to Rich, a forced smile on my face. "I'm only sixteen."

"Oh. I guess you'll have a Coke."

"Sure."

Dad lifted his glass off the bar and looked at Rich. "It's good to see ya again, son."

"It's good to see you, too. Two times in two weeks is a world record."

Dad winked at me. "So, ya gonna drink with your ole man?"

I counted to five. "Not really. I just came for the ride in Rich's GTO."

He slapped me on the shoulder. "His car's slick. But, ya know I'm the best driver in the world, dontcha?"

"I guess."

"Yeah, I am. I found that out the year your mother and I got hitched. It was on her 20th birthday. Next thing we knew, your brother Rich came along. My first job was as a stunt car driver with Jack Kochman's Hell Drivers. We rode up and down the east coast from Maine to Florida that year. Every night your Mom would be standing in the pit at a track with Rich on her hip and a Kent in her mouth. She rooted for me because I was the best driver in the show."

"Mom has an old program, signed by all the drivers, in a box with all of our family photos. We kids would look at the program and see you standing beside a stock car. You looked happy." Rich bit his lip in reflection.

"I loved driving. It wasn't work to me because I was good doing tricks with cars; balancing on two wheels, jumping over six wrecks and flying thirty-feet through the air from one ramp to another. Your mom got tired of living out of the trunk and with Rich and all, so we went back to her hometown, Teaneck."

Rich slapped Dad on the shoulder. "It sounds like you got off to a fun start, traveling and being free."

"That first year was a doozie for the three of us. Then, Sue came along. A few years later Danny, Ray and Eileen. Before we knew it, ten years had come and gone and we had seven mouths to feed. I was bouncing from one job to another while your mom took care of you kids."

Rich took a swig of his beer. "I know it wasn't easy."

Dad reached over and tousled his hair. "You were a terror as a kid."

Then, he pointed to me. His smile revealed a void between his front teeth, just like Rich's. "But, you were a good boy, Danny."

Dad grabbed Rich's bicep. "So, you're going to Viet 'Nam. Keep your head down and don't be a hero. There are too many dead heroes if you ask me."

"I will, Dad."

I put my hand on Rich's shoulder and looked him in the eye. "I'll pray for you every night, Rich."

He pulled me close. "You may also want to pray that you go to college. You'll be much better off."

It was clear to me that not everyone's brother returned from Vietnam. I was frightened for Rich even though he displayed his signature sense of being calm and in control. I hoped to hell that someday I wouldn't have to fight in the war, too. Later that night I hardly slept hearing Dad's raspy voice, "Keep your head down, son. Just keep your head down."

Chapter Fifty-Two

Rich and Dad remained at the bar, drinking and chain smoking. I headed to a darkened corner, picked up a few darts and played a solitary game, waiting for Rich to give me the high sign. Someone kept putting one quarter after another into the jukebox, replaying Creedence Clearwater Revival's "Fortunate Son." All I could think about was how the lyrics of that song related to me and Rich.

It was after ten when Rich nodded in my direction. "We better get going. We got a long ride ahead."

I shook Dad's hand but avoided his eyes. "See you." I walked back down that darkened hallway hoping I'd never see his sorry ass again. My stomach was queasy from inhaling his constant stream of smoke. *Why didn't he ask me how I was doing in school or work?* It was all about him. I'm glad Rich sat next to him at the bar, not me.

I was tired, but perked up when we stepped out of the bar into fresh air and Rich asked me to drive. "You know, I've been dying to get behind the wheel of your GOAT since the first time I saw it. Can we take the top down? It's a beautiful night; I could use fresh air after three hours in there."

Rich slouched in the passenger seat, reached under the dash and flipped a switch for the convertible top. "Sure am glad you can drive, because I sure can't."

With my recently-issued drivers permit in my wallet, my driver's ed training kicked into gear. I adjusted the driver's seat, buckled up and glanced at the rally tach dash. My friend Tony had shown me how to drive a four speed. I started the engine, gripped the four on the floor, put it in first and slowly released the clutch. I gave it some gas, then shifted through

181

second, third and fourth. We were on our way home, the headlights piercing the pitch black darkness of the night.

The damp evening breeze cascaded over the top of the windshield. Rich slurred... "What did you think about our visit?"

"It was surreal. He was a total stranger, and I couldn't relate to anything he said. All he talked about was himself. I wondered why we had come in the first place. He's never come to see us."

"Seeing Dad was that good, huh?"

"One thing caught me by surprise. I was amazed to hear Dad say, 'Your mother was a wonderful woman to have raised the five of you all by herself.'"

"He left out the part about Mom and us not getting any cash from his cheap ass."

"Was he trying to apologize when he told us, 'It was me who screwed up. I couldn't get my drunk ass off the bar stool long enough to be the father your mother wanted me to be.'" The corners of my mouth turned down. "Do you think that was what Dad learned during the past ten years of being out of our lives?"

"Who knows? He seemed glad to see us, but all he did was sit on that bar stool all night. I should've known I was drinking and smoking out of my league." Rich sprawled in the passenger seat.

"Do you think he ever tried to find us?"

This question had plagued me for years. *Why wouldn't he have tried to locate or at least talk with us?* All he had to do was get our phone number from Gram or Uncle Ed and Aunt Eleanor. They would have given it to him. *What else was so important to him other than contact with his kids?* Well, I really knew the answer to that.

"Hell no, brother. First off, you can generally tell what someone thinks is important by how he spends his time. Not much of Dad's time was spent at home. I'm pretty sure he didn't give a shit about us. Come to think of it, I'm more than pretty sure, I'm certain."

No other cars were visible in either direction. I yawned and reminded myself to keep my eyes wide open, focused on the moving path of light just in front of us. I cracked open the butterfly window. "Do you ever wonder what Dad thought about at times like the beginning of school, our birthdays, Christmas?"

"Your guess is as good as mine. He probably did the same thing he did every day—drink. He may not have had his family, but he had his constant companion."

Maybe he needed to drink to erase his memories and deaden his pain. *Did he look at his reflection in the mirror and see an image of a lonely broken man?* I hoped so. The night was as dark as a cave that we seemed to be exploring deeper and deeper.

I glanced at Rich, encompassed in shadow. His body lit up from headlights of an oncoming car as it approached, then, became cloaked in darkness as the car passed by. "Aren't kids supposed to look up to their fathers?"

"Hell, yeah! Some kids even see their dads as heroes."

My jaw tightened and I ground my teeth. "My hero?"

"Guess not. Maybe he thought he did the best he could."

I yawned and wiggled my jaw. Isn't it more important what other people, especially his family saw in him? That's how I think his life should be judged."

Rich lay his head back on the seat. "Don't worry. He'll be judged someday, and he'll pay a hell of a price."

"Right." I peeked over at Rich; he was passed out, his head turned toward me with eyes half-open and mouth half-shut.

I drove alone for the rest of our ride home from the bar and thought about Rich's "do-over" comment. *Had my opinion of Dad changed?* Not really. *Had it been worth my time to visit him?* I didn't think so. *Would I want to do it again?* Hell, no.

Just before Route 70 forked to the north, I pulled onto the shoulder of the road, got out and walked to the rear of the car. I leaned against the trunk straining to look back and recall the past—the route we had just traveled. But, it was gone.

Before I knew it, Rich shipped out to Vietnam. I had no idea when, or if, I would ever see him again. I certainly could not have predicted the impact that year would have on him.

∞

"Hrrnnaha. Hrrnnaha. Hrrnnaha." I was startled by six horses and riders as they trotted single-file past the car along a path leading to the Buffalo Valley Ranch. I knew I was just a few miles from the Grand Tetons National Park. But, I wasn't feeling motivated to leave the café parking lot just yet.

Chapter Fifty-Three

I didn't care if visitors saw me in the GTO when they entered the Buffalo Valley Ranch Café and then again when they exited. I slouched in the driver's seat as beer-stained scenes of our bar room visit with Dad surfaced. Maybe I'd get reenergized if I took down the top? I unlocked the roof hinges, reached under the dash and flipped the switch. "Hmmm. Hmmm. Hmmmpp." The top folded into its storage well, the midday sun's rays beat down, and I began to sweat. I put on my Red Sox cap and sunglasses.

How about some music?

I turned on the AM radio and scanned stations until one came in clear. Bobby Vinton sang his oldie, but goodie, "Mr. Lonely." I had heard the song several times before but never concentrated on the lyrics until that day. I've had the same experience with other songs, too. "Did you ever feel that way, Rich?"

If you mean was I lonely in 'Nam half a world away from home? The answer is "yes." When I returned everything had changed and I was even lonelier.

After Rich's discharge he stayed out late and seldom slept in his own bed.

That's right, man. I couldn't sleep then and can't sleep now. When I do, I'm spooked by bad dreams.

"Honk! Honk!" A trucker blasted his air horn at a driver who had slowed down to turn into the Café's parking lot. Rich took a deep breath, peered straight ahead and stopped his erratic hand motions. Then, he closed his eyes and they flitted behind his eyelids, a telltale sign that he was having another episode. I could only imagine what he was dealing with.

∞

He was in the back seat of a cab as the driver zig-zagged his way through the Holland Tunnel. When the cabbie emerged at the NYC end and cut in front of a truck, Rich was startled by an air horn blast. "Pull over," he said. He paid the tab and jumped out as the cab was rolling to a stop at Varick Street. He ran to the Canal Street Subway Station, hopped down the escalator and vaulted over the turnstile. His knees buckled and he struggled to catch his breath. He looked at the map and turned in a circle. Which train should I take? He boarded the first one, a deserted M1 uptown train. He heard the clackety-clack of steel wheels as they crossed the seams.

His heart fluttered and vision blurred as the conductor announced: Houston Street, Christopher Street, 14th Street, 18th Street, 23rd Street, and 34th Street-Penn Station. "Finally!" He stood, looked around and saw that he wasn't the only person onboard. A man in a hooded black sweatshirt was at the back of the subway car. As the train approached the platform, Rich inched toward the door. Out of the corner of his eye he saw that the man mirrored his movements. Rich's legs were wobbly and his palms were sweaty as he stepped onto the empty, poorly lit platform. He turned hoping to find someone, besides the man who had stepped off behind him.

With each step forward he repeated, "Follow the Arrow to the Exit, Follow the Arrow to the Exit." Damn. The escalator was broken. He began a step-by-step ascent of the stairway. He saw light at the top, but his feet wouldn't propel him faster than a crawl, as if he were trudging uphill through mud. He urged himself onward, "Just one more step. Just one more step." His hands grasped both sides of the railing, and he pulled himself to the last step. "Phew!" He took a deep breath and turned to get off the stairway when the hooded man slammed into him. He tumbled backwards, hitting the stairs with each flip of his body, until he lay bloody and broken at the bottom.

∞

"Wake up, Rich," I screamed.

Rich gasped for air, shook his head and his brown eyes brightened from cloudy to clear. *Where am I?*

"You're here with me. Brother Dan."

He nodded and looked my way. *Thank God.*

"Holy shit, Rich. That's one hell of a nightmare."

He let out a sigh. *It scares the hell out of me every time I have it.*

"Who the hell is that guy, and why he is he after you?"

Chapter Fifty-Four

Rich looked at me and clutched my shoulder. *He was a boy, like me. One of the VC I killed.*

"You didn't have a choice. Did you?"

No. It was kill or be killed. After that, my hands started shaking every time we had to go out on patrol, as if I knew by the end of the day I might be dead.

Rich slumped in the passenger seat, closed his eyes and found himself back in Vietnam.

∞

The Vietcong had an underground maze of tunnels and fortifications throughout Vietnam to hide their Ops in the light of day. All over the jungle there were hidden entryways to their underground world. Rich and his squad were dropped about ten miles into enemy territory, walking single file and scanning their M16 rifles. He looked ahead, gazed right, then left and stopped every ten steps to turn and glance behind. His jaw began to tremble as he imagined a sniper camouflaged in a distant tree with his head in the crosshairs.

When a squad of eight Vietcong appeared about twenty feet from the trail, Rich's squad slammed to the ground and began crawling toward the enemy, until they reached a small clearing. The VC had disappeared.

The Squad Leader stood and motioned for everyone to remain still. He poked his bayonet into the ground, turning over jungle vegetation until he struck something that sounded like a knife thrown into a wooden door. He raised his hand while using his bayonet to turn over a small wooden hatch. He bent down into a kneeling position with his rifle pointing into a tunnel. He motioned for Rich to kneel beside him.

"You're our Forward Observer Duffy. So, I want you to shimmy into the tunnel and look around."

Rich's stomach curled into a tight knot. "Yes sir. Can I take my rifle, Sir?"

"Leave your helmet and rifle behind. Keep your sidearm holstered."

Rich was too scared to refuse. All he could think about was how he could possibly get to his gun. "Yes sir."

"The rest of the men will crawl behind you forming a human chain."

Rich took off his helmet and placed it on the ground next to his rifle. "Yes sir," he repeated for the third time.

He tried not to think about the tight quarters despite the dank fetid earthiness all around him. He took short shallow breathes, his lungs squeezed against his ribcage. He pulled himself along, and his fingers bled as he scratched into the dirt for handholds. He saw a ray of light on the ground ahead and realized it was from a small bamboo pipe that breeched the surface to allow air into the passageway. The tunnel widened enough for him to crawl with his elbows tucked beside his body. It was pitch dark just beyond his field of vision. He sensed, rather than saw movement advancing toward him as if he were tied to a rail bed with a train approaching in the dead of night.

Rich's mind went into overdrive. There were so many things to think about in so little time. He couldn't back out and couldn't go forward. He wanted a weapon but couldn't reach his side arm or knife. He felt a slight movement of air against his cheek and put his nose to the ground. Bam! He and the enemy collided, and all he could do was raise his head and scream, "GOOK! GOOK! GOOK!" Rich was eyeball to eyeball with the VC and could smell his spicy breath. He sneered and Rich sneered back, head bumping him. The VC spit in Rich's face. Then, Rich bit off the VC's nose and spit it on the ground. The VC's eyes flared when he saw his blood gushing onto Rich's face.

A bloody scream erupted in the tunnel. Rich realized it was coming out of his mouth. He kicked his feet and two hands surrounded his ankles. He was pulled out of the abyss puking at the sight of what he had done. All along the passageway Rich retched a half dozen more times, mostly bile and dry heaves. When he was finally pulled into the open, he gasped for air trying to wipe blood out of his nose. A Corpsman poured water over Rich's head and took off his tee-shirt to wipe Rich's face of blood, sweat and vomit. Rich curled into a fetal position, wrapped his arms around his knees and began rocking.

∞

"Rich? Rich?" I screamed. "Wake up!"

Rich's body jerked as he opened his eyes and shook his head.

"Are you OK, Rich?"

What? Yeah. I'm OK.

I shook my head. "God..." My hands trembled and beads of sweat surfaced on my forehead.

You know what? Afterwards, no one asked me what happened in that dark tunnel. So, I never told anybody.

"I'm so sorry..." I covered my face with my hands and gagged. Then, opened the door and barfed fragments of my lunch on the Café parking lot. I gulped a mouthful of warm water, swished it around and spit it on the ground. I wiped my mouth with my arm and looked Rich in the eyes. "War really was hell, wasn't it?"

Yeah. I had to go back on patrol, too. They didn't give a shit about me in that hell hole.

I took a swig of water and swallowed hard. "You had to go out again?"

Everyone had to. I don't know how I did it...

Drums, bongos and a cowbell beat from the rear speakers introducing Santana's, "Evil Ways." "Dun, dun, dot, do, do, do..."

I put my hand on Rich's shoulder and squeezed. "I don't know how you did it either. Brother, you know I love you, right?"

DAN DUFFY

Chapter Fifty-Five

I couldn't shake the gruesome scene of Rich in the tunnel. I drove south toward my destination, Signal Mountain, twenty-five miles away. I was quiet for the rest of the morning's ride. But, my stomach felt like a tightly-coiled spring. I watched for possible turnoffs in case my stomach cramps erupted into more spasms of puking. I opened a can of orange seltzer and took small sips that tingled in my mouth and throat. When the can was empty, I belched and let out a sigh.

My spirits brightened when I entered the national park of the most majestic mountain range in North America, the Grand Tetons. I fell in love with them during a college photography course. Ansel Adams black and white image of *The Teton Range from the Snake River Overlook* introduced me to the spirit of the wilderness. I was captivated by the magnificence of the rugged snow-crusted mountains framed by the winding Snake River—nature depicted in stunning shades of black, white and grey.

Just outside of Jackson Lake Junction, I saw the turn for Summit Road, took it and downshifted into second. I followed the steep narrow road as it threaded through the dense forest in its ascent to the peak. The mountain air flowed over the windshield and buffeted my face. I couldn't help but smile. "Hey Rich. Do you think a stunning view of Mother Nature will perk us up?"

I hope so. There's nothing better than to see God's creation from a mountaintop.

I pulled into the overlook parking lot and stood on top of a dry-stacked wall. I was overcome with the beauty and sheer majesty of the panoramic view. It left me breathless.

I'm blessed to be here with you. But are you a believer?

"I believe in a lot of things...the great outdoors...being with you on our trip. Though, I'm not the same kind of believer as you."

Too bad. Maybe one day you'll become a true believer.

I shook my head knowing that I would never be able to bridge the spiritual chasm that separated us. I just didn't believe in surrendering control of my life to something outside myself. My mantra had always been, "If it was to be, it was up to me." We sat beside the trail meditating with eyes open, enveloped in Mother Nature's womb of peace and tranquility.

The prevailing winds in the Grand Teton Valley were from the southwest. Yet, a summer storm was beginning to brew in the east.

"Rich, I've been meaning to tell you something."

What's that?

"When Mom told me that Diane left you, I couldn't believe it. How could she? I was so angry. I went straight to my room, fell on the bed and cried in my pillow."

∞

Eric Clapton's guitar and Jack Bruce's lead in Cream's, "In a White Room" blasted from my bedroom speakers. I listened to the lyrics and sensed myself spiraling down into a vast darkened tunnel. I didn't know if I was crying for Rich or for me, or for both of us. I loved Diane too. Now she was gone.

My sadness was fragmented with memories of joy. Rich's life and mine had changed for the better, after he began dating her. We cleaned up our outward appearance and masked our impoverished background, which also seemed to transform our inner sense of ourselves. Rich wasn't as restless, became more patient and soft spoken. I tried to emulate him.

It was late afternoon before I decided to stop wallowing in my anguish. I got out of bed and dried my eyes on my sleeve. I put on Rich's bright orange USMC boot camp tee-shirt, drove downtown to Main Street and parked behind a historic home that housed Toms River Title Search. My palms were clammy as I clenched the wheel, staring at the back door. I knew it was Diane's boss because he was the last to leave. He locked the door and strode toward the only other car in the lot—a big, black four-door Lincoln Continental.

I stepped out of my Corvair convertible with my stomach as tight as my fist. I made a direct path to intercept him on his way to the car. When he saw me, he quickened his pace. Reaching his car, he got inside and clicked the doors and windows shut. He looked out his window at me, like a trapped rat, staring at the four-inch letters across my chest—USMC. I really didn't know what I was doing there or what I was going to do next. I'm not sure what overcame me because I glared at him and began beating his window with my fist. My right hand began to throb so I stood there giving him the evil eye thinking, *Why didn't I bring my bat?*

Tears began to stream down my cheeks. "How could you do this?" I shouted. "You bastard! You stole my brother's wife when he was off fighting in the war."

He leaned forward and cracked open the butterfly window. "I didn't mean to hurt your brother or your family."

"But, you did! God damn you! I can't wait for Rich to get home. He's gonna kick your ass!"

He started his car, put it in reverse and backed away. I walked next to it, continuing to glare at him. I raised my fists, this time hitting both against his window. I lifted my middle fingers, a pane of glass separated my hands from his face. "Fuck you!" I sneered, curling my lip. He shifted to drive and peeled away.

I was lightheaded as I walked back to my car. I stopped, put my hands on my knees, took a few deep breaths and picked up a stone. I tossed it from one hand to another before looking at it in my palm. His fucking face seemed to be looking back at me. I gripped and stretched my arm back throwing it high in the air. I watched it arch toward the house. When I heard glass shatter, I knew it hit its mark. "Take that you bastard." I smiled and hoped that tomorrow morning he'd see a reminder of my visit sitting in the middle of his office.

Holy shit. You did that for me? Thanks.

∞

Rich's eyes glazed over while the Jimi Hendrix hard rock song "Hey Joe" boomed from the car stereo. *It was a bitch being alone in my bunker after reading her letter. You know what's funny? I thought I could go away for a year, come back and pick up where we left off. But, it wasn't going to happen. In an instant, my life changed and I didn't give a shit if I lived or died.*

∞

Rich knew his marriage was dead, like a copter pilot struggling with the pitch control knew impact was inevitable. In the weeks that followed, he became detached, his mind disjointed from his body, his actions disassociated from his conscience. He shadowed his hooch mate Newman, day and night, just going through the motions. One day he stood with his squad in front of another nameless Ville. Directly in his path were four thatched huts tied together with palm leaves and bamboo. Someone shouted, "Mad Minute." Rich and his buddies opened fire with everything they had for two or three minute's straight. Rich shot his anger out the barrel of his M16. Someone cried, "Cease fire," but Rich kept his finger on the trigger until his clip was spent. Silence was the only sound as flames leapt from hut-to-hut illuminating the night and obliterating lives once lived.

∞

Rich came back from the bush of Da Nang and looked at me. There was nothing I could say as the sky darkened. I started the car. A bolt of lightning streaked across Signal Mountain followed by a loud thunderclap. We were pelted by raindrops the size of M16 bullets as the storm front passed.

Rich touched my shoulder. *You know something? Afterwards, I was never the same.*

I looked at Rich tight-lipped, nodded and turned the tape deck on. We drove in silence, tormented by Three Dog Night's haunting lyrics to their song, "One."

Chapter Fifty-Six

I sat beside the campfire and west of me the spectacular Teton Range rose knife edged from the valley floor. South, Middle and Grand Teton peaks jutted two and a half miles into the sky. I whispered, "sacred, revered, spiritual" as I opened Rich's journal to his next entry,

Day #29, July 19, 1970 (Grand Teton National Park, Signal Mountain Campground)
At sunrise I visited the Chapel of the Transfiguration, sacred ground with spectacular views of towering mountains. It was just like the Bible story, from Luke, when Jesus was illuminated, his body radiated light from a thousand suns. Rays of sunlight streamed to me from heaven as I prayed in the chapel. And just like in Luke, I believed the voice of God when he said, This is my beloved son. Hear him.

My body flinched when I heard a branch snap in the woods just beyond my campsite. I held my breath, closed the journal and turned on my flashlight. A mule deer with nubs as antlers was foraging among the bushes. It ignored me, turned and strutted off. It was getting late, so I found a stick and spread the glowing remnants of my fire. I watched the embers pulse as they were fanned from the breeze. I decided that tomorrow would have to be an early start if I wanted to see the sun rise from the chapel, just like Rich.

Hours later in near darkness, I followed a path through an arched wooden gate and covered bridge. I pictured early settler families on horse-drawn wagons as they arrived for church. Inside the log cabin chapel I sat on a rough-sawn bench that served as a pew. One end was pressed against a log wall; the other framed a center aisle. Saplings provided back support and reminded congregants of the beauty and function of nature. There were no stained glass windows or images of Jesus, only a simple wooden cross centered on the altar. This was indeed a holy shrine.

I saw Rich in his Moses robe shuffling down the aisle. He held his head high captivated by the radiant rays of light streaming through a picture window centered in the front wall. He stopped before the altar and gazed out at the regal sun—lit peaks of the Grand Tetons. A low layer of clouds blanketed the tops of white river birch and lodgepole pine surrounding the foothill free range.

Rich dropped to his knees in prayer. *Only God could create such a masterpiece.*

I stood beside him, looked at the horizon and watched the sky as it turned from garnet to orange, then bright yellow. I placed my hand on his shoulder and sensed Rich's sentiment of God's presence and grace.

My focus shifted from the peaks to the valley floor as the scene faded. I became aware of sagebrush dominating the landscape amid wildflowers, streaks of yellow, purple and gold. I glanced down, but Rich was no longer kneeling beside me. I turned, fell on my knees and whispered, "Come back, Rich. Come back." But no one was there except me and utter silence.

Chapter Fifty-Seven

It was quiet during my half-hour ride back to Signal Mountain Campground. No radio. No tape. No Rich. The imposing Tetons reminded me how small and insignificant I really was. *"Larger than life" came to mind as an apt description of the wilderness, but was I becoming a true believer because of it?* Well, if believing in a higher power meant being astonished by the beauty of nature—its rugged mountains, crystal clear rivers, lakes and infinite sky, then, yes, I was a true believer. That was the only point where Rich's and my spiritual beliefs intertwined.

I pulled into my campsite overlooking Jackson Lake, put down the top and the scent of evergreen floated through the air. I was overcome with a sense of being alone in a forest and isolated in the midst of this wild and uninhabited territory.

Don't worry, Danny. I didn't abandon you.

Hearing Rich's voice again, I let out a sigh. "It's lonely here."

But you're not alone. You've got friends everywhere.

"You're right. Lately I've been immersed so much in nature that I haven't thought enough about my family and friends."

Put on Joe Cocker. He'll remind you of what matters.

I played the title cut of Joe Cocker's album, *With a Little Help from My Friends.* I first heard him sing the song live the summer after I graduated high school.

"Do you remember the summer of '69, Rich?"

Absolutely. I got back from 'Nam earlier that spring. I was done with being a Marine, but they wouldn't discharge me until my time was up. So, I went AWOL. They caught me, cut off my hair and threw me in the brig for thirty-days. Right before I was discharged the VA Doctors told me the shaking in my hands would go away if I took their medicine.

"Did the medicine help?"

Hell, no! That stuff made me feel like I was sleepwalking in the middle of the day. Besides, I didn't want their poison in my body.

"So let me get this straight. You didn't want the VA's substances in your body, but pot and acid were OK?" His logic just didn't sit right with me.

They helped me forget the past and opened my eyes to the future.

"Really? Did anything else help you?"

My Bible. It was with me everywhere I went. I read it and preached the word of Jesus to anyone who would listen. I got by with a little help from my friends, too. Just like Joe Cocker.

I'm glad the Bible brought Rich comfort; however, when he returned from the war, his continual quoting of scripture had annoyed me. I learned to half-listen to his rants. He kept warning me to accept and be saved by Jesus because the Day of Judgment was soon to arrive. I made no effort to confront Rich about the effect drugs were having on him. The brother I had known before he left for Vietnam had disappeared, and I didn't have a clue how to get him back or how to help him.

Play it again, will you? Don't you love it?

"I sure do." Even though Rich and I were worlds apart on many levels, we connected on one: rock and roll music. "Do you remember seeing Joe Cocker on stage that summer?"

At the AC Pop Festival. Rich's eyebrows arched and his mouth formed a Cheshire-like smile.

"What's so funny?"

Well, did it really exist? Most people don't think so. Because two weeks later Woodstock happened and that's the only thing everyone remembers.

"Of course it existed. We were there."

Chapter Fifty-Eight

A few weeks before graduation, my friend Stu asked if I wanted to go to a weekend concert at the Atlantic City Racetrack. I wasn't sure what I'd be getting into. I knew he smoked weed with some of his neighborhood friends, but he had never pressured me to join him. I figured it would be OK.

"Who's playing?" I asked.

Stu's long, black curly hair skimmed over his shoulders as he turned to face me. "Just about every band you ever heard of."

I raised my hands in the air. "The Beatles?"

He shook his head. "Just about I said but not every fucking band is gonna be there. Try again."

"How about The Byrds? You like 'Mr. Tambourine Man', right?"

"Yep."

"Chicago Transit Authority? John turned us on to 'Does Anyone Really Know What Time It Is.'"

"Yep."

"How about Three Dog Night? 'Eli's Coming...'"

"Stop! I didn't ask you to sing their song. But, you're right. Look at this." He took a flyer out of his back pocket, unfolded it and handed it to me.

I scanned the list of over thirty acts. "Wow!" I didn't know all of the bands, but I loved Janis Joplin and Joe Cocker. "I'm in."

"We could pitch tents at a campground."

"Sounds good to me. Who else is going?"

Anthony said he'll drive us. Did you know he's got a '60 four-door Benz? You'll feel like a diplomat when you're riding in the car with him."

"Sounds good." I did an air drum roll and hit an invisible cymbal. Stu looked at me and shook his head.

∞

The Friday morning of the concert weekend Stu and I left our cars in front of Anthony's house. We threw our sleeping bags and backpacks in his trunk. I brought a change of clothes. Who would've known that a shower wouldn't be an option. Maybe everyone but me.

On the ride down, we listened to a tape of The Band. I hoped to hear "Up on Cripple Creek" played live sometime over the next few days. It wasn't a long drive, first south on the Garden State Parkway and then west on the Atlantic City Expressway. Anthony hit the brakes hard as the racetrack exit turned into a single-lane parking lot. "Where'd all this traffic come from?"

We were entering the Pine Barrens where there were usually only trees, but this time there was an endless line of bumper-to-bumper vehicles ahead of us. We crept along as if we were day trippers schlepping to Seaside Park for a day at the Shore. As we inched along the roadway, I was amazed to see one painted neon psychedelic van after another parked along the shoulder. Many had American flags draped over their side and rear windows. We finally arrived after three hours and parked in a grassy field. Within minutes, we were boxed in by countless other cars parking erratically around us.

"Looks like we can forget about camping in Mays Landing," Anthony said. "We're not going anywhere until the concert's over."

"It'll be cool," said Stu. We all got out and joined hundreds of other concert goers.

"Guess we follow the crowd." Jeez, I thought. *What the hell am I doing here with all these long-hairs?*

Chapter Fifty-Nine

Rich punched me in the arm, startling me back to my driving. I heard Steppenwolf's "Born to Be Wild" blaring from the speakers. *You were the Jack Nicholson dude in Easy Rider.*

I was the straight guy who wore jeans and a tee-shirt with no socks and penny loafers. My Princeton haircut and lack of side burns set me apart from the crowd.

I bet everyone you saw was a long hair.

"Never saw so many hippies in one place. Guys with beards and girls with long flowing dresses and flowers in their hair. Everyone was giving me the peace sign and smiling."

They were happy because of the drugs.

"I wasn't looking for drugs, but that weekend was an eye opener for me. Sure, I knew about pot, but everything was there—acid, hash, peyote. Guys and girls were walking around like zombies.

∞

Each day we sat in the grandstand, giving us a view above and in front of the stage. One act after another played without delay because the middle of the stage rotated, allowing one band to set up while the other performed. Friday night Chicago Transit Authority played "Only the Beginning" and Procol Harum sang "A Whiter Shade of Pale." On Saturday, Jefferson Airplane played "White Rabbit" and the Byrds sang "Turn, Turn, Turn." On Sunday I loved when Canned Heat played "Goin Up The Country" and Three Dog Night sang "Easy to Be Hard."

At night there were campfires all around the field we had parked in. The smell of smoke was laced with the sweet aroma of marijuana. We opened cans of Spaghetti O's, Chef Boyardee ravioli and Dinty Moore stew and put them in the coals of a nearby campfire. Anthony balanced the sizzling hot cans with two pieces of kindling and dumped them out on paper plates.

Stu disappeared for a few hours. When he returned I didn't need to ask him what he'd been doing. He smelled like a mix of the smoke that was in the air. I wasn't tempted to experiment with drugs that weekend because I saw how they were screwing up Rich's life. I wasn't willing to take the same risk.

Anthony said we could sleep in his car. Stu crammed his pillow between the front bucket seats, unrolled his sleeping bag and lay it on top. I was so hot I stripped down to my underwear and crawled onto my bedroll on the massive rear bench seat. Anthony squeezed into the trunk—his feet hanging halfway over the bumper. Throughout the night, I heard people stumbling between vehicles as they went from one campfire to another. Music played from car stereos as the soundtrack to the day's events.

Chapter Sixty

What a contrast. Reminiscing about classic rock and roll music from '69 while being with Rich amid the deafening silence of the wilderness. He and I continued our conversation into the past.

Well, I had a fucking fantastic time, he said. *It was a three-day coming out party for me. My freak flags were flying. I had two firsts that weekend. I dropped L.S.D.— psychedelic, man. I was so high, tripping for three days and nights. The music came alive right before my eyes.*

Even though Jimi Hendrix didn't play that weekend, I heard him singing about Rich. "Are You Experienced?" "I saw a lot of starry-eyed hippies strung out like you. So, what was your other first?"

I had a threesome in a van.

"A threesome?"

Sex with two women, man.

"I know what it is." I just couldn't believe it, and maybe I was a little jealous, too.

It's true, Rich continued. *Judy was a chick from California, visiting her cousin Denise. They heard about the festival and just had to be there. Judy's van was a sex machine with a built in bed from side to side. I never knew sex could be so good on psychedelics.*

I shook my head and looked away from Rich. "Oh, Really?"

At first we were all sitting in a field, stoned and listening to the music. Next thing I knew both chicks asked me to join them in the van. I didn't know what I was in for, but

206

my eyes lit up when I stepped inside and saw they were already bare assed. They stripped me, laid me on the bed and climbed on top. We were up most of the night, screwing our brains out. I tried to keep the beat of the music that was playing, but couldn't. Who the hell could have sex to Iron Butterfly's "In-A-Gadda-Da-Vida?"

I laughed at that image. "It's probably why I didn't see you that weekend."

We hardly left the van, Rich scratched his scalp and shook his head. *We did it in more combinations than I ever thought possible. It was quite a scene and a weekend I'll never forget.* Rich seemed pleased with himself as he sat back in the passenger seat.

"I guess it's true what they said about free love in the '60's?"

Free it was. You were too straight to get any tail, but any hippie chick would have parted her legs for you, Rich chided.

"Really?"

True hippies lived their lives in body and soul. We accepted and loved one another and our spirits soared as one. When we were together we could become anything we wanted to: a flower, snowflake, star, rainbow or a musical note that blended into a kaleidoscope of color.

He was really painting me a psychedelic image with his acid talk. "That doesn't sound anything like me."

Amen. You needed to find yourself a nice college girl to get your Willie wet.

I looked at Rich and nodded. "I eventually did."

Rich's mouth turned up in a half-smile. *Hey, I heard you were stoned the whole weekend, too.*

I didn't take anything that weekend or since. I was afraid if I got stoned my life would morph into Rich's. That was the last thing I wanted to happen to me.

Too bad. You missed a chance to kiss the sky.

Chapter Sixty-One

"Boom, Ba. Boom, Ba. Do, do, do... Do, do, do..." The opening chords of Jimi Hendrix playing "Purple Haze" began to pound through my skull. I didn't need to kiss the sky. I liked solid ground beneath my feet. I was at the concert to enjoy the music, not to screw up my life. I had dreams of going to college in the fall.

That was your choice, not mine. So what if you were straight. Who cared? I didn't. Did you dig it? Joplin, Cocker, Canned Heat, Creedence and all the rest. It was heavy man.

I still remember Janis Joplin singing on stage in her tight purple pants, dancing with her back to the audience and boogying with her Kozmic Blues Band. I expanded my taste in music. Before that weekend, I hadn't even heard of groups like Santana, Iron Butterfly, Chambers Brothers or BB King. Yet, there I was, seeing them perform live.

It was a real happening. So many people from all over America hanging out with each other, just listening to great music.

"They were hanging out all right. I saw guys climb light towers holding on tight while grooving to the music. Girls were swimming naked in the racetrack infield lake and jumping up and down with a lot of soft white body parts bouncing all around."

Their skin was as white as some of the day-trippers we used to see on their first day at the beach, joked Rich.

"Even the chicks who wore clothes were fun to watch, braless in their tee-shirts. I didn't know any girls from high school who let it all hang out like those girls did."

See what you missed? Hippie chicks were everywhere that summer—on the boardwalk, in head shops and at concerts.

"Speaking of concerts. Did you go to Woodstock two weeks later?"

What's that man? Another festival on a farm in upstate NY? With Hendrix and The Who. I wanted to go, but couldn't catch a ride. What a bummer.

"I didn't go to Woodstock either. I enjoyed the music in AC but knew I wouldn't be able to handle another weekend of free spirits, drugs and sleeping in the car," I confessed.

So what if I didn't get to Woodstock. I enjoyed the hell out of my AC weekend. It was far out! Many of my friends never even heard about it. Too bad, they missed out on a real trip.

"What can I say? As straight as I was, I was lucky to have been there, and I'll never forget it."

Do you know what I remember most about that weekend?

"The drugs? The sex? The music?" I offered.

When I woke up Sunday morning, it was raining. The sun broke through the clouds, and it dawned on me. I didn't have any 'Nam nightmares the whole weekend.

"Well, that was good."

I figured if marijuana and acid could drive away my demons, I'd have to do them more often.

I wondered why it hadn't occurred to me before that Rich was self-medicating to ease his pain. He never told me back then what he had gone through in Vietnam or how abandoned he felt when Diane left him. It just wasn't what brothers talked about, but I wish we had. The drugs he took were illegal but helped him cope. *Isn't that what he and I were both trying to do with our lives—deal with the circumstances we faced as best we could?*

I nodded at Rich as the Byrds song, "Turn, Turn, Turn" reverberated through my mind.

Chapter Sixty-Two

Hours passed and I pushed back the driver's seat to stretch my legs. I listened to Led Zeppelin play "Good Times, Bad Times" before turning down the volume. I was absorbed with thoughts of Rich's behavior after the weekend festival. I saw him slide deeper and deeper into an abyss. I remembered giving him a ride to the liquor store for a bottle of cheap apple wine and then dropping him off at his friend's house for the night. We talked but seldom spoke of what was truly on our minds.

One day my friend Stu and I were giving Rich a ride to Riverwood Park. Rich sat in the back seat of my '66 Corvair. I looked in the rearview mirror and saw him smiling back at me. "Why are you growing a beard?"

Rich arched his eyebrows and grinned. *A cat has hair. I have hair.*

I shrugged my shoulders and looked over at Stu in the passenger seat. He turned my way and mouthed a silent, "Meow."

Throughout the winter and spring Rich would stay out all night and stagger through the door each morning reeking of booze and marijuana. His disheveled hair and glassy eyes made him look like he had just awakened from a bad dream. He'd sleep all day. This pattern continued for weeks.

One afternoon, I sat down with him at the dining room table before he disappeared for the night. I was drawn into his brown eyes and imagined his irises connecting a pathway to the ever expanding cosmos of his mind.

No, that wasn't right. Cosmos implied harmony. He was experiencing the antithesis—inner chaos—as all that he had known, no longer existed. He had chosen only to reveal fragments of his mental anguish, aspects of himself that he deemed decipherable to me. So what if I didn't know firsthand how terrified he was in Vietnam, didn't understand how devastated he felt when the love of his life deserted him, or couldn't relate to his feelings of despair upon his return from an unpopular war, unrecognized for his sacrifices. *What prevented him from sharing his thoughts, fears and worries?* I was his brother. The same ancestral blood circulated through our veins. The more I considered it, I realized he probably thought I would be too judgmental, unable to empathize. I probably was then. But, not now.

Eventually, Rich stopped coming home. One morning Mom told me, "Last night Rich was arrested by the Dover Township Police. He was walking naked along the shoulder of Route 37." I looked at Mom speechless. *Walking naked?* I tried to imagine why Rich would do such a thing. Drugs were the only explanation. I shook my head realizing Rich and I were on opposite sides of a four-lane highway accelerating rapidly and pulling away from each other. I knew something was drastically wrong with him but didn't know how to share my concern or do anything about it.

Right before his scheduled court appearance in late June, Rich left with his friends for Corrales, New Mexico. He scribbled Mom a note with his new address and asked her to forward him his monthly VA check.

∞

Rich looked out the windshield at the reflection of Eagle Rest Peak and Mount Moran in Jackson Lake. He shook his head. *Yo, bro'. There really wasn't anything you could do. If there was, I wouldn't have listened or let you do it.*

"I should have tried anyway. You were my brother. I loved you."

You know what? I found out that changing my life after 'Nam was easy. I just turned left; not right and kept going 'til my past was outta sight. I had to become someone else because I was ashamed of who I became in 'Nam. I needed to forget the evil things I did as a Marine. If I could have turned back time, I would have. But, I couldn't. So, I shed my old skin and followed Jesus.

Rich changed the subject. *Hey. Do you hear what's playing on the radio?*

The Grass Roots sang "Live for Today." I loved that song, but deep down in my heart I didn't quite believe it. *How could I live for today? Didn't that imply not working?* Hell, I've worked since seventh grade. Though, it seemed like I had been living for today since my trip began.

Of course you have. Because you've been with me. It's what freedom's all about. Not worrying about tomorrow.

Even though we were parked, it was sunny and the top was down. I turned up the volume, nodded at Rich to the beat of the music. We began singing along. Maybe there really was something about enjoying all that life has to offer each day.

Chapter Sixty-Three

I was already missing the Grand Tetons when I pulled away from my lakeside campsite. It would be another day on the road for me, traveling from Jackson Hole, Wyoming to Elko, Nevada. I came into town and saw tourists posing for photos under the elk antler arches that curved over each corner of the town's square. I passed the Million Dollar Cowboy Bar and regretted not driving by at night to see the rooftop neon sign lit of a cowboy riding a bucking bronco. It would have been my second Wyoming cowboy bar.

It drizzled on and off throughout the day as I drove across the expansive rugged landscape. Hours and miles went by as I traversed the high desert plains, passing through the towns of Soda Springs and Malad City, Idaho. There was a deserted stretch of Utah highway with no civilization in sight for miles. I journeyed into Nevada and was steeped in the Great American West, cattle ranch country with hot air balloons rising above the Ruby Mountains in the distance.

In traversing three states today, I realized that wherever I was it seemed I was always far from someplace else, isolated and distant. The same way I was feeling about Rich and me—together, yet still miles apart. Throughout the afternoon I drove in silence and thought about what I could possibly do to bridge the distance between us.

It turned into a crisp and clear night beside the campfire as sparks floated amid the swirling up draft. Diffused light from millions of distant stars formed the Milky Way, visible as clouds of stardust on this moonless night. I turned my LED headlamp on, opened Rich's journal and began reading his next entry,

Day #31, July 21, 1970 (Elko Motor Vu Drive-In)
Amazing! We've been on the road for a month. The good
news is... I led the way today. The bad news is... We lost
Ken and Sally. Ginny noticed they weren't following
anymore so we pulled over and waited for them to catch
up. When they didn't show after an hour we turned
around on I-86 and went looking for them. Another hour
later we still couldn't find them. They just disappeared.
We're bummed about being back on the road by ourselves
and hope we see them soon. Today's seven hour trip
turned into a nine hour one. We were exhausted when we
stopped for gas in Elko. It was late and before we knew it
we were parked in the back row of a drive-in theater. I
didn't get to Yasgur's Farm last summer, but when I
saw WOODSTOCK written in foot-high letters on the
marquee, I pulled in for the night.

As I continued to read, Rich's words morphed into a
scene that appeared before me.

∞

Rich was driving and Ginny was beside him as the van's
tires crunched gravel. They rolled over one small hill after
another before turning into the last lane.

"It'll be private back here." Rich parked in the end spot,
next to a metal post holding a corroded cast-aluminum
speaker the size of a toaster. As his front wheels crested the
ridge, he stopped. "What a view! I wish Ken and Sally were
here."

"Me too. The screen is so big it would've seemed like we
were all at the concert," said Ginny. "Guess, it'll just have to be
us."

"I already miss them." Rich held the speaker in his hands before hooking it to his window and rolling it back up. "It's not going to be stereo music."

"That's OK with me. It'll be cool just to hear the bands and see what we missed."

They'd imagine they were at that event when the sun, moon and stars were in alignment for three days of freedom filled music and peace on a farm in upstate NY. Hippies came out of the woodwork seeking community, love and peace, and to groove to music while high on whatever drug they could find—marijuana, speed, or acid.

Rich lit a joint, took a deep drag and handed it to Ginny. They passed it back and forth until only a roach remained. Rich held it between his tobacco stained fingers and sucked long and hard. "Ouch." He dropped it to the floor. "I'll get it in the morning. Besides, the movie is about to start."

"Wow! Split screens," Ginny said. "What beautiful images." Thousands of hippies everywhere were grooving to the music. Too much was happening for Ginny to take it all in at once. "We'll have to see this movie again."

Rich smiled at Ginny. "It's a Garden of Eden filled with innocence and joy, plenty of mud, too!" As Rich watched, the sounds and sights of the movie transported him into the experience, just like that weekend at the Atlantic City Pop Festival. After Richie Havens sang "Freedom" on his acoustic guitar, Rich couldn't stop smiling. Maybe it was the music or the dope, or a combination of the two. He pulled off his robe and threw it on the middle seat. No longer watching the movie, Rich and Ginny heard The Who being introduced. The prayerful beginning of their hope-filled song began. Rich pulled Ginny closer and she let out a whimper as her body enveloped him. They kissed and held each other while rocking to the opening lyrics of "Pinball Wizard."

Sometime later they joined a chorus of moviegoers who were singing with Country Joe McDonald and The Fish, as they followed the bouncing ball on the screen. Rich wondered once again what we were fighting for. "Man! What a statement against that fucking war! If Country Joe played their "Fish Cheer" and Crosby, Stills and Nash sang, "Find the Cost of Freedom" to troops in 'Nam, we woulda thrown down our weapons and screamed to be sent home."

Ginny hugged Rich and whispered, "I wish that had happened for you. I really do."

"Me too. But, everything came together for those long hairs that weekend. Didn't it? Hippies did whatever they wanted to, and no one hassled them. Freedom, man, freedom. What a far out movie!"

Not only did Rich and Ginny see and hear great bands, they witnessed a half million stoned young people dressed in jeans and tee-shirts living peacefully.

"Can you imagine dealing with all the mud and sharing food while having sex and sleeping under the stars?" Ginny asked.

"I sure can. It was far fucking out! I can't wait to see it again."

Chapter Sixty-Four

I awoke to a hot and dry morning. I hadn't been in temperature like that since the last time I stepped into a sauna. It felt like fire in my lungs when I inhaled deeply. So, I settled on short, shallow breaths. Rubbing my eyes and yawning, I stretched my legs in front of the camp chair I'd slept in all night. That felt better. Rich's journal was on the ground beside me and traces of charred wood and ashes from last night's campfire were in the pit.

I picked Rich's journal up and paged to the spot where I had left off,

Day #32, July 22, 1970 (Haight Ashbury, San Francisco)
We awoke this morning as two naked jay birds, lying in each other's arms in the middle of a deserted drive-in.

A setting emerged of a solitary psychedelic van parked in the last lane of a drive-in next to row after row of speaker columns all in alignment, like gravestone flags on Memorial Day.

∞

The high desert summer sun had just crested the ridge of the Ruby Mountains that surrounded the VW van, baking the inside to over 90 degrees. Perspiration dripped from Rich's brow, and his skin was stuck to Ginny's. They lay on the front seat, their bodies interwoven as tight as a macramé knot. "I can't breathe," Ginny said.

Rich pulled a lever, the door opened, and they both fell to the ground.

"Ouch. That was a bumpy ride." Ginny reached into the van for her jeans and top.

Rich stood, arched his back and surveyed the distant mountains all around them. "I guess we fell asleep."

"We did. Here's your robe."

"I had a dream that Ken and Sally were parked right here. I miss them."

"Me, too. Maybe we'll see them before we get to New Mexico."

"I hope so. I know Sally would have gotten naked last night and sang along with the music. We would have joined her because that was a far-out movie. I'd love to see it again tonight. Wouldn't you?"

"Yes, but, it's hot as hell out here in the desert. Don't you think it will be cooler in San Francisco?"

"Probably. It's close to the ocean. We'll have a long drive today. We've got to see that movie again when we get to New Mexico. Don't we?"

"We sure do."

∞

Later that afternoon I found myself in the backseat as they arrived in the hippie center of the universe, "Haight-Ashbury." They parked a street away from the narrow strip of parkland called, "The Panhandle," one block wide and eight blocks long. Many young people seemed to be squatting there, taking up residence on blankets and in tents. It merged with Golden Gate Park, allowing intrepid visitors to feel grass between their toes all the way to the Pacific Ocean. Rich and Ginny put their sleeping bags on their backpacks and walked over to a crowd of long-haired young people congregating on the grass. Several held placards that read, "Get US out of 'Nam," "Drop Acid, Not Bombs," "Kent State" and "Withdraw US Troops."

A young woman with close cropped red hair shouted into a bullhorn, "There's a happening in the park. Let's get going." She held a portable tape deck up to the mic and Buffalo Springfield's "For What It's Worth" became the score for the anti-war protest.

As they began walking, Rich saw a guy holding the "Kent State" placard and asked, "What's Kent State?"

"What rock have you been living under? You don't know that the fucking Army National Guard killed four students in May?"

"Why'd they do that?"

"Who the hell knows? It's just like soldiers in 'Nam. Killing innocent civilians."

Several possible responses flooded Rich's mind. What the hell would you know? Why weren't you in 'Nam with me and the rest of us? None of them understandable to anyone other than a soldier who had been there. He looked the guy in the eyes, nodded and walked away as he heard chanting, "Four dead in O-hi-o. No more! Four dead in O-hi-o. No more!"

∞

I never spoke with Rich about how important Kent State would become to me. It was the end of my freshman year in college when I heard the news that four college students had been killed on that dreadful day of May 4, 1970. I had just celebrated my eighteenth birthday the month before. Those innocent students should have been busy thinking about and preparing for exams, not, lying on the ground bleeding to death. It was incomprehensible to me what was happening in America. I couldn't get the image out of my mind of the grief-stricken girl kneeling beside the body of Jeffrey Glen Miller. I had learned more about life from that photo than from my first year in college. Here we were living in the land of the free where students were exercising their First Amendment rights, and they were killed. *For what?* America as I had come to know it, changed—never to return to my original conception of it.

The next day, it was announced on campus that Ocean County College President, Dr. Moreland, would address the college community. I was among several hundred students, faculty and staff sitting on the grass in front of the College Center. A podium had been set up on the stairway, and I was anxious to hear his thoughts. News circulated among us of college campuses being shut down around the country. We were silent when President Moreland approached the microphone. He began, "War is immoral." His words echoed through my mind, blocking out much of the rest of his comments. Yes. War. Is. Immoral, I thought, happy that Rich was no longer caught in its grasp.

Two months later, college classmates and I found out our fate when we watched the military draft lottery on TV. My friend Ray's birthday was selected as #1. Another pal Casey's birthday was picked as #14. Both decided to enlist, rather than get drafted. Those two guys spent the next three months traveling around the country before reporting to boot camp. I breathed a sigh of relief when my birth date was selected as #252. I wasn't a math major but knew enough to realize that about 75% of my cohorts would be drafted before I would.

No one from my family asked me how I did in the draft lottery. Maybe they were busy with their own lives or didn't realize how important an impact it would have on mine. Perhaps they were trying to stay in denial. They didn't want to know.

Chapter Sixty-Five

Rich and Ginny heard music playing in the distance as they entered Golden Gate Park with me following close behind. Rich thought, Was it rock? Not exactly. Folk? Nope. Blues? Kind of. Jazz? Not quite. Country? Nah. How about bluegrass? Not really. How could a band sound so good but be beyond description? Everyone around Rich was grooving to the music while marching and carrying signs. Others joined in along the way. Ahead he saw several other groups of marchers intersecting the park from different directions. The music seemed to be drawing them to its epicenter.

"Groovy music!" Rich said to a woman holding a "Withdraw US Troops" placard. "Who are they?"

"The Dead."

"The Dead?"

"The Grateful Dead. They play in the park all the time. Everyone loves 'em."

"The music touches my soul."

"Maybe you're a dead head?"

"A dead head?" said Rich.

"More than a fan. Something like a believer."

"I believe in Jesus. I'm not sure about believing in a dead band."

They arrived at Hippie Hill, and Rich finally saw who was playing the awesome psychedelic music. Six guys were jamming from a raised bandstand on wheels that looked more like a flatbed truck. The musicians were having as much fun playing as the several hundred spectators who were listening and dancing.

Rich was drawn to the lead guitar player, a big teddy bear guy in a flowing robe outlined in fringe. He wore aviator glasses as black as his unruly beard and head of curls. Rich and Ginny unrolled their sleeping bag and sat down, snapping their fingers and shaking their bodies in sync with the rhythm of a song called, "Truckin."

"We're gonna take a break, be back again in a few," said the lead guitarist. As band members left the stage, a woman with flowers in her hair approached the mic.

"Hey, Deadheads. We'll soon hear more of that psychedelic music. First I'd like to introduce you to Tom Hayden, leader of Students for a Democratic Society."

Rich's gaze followed the lead guitarist as he walked toward several folded tables stacked with 8-track tapes and tie-dyed tee-shirts. "I've got to meet that dude. Do you want to come?"

"You go. I'll stay here."

Rich smiled at the lead guitarist. "Your music's bitchin'."

"Thanks. We love it when our music flows, pure energy."

"Psychic energy. You guys turned me into a dead head with the first song. Something about 'Sugar Magnolia.'"

"We got more music coming later. Love your robe, brother."

"I love yours too. I can't wait to hear more music."

"We'll carry you away. Especially if you have some of our electric Kool-Aid."

"Electric?"

"We mix up a garbage can batch of Kool-Aid with tabs of acid. Then, your journey begins, mind and music fuses as one."

"This is a beautiful place for tripping. First, I'd like to get an 8-track and a couple of tees."

"My mountain girl, Carolyn, can help you."

Rich tip-toed toward Ginny, a paper cup filled with Kool-Aid in each hand, a tee-shirt draped over each shoulder and an 8-track tape wedged between his teeth.

Ginny took the tape cartridge out of his mouth and gave him a kiss. "You look pretty silly."

"That dude's far out. He gave us some electric Kool-Aid."

"Really? Kool-Aid and acid?"

"Yep. Let's drink it now, so we'll be tripping when they play again."

"Cool." Ginny raised her cup to Rich and swallowed it in one gulp.

Rich drank his, kissed Ginny and sat crossed-legged on the ground. "See you on the other side."

Next morning Rich opened an eye, glanced around and listened. Silence. It was morning and all he sensed was the pressure of Ginny's body against his back and her rhythmic breathing. Their sleeping bag enveloped them like a cocoon. Other couples were snuggled together on sleeping bags and blankets, spread out on the knoll surrounding the stage.

"I've got to pee," Rich whispered. When he rolled onto the damp grass, his naked body jerked to alertness, and he jumped to his feet. He shook his head. "That's one way to get up."

If Ginny had awakened, she would have witnessed Rich's acid head look, wild hair and beard ablaze all over his face and head. But, she didn't see him or his troubled eyes burning a path to his restless soul. After peeing behind a cluster of trees, he walked along a paved path, unclothed and uninhibited as if he were going for a Sunday morning stroll. He stopped when he heard a hissing sound all around him, like the rhythm of distant chopper blades. He hit the ground hard with his hands shielding his face. He turned and listened as dozens of sprinkler heads popped out of the ground.

"Tee, tee, tee. Jussssh. Tee, tee, tee. Jussssh."

"Phew," he whispered. He stood, raised his arms and opened his mouth as he ran into the mist, turning in circles while singing The Grateful Dead song, "To Lay Me Down."

∞

The spray cascaded over me and the image of Rich running through the sprinklers dissolved before my eyes. I jumped up from the grass and ran toward the paved path. Once out of the sprinkler's range, I sat down on a wooden bench and looked back at the field before me. I was soaking wet and thought Rich was too. But, he was nowhere to be found. The persistent triggering of metal against pressurized water was the only thing I saw or heard.

Chapter Sixty-Six

When I got back to "The Panhandle" section of Golden Gate Park, I searched for the van. I wandered along Page Street where I thought Rich had parked it. I stopped, stared at the car in the parking space and shook my head. There sat Rich's '66 GTO. Seeing is believing, I told myself as I opened the door, tossed my backpack in the back seat and took down the top.

My GPS showed it would be a four and a half hour trip to my next destination, Yosemite National Park. As I drove though the San Joaquin Valley, I passed a billboard, "Welcome to The Food Basket of the World." On both sides of me were mile after mile of lush vegetable fields—tomatoes, asparagus and sweet corn. The snow-capped Sierra Nevada dominated the eastern horizon.

By sunset, I was fully relaxed, lying beside Yosemite's Mirror Lake. The sun's rays simmered in shades of orange and red. My eyes were drawn to the western horizon where I could see Earth's sister—the goddess Venus, glistening over the water, as if she had risen from the depths. I opened Rich's journal and began reading. In my mind's eye I saw him sitting here beside me in another time. I heard his thoughts as the peacefulness was shattered when a nearby camper's bottle rockets exploded overhead. While I witnessed the rhythmic detonation of fireworks—cascading entrails of fire and ash— the weight of one of Rich's distant memories descended upon me. "Tell me," I said.

∞

It was a long time ago, yet, like a recurring infliction, it was real right now, forcing dinner up Rich's throat. His hands began to tremble, his mouth was dry, as he tried his damnedest to keep it together. He knew they were here, but couldn't see his buddies beside him in the gloomy mortar pit, enveloped in the suspended reality called 'Nam. Like the tip of his bayonet, the silence was piercing. No birds, animals or insects dwelled within this desolate expanse. One of Rich's hooch mates, Anderson, had just launched an illum round—overpowering the darkness with an eerie luminescence—as if an acetylene flame was adrift in the sky.

He heard the screeching descent of an enemy mortar round and someone shouted, "Incoming." Rich hit the dirt, putting both hands on his helmet. He prayed that the shell wouldn't find him. But, it did. The explosion imploded the sandbag walls, leaving a six-foot crater where his buddy, Baker, had just been. In a millisecond, Rich was hit with a knockout punch. A burst of gunpowder mixed with a mist of blood and fragmented body parts. Rich was thrown on his back and landed on something soft, oblivious to his surroundings. Then, darkness. He couldn't catch his breath as he fought to free himself. He managed to unbuckle his helmet and slide his head to the side, finding an air pocket. He drew shallow breaths and tasted the caustic smell of death. His fingers clawed the sand and scraped through to the surface sending smoke into his lungs. As he blacked out, someone grabbed his hands. A sudden tug then pulled him forward through the mire as the ground surrendered his body and legs from entrapment. He lay face-down in a pit gasping for air.

∞

I was startled back to my camp by the incessant bursting of fireworks. "Holy shit, Rich. Were you OK?"

"Even though I was going in and out of consciousness, I heard someone shouting on the radio."

"We've been hit with a mortar round. Do you read me? I repeat. We need dustoff immediately to evacuate wounded."

"I was stabbed with sharp chest pains, and was lying on the ground gasping for breath. I heard myself cry out for Mom. Someone said, 'Hang in there Duffy.'"

Rich wasn't sure how much time had passed. He was hoisted through the air as wave after wave of turbulence assaulted his body like being caught in the jaws of a nor'easter. He came to when a chopper Corpsman jammed smelling salts up his nose and pressed gauze over his ribs. "If you die on me Duffy, I'll kill you."

When Rich heard the Corpsman, he snapped out of it. He was dizzy and his heart was pounding trying to bust out of his chest. He couldn't catch a breath. He dreamed that a woman put a moist cloth on his head. She held his hand and said she loved him. He felt her breath on his face as she kissed him.

"Diane? Is that you?" Rich moaned as the scent of Ambush drifted in the air.

"Just sleep," she purred, like a gentle breeze floating over tranquil water.

But Rich couldn't sleep. A haze fractured his thoughts. He saw wreckage of his life strewn in the air, as if he had just stepped on an M-14. His mind and body became a diffused cloud of blood and smoke.

Days later he awakened. "Welcome back Corporal."

"How long was I out?"

"Three days. A Medevac chopper brought you to the 95th Evac Hospital. We may not look like much, being just a tent hospital, but, we have some of the best trauma surgeons in the world."

"What did you do?" Rich managed to ask, in spite of the intense pain stabbing his chest every time he took a shallow breath.

The surgeon handed him a melted piece of metal the size of Rich's wedding band. "I operated on you for two hours and removed this piece of shrapnel that was lodged between your skin and ribs. It collapsed your right lung."

"No wonder it feels like I'm trying to breathe underwater."

"It'll be uncomfortable for several weeks. The tube in your chest will help you breathe."

"Thanks for saving my life, Doc."

"You're welcome. We're just sorry we can't save every soldier."

Rich nodded. "I know what you mean. There wasn't any hope for my friend Baker. Me and my buddies deal with a lot of shit out in the bush."

"That's the most heart wrenching part about being a surgeon here. Trying to play God in a place we call 'Hell on Earth.' Except your case is different, you got here in time."

"God bless you, Doc."

"Now get some rest and let our capable nurses' help restore your body."

"Yes Sir," Rich moaned, as he closed his eyes and surrendered his mind to the blissful nothingness of sleep. Losing consciousness, Rich heard Country Joe and the Fish counting off their "Fish Cheer" while he and millions of other soldiers joined in to sing along.

∞

I lowered the volume on the tape deck and "I Feel Like I'm Fixin To Die Rag" became the soundtrack to my thoughts. I mulled over my encounter of Rich's near-death experience. "Hasn't he had enough?" I uttered. *How could my brother have endured all the shit thrown at him and keep it together without losing control?* His mind and body sure got fucked up.

Chapter Sixty-Seven

I had been driving from Yosemite to the Grand Canyon for hours, road weary and as tired as a long-haul trucker halfway to his next pick-up. No rest area was in sight, only mile upon mile of green desert sagebrush. My eyes lit up seeing a sign, "Truck Stop, 5 miles." I pulled in and parked within one of six spaces reserved for cars. A guy who trailed me the past twenty miles pulled in beside me. I nodded in his direction as we both got out. After stretching my legs and using the bathroom, I got back in the car. I shifted into second and passed a line of eighteen-wheelers parked diagonally just beyond the gas station. *Maybe a nap would get me energized?* I pulled into a roadway that paralleled the exit ramp and parked beside a grove of picnic tables shaded by evergreen trees. I took my sleeping bag, pillow and blanket out of the trunk and walked into a cluster of palm trees. *Palm trees in Arizona?* In a clearing, I lay down on top of my sleeping bag and fell asleep.

I was awakened by the blast of a trucker's air horn and figured it was time to get back on the road. I didn't realize what time it was until I put my gear in the trunk, and a man got out of a car parked next to mine and said, "Good Morning."

"Good Morning. What?" I mumbled. *Did I really sleep through the night?* I took two granola bars out of a new box, splashed water on my face, right out of the bottle and got back in the driver's seat. There were a few tandem trucks on the interstate when I pulled out. Those guys must have been driving all night trying to avoid tourists like me who got in their way during daylight hours.

The sun was directly above me when I saw a sign, "Flagstaff, 75 miles." I estimated getting there in about an hour

231

and a half. Then, I'd take 180 north another 60 miles to the south entrance of Grand Canyon National Park. So what if it would be in the heat of the day when I arrived. Maybe I'd have time for another nap before seeing my first canyon sunset.

That afternoon I sat on the bumper under the open trunk, its shadow a welcome relief from the sun. Another day had passed and I hoped I was moving forward. It seemed just like that day I had found Rich's GTO. It had started out as another familiar day but became something unworldly. *Maybe I'd have the same luck today if I went through everything in the trunk? Hadn't I delayed long enough?* I soon found myself sitting in the middle of the trunk on top of boxes. I glanced from one item to another, everything within reach. *Where do I start?* I looked around and saw something wedged between the spare tire and side of the trunk. I pulled the tire away from the side and squeezed my hand around a crushed shoe box. *Why hadn't I seen it when I changed the flat in Cody?* Damn if I knew.

"Could this contain some of the treasures Rich spoke to me about that day in the storage compartment?" I whispered to myself.

Rich's voice came out of nowhere. *It sure could.*

"If it was so damn important, why didn't you tell me about it in the first place," I shouted. I waited in silence, uncertain if my question would be answered, or if it had even been heard.

It's not my puzzle to solve. It's yours, remember?

"I remember all right. I've grown tired of your cryptic answers. Because there have been times, like right now, when I wonder why the hell I ever allowed myself to get sucked into the black hole of your disappearance."

I've wondered about that too. What are you really seeking?

"Closure, Rich. Closure."

Maybe something in the box will help you.

I broke the tape, tore off the cover and found a handwritten note placed on top. It said,

Mrs. Duffy,
I'm sorry but I can't speak with you in person. I'm still so upset about Richie. I loved him, and know that he'd want you to have his Bible and journal and other things he left behind. I hope they bring you PEACE.
Ginny

I let out an audible sigh. *His Bible and journal?* I'd already found them in the GTO when I visited EZ Storage months ago. *If Ginny had dropped them off to Mom in the '70's, how'd they get out of the box and into the trunk? Could Mom have rooted through everything Ginny had left, found Rich's journal and read it? If so, then why'd she leave it for me to discover after her death? Did she create this tomb to remember Rich or to forget him?*

I thought you were looking for answers. Not more questions. Rich sounded irritated.

"It seems I wasn't the only one looking for closure." I just couldn't understand why Mom hadn't told me about getting Rich's things.

Maybe my stuff brought her peace.

"Or, maybe more pain. Maybe more pain." I frowned, shook my head and stared at the box that awaited my exploration. *Could all of Rich's worldly possessions be condensed into the confines of a simple cardboard box?* I knew mine couldn't. His life was a paradox; an outward appearance of scarcity and inward expression of abundance.

One's fortune really should be comprised of the intangibles of life—love, faith, family, health, and friendship, right? Aren't these key measures of a satisfying and fulfilling life? Enough with the questions. Besides, I knew the answers to these were an emphatic yes, yes and yes. *So what about considering a more difficult question? Will anything in this box lead me any closer to finding clues?*

My legs were cramping so I got out of the trunk. I opened the driver's door, slumped in the seat and placed the box on my lap. My hands trembled as tears filled my eyes and streamed down my cheek, one after another. I gently held the box and bowed my head over it. "I hope this contains answers I've been looking for."

There's only one way to find out.

I removed one item at a time, placing each on my lap. What I saw were slices of Rich's life, memorabilia—family photos, Polaroid shots from Vietnam, an Indian bead necklace and headband, an MIA bracelet and a dozen letters addressed to him. I shuffled the letters, one behind another, seeing that most had been sent to Rich in Vietnam and a few had his Corrales, New Mexico address. One stood out from the others, written in Rich's tiny block-lettered printing. It simply said, "Mom." I saw that the seal had been broken and wondered how many years ago it had been opened. I read his note,

Dear Mom,

Don't worry about me or how I'm doing. Jesus is my savior and companion. I LOVE YOU and can't wait to see you some day in God's cathedral of the sky—Heaven! Bless you.

Your Loving son, Rich.

I tossed the letter back in the box. "There you go again, being mysterious."

I thought I spoke from my heart.

"From your heart? Hell, I would've freaked out if I was Mom reading your note soon after you disappeared. It sounds like one of those letters G.I.'s wrote to be sent home if they didn't return."

I wrote one of those in 'Nam. All my buddies did.

"Hell, I'm so glad Mom never had to read your "letter" from Vietnam. Although, this one seems just as bad. It's as ambiguous as the postcard Mom received from Ginny."

∞

I struggled to make sense of Rich's belongings, failing to piece them together into a coherent whole. Maybe some puzzle pieces weren't meant to be joined with others.

Perhaps they could stand alone, each one's beauty admired as if it were a solitary mosaic tile.

Sure. Just sit there admiring all my shit. Where's that gonna get you?

Nowhere fast, I thought. Maybe I'd learn more if I took time to examine each item individually.

Sounds like a gas, said Rich as The Rolling Stones song "Jumping Jack Flash" buzzed inside the trunk.

My stomach burned in angst. "A real gas. Thanks for leaving me a lot of fabulous clues." I muddled through the Polaroid shots of Rich in Vietnam. He and his fellow Marines were burrowed down in mud bunkers living like wild dogs. A primitive existence in a mortar-cratered landscape with little or no hope of surviving until "wake-up day."

"How'd you get through those twelve months?"

I took 'em one day at a time, praying to Jesus to get me though it all alive. During patrols I counted on my buddies to cover my back and I watched theirs. One day my radioman McManus was kneeling beside me calling coordinates into Command. A few minutes later all hell broke loose. The VC had us surrounded and were closing in fast. McManus called for a dustoff as we ran for cover. The chopper got there and in all the confusion McManus didn't get on board. I jumped out and ran back to where he had been and couldn't find him. We had to leave without him, something Marines just don't do. He was listed as MIA and I never saw him again. Rich cleared his throat. *He was only nineteen. His whole life was ahead of him. When I got back to the states, I wore his MIA bracelet every day.*

I picked up the stainless steel band, traced the engraving with my fingers: L/CPL TRUMAN J. MCMANUS-

06.05.68. I wrapped it around my right wrist, got out of the trunk, and sat in the driver's seat. Rich was beside me in shadow, his head and shoulders slouched. Another time Rich had come close to being killed. To make things worse, he left his buddy behind. What a hell of a burden to carry. Another unspoken horror.

Rich rubbed his eyes with both hands. *It sure was.*

I pursed my lips. "I'm so sorry that war had to define you as a young man."

It was a bitch. But even though it stalked me, I refused to surrender the rest of my life to it. He reached over, squeezed my shoulder.

"Good for you." I wrapped my arm around his neck and pulled him close. "Good for you."

What had I found? I still hadn't deciphered any pattern or found any answers that made sense. *Hell, did I really think the mystery of Rich's disappearance was going to be revealed from the contents of a shoebox?* I didn't know what I expected to find. Maybe there just weren't any answers.

Chapter Sixty-Eight

I followed Rich and Ginny's neon painted van as they exited the south entrance of the Grand Canyon. I could have driven blindfolded sixty miles to Williams, Arizona; Route 64 south was practically a straight line. But, I couldn't concentrate on my driving. All I could think about were my brother's words. I tried to wrap my head around what he had said so clearly, "Even though it stalked me, I refused to surrender the rest of my life to it." Perhaps I could learn from him by refusing to surrender to something that had stalked me, too. Maybe this would be a good time to not just talk, but begin communicating with Rich. Nah, not yet. I wasn't sure I was ready for it yet. I had held onto it for this long. *What difference will another day or two make?* I still needed time to think.

I stopped in the middle of Route 64 when Rich hit the brakes and pulled his van onto the gravel shoulder. There wasn't a car in either direction for as far as I could see. Ginny got out and slid open the side door. I saw her and a long-haired guy help a pregnant girl into the van and then load a few bags.

The girl tossed her fringed suede shoulder bag on the seat beside her. "Thanks, Buddy." She gripped the hem of her denim jumper and waved it up and down as beads of sweat dripped from her chin. The guy threw his back pack on the floor, sank into the seat and wiped his brow with a red bandana. He handed it to her, and she dabbed her chin. Then she held each end, spun it until it was tight and wrapped it around his head. She tied it in a knot as his long blond hair puffed out from under it.

"What are you two doing in the middle of the desert?" Rich asked.

The guy tightened his headband. "Waiting for you to pick us up."

"I guess it's your lucky day. I'm Ginny and our good-looking driver is Rich."

"Nice meeting you. They call me River and my wife here is Sky."

"If you're thirsty, help yourselves to the jug of water. Where are you headed, anyway?"

"We're going to Jerome."

"You're going to meet someone?"

"No. It's a town. A ghost town."

Ginny turned and looked at them. "Really? A ghost town?"

"We met a couple at our Grand Canyon campground who were heading to California. They told us all about the deserted town they had lived in for months. Everything's free."

"You can't get better than that," Rich said. "Why'd they leave?"

"They wanted to go to Mecca... Haight-Ashbury."

"I guess it is Mecca," said Rich. "But, what about you two?"

"We're going to find a deserted home and fix it up. We've got to settle down; Sky is expecting in a few months."

"I can see that. How far is this place?"

"It's about two hours away," said Sky.

Rich raised his eyebrows and looked at Ginny. "What do you think?"

"Let's go."

∞

They followed 89A along Walnut Creek as it curved, climbing in elevation. Their right tire clung to the edge of the road as they slowly ascended the slope to Jerome, an 1800's copper mining town perched on top of a mountain. The ride was like being on the *Wild Mouse* in Seaside Heights with steep inclines, abrupt dog-leg turns and sudden sprawling views. The last mile was steep so Rich kept the van in second gear. At the top of the hill the road made a hairpin turn into town, bringing them smack dab into the middle of the 1960's.

"This is hippie heaven," said Rich.

Psychedelic painted Volkswagen's were everywhere. Beetles were squeezed on one side of a narrow street. About a dozen VW buses and campers were parked erratically on the only flat space available—a gravel lot the size of a large community garden. Long-haired young people were hanging out; sitting on front steps and bursting out of vans with their doors wide open. The pungent spicy aroma of pot drifted through the air along with the bubblegum pop sound of The Friends of Distinction singing "Grazing in the Grass."

"This town really is a gas. I can dig it," said Rich. He pulled the van behind another and parked in front of a head shop called, Mile High. "This shop should have everything we need."

"Or someone will know where we can find it," said Ginny.

Rich and Ginny stood in front of a glass counter filled with Zig-Zag, e-z wider and Rizla Double Wide rolling papers, handheld bongs, pipes and other cannabis paraphernalia. On top of the counter, the warm, sweet earthy scent of Patchouli Noir seduced them from an incense stick balanced on the end of a bamboo stick.

"What's happening?" Rich said to a burly bear-like guy behind the counter wearing bib jean overalls. His light brown curly ringlets and beard sprang out in every direction framing his head.

"Welcome to Jerome."

"You've got one far out town."

"We like it. No one hassles us here."

"No cops?"

"Nope. We're on our own and like it that way. What can I get ya?"

"We'll have a couple packs of e-z wider and would love to get something to stuff inside."

"You came to the right place. I got nickel bags of Jamaican Gold."

"We'll take six of 'em."

"Sure 'nuff. The papers are on me."

Ginny counted thirty dollars onto the counter. Burly Bear pocketed the cash. He stuffed the pot in a brown paper bag, handed it to Rich and winked.

"See you outside," Rich said to River and Sky as he walked past them and they approached Burly Bear.

"Are you two here for the same goods?"

"No. We're looking for a place to crash," said River.

"You mean more like somewhere to squat," added Sky.

"Ohhhh. Squatters."

"Sure would appreciate your help."

"You're not trouble makers, right?"

"No. We're peaceful and want to put down roots 'cause we're going to have a baby," said River.

"What will you do for money?"

"I have leather-working tools to make belts and handbags," said River.

"I've made and sold all kinds of silver jewelry, earrings, necklaces, bracelets and rings. I've even pierced ears," said Sky.

"Sounds like you two are a good fit for Jerome. I've got some extra space. Would you like to set up shop here?"

"Really? That would be fantastic." Sky nudged River's arm.

River shrugged. "It's just that we don't have a lot of money."

"Tell you what? Think about what supplies you'd need to start making some of your own stuff and we can talk more about it."

"That's cool."

"I'll think about it, too. Maybe I can loan you some cash to get started. The first month's rent would be free. You'd have to pay from that point on."

"We'd be glad to pay our own way," said Sky.

"Now, let me think of a place for you to crash. There's an abandoned church over on Hill Street that a group of squatters call Mountain View Café and Hostel. They removed the pews so guests can spread sleeping bags on the floor. It's not very private. But, you don't have to pay if you help prepare or serve meals."

"Sounds fine. We'll check it out and get back to you about your offer." River took Sky's hand and they headed to the door.

The next morning Ginny and Rich sat across from Sky and River on a wooden booth under a high arched ceiling. In the background, Sly and The Family Stone sang, "Everyday People." Muted sunlight flickered through a stained glass window casting shadows on the table.

Ginny licked her fingers. "These pancakes are amazing. I didn't know blueberry syrup could taste so good."

"I spoke with the manager last night about being a waitress here," Sky said.

"What did he say?" asked Ginny.

"He said I could work until my baby is born. He also told me that several mothers in town have formed a childcare co-op."

"Things seem to be falling in place for you two," said Rich.

"Do you think you'll be staying for a while?" asked River.

"No. Ginny and I talked this morning about getting an early start today. It's a full day's drive to Zion."

Ginny placed her hand over Sky's and looked her in the eyes. "We're on our way to our future. We're excited that we were there when you found yours. Maybe we'll stop back someday and visit you and your baby."

"We'd like that," said Sky. "I hope we find a place to squat before you come back."

"We hope you do, too. It's a brand new start for all of us," said Rich. "We better get going."

Rich and Ginny stood and gave River a hug. Sky wrapped her arms around all of them and whispered, "We won't forget you."

∞

I put the top down and the early morning sunshine warmed my face. I pulled onto 89A ahead of Rich and Ginny and kept it in second gear as the road twisted down from the mountaintop. It seemed just like Rich's luck. And, mine too. A two-hour Good Samaritan detour had turned into a 325-mile, six-hour trip from Jerome to Zion National Park. I couldn't wait to get back to the wilderness.

Chapter Sixty-Nine

As I passed through Flagstaff on Route 89 north, I thought of Rich's comment, "a brand new start." This would be a perfect time for me to clear the air with Rich about something that has been bothering me the whole trip.

"All this driving is giving me way too much time to think."

It don't matter if you're driving or standing still. You do way too much thinking period!

"I'm trying to have a serious conversation, and you're joking around."

So what. I get a kick out of pushing your buttons. Haven't you figured that out by now?

"I guess I should have seen that coming. There's something I need to tell you."

Go for it. Besides, we'll be together in this car for many more miles. Won't we?

Where do I start? I guess at the beginning. "Well, it's something that happened when you were in Da Nang. For most of that year Diane spent a lot of evenings, weekends and holidays with us."

She wrote me about spending time over at the house. It helped her feel closer to me.

"It must have. Anyway, she came over for Thanksgiving. After dinner, we were all in the living room watching TV. She sat in the wing chair with her feet on the ottoman and I sat on the floor, leaning against it."

Sounds cozy.

243

I clenched the steering wheel and paid no attention to Rich as broken white lines whizzed by. "It was." I hesitated a moment to take a deep breath before continuing. "Until Diane took off her shoes and began rubbing her toes against my back."

Oh?

"I just froze. Didn't know what to do. During a commercial I got up and went to the bathroom. I didn't have to pee, so I sat on the edge of the tub to think about what had happened. When I returned to sit on the floor, I glanced her way and she gave me a big smile."

You got a toe massage from my wife?

"I don't know why I didn't just move to another spot."

Maybe you liked it?

"Yeah, I did. But, I knew it wasn't right. Another night in December we were sitting on the sofa watching a movie on TV. Mom and Sue had left earlier to go Christmas shopping. It started again. This time she took her shoes off and rubbed her foot up and down my calf. I couldn't stop myself and guess she couldn't either. Next thing we were kissing. She kept murmuring, "Richie. Richie.""

Then what happened?

I heard stones crunch on the driveway as Mom and Sue pulled in. I jumped up, ran into the bedroom, got under the covers with my clothes on and pretended I was asleep. Didn't even say goodbye to Diane. A few weeks later we were at her house for Christmas, and we both acted as if nothing had happened.

That's it?

"Nothing else. I pinky swear that if I could go back and undo it I would. Please forgive me."

Rich shook his head. *What's to forgive? You were sixteen, right? She was twenty. She hadn't seen me for six months. It was just something that happened. Anyway, Diane told me about it when we met in Hawaii for my mid-year R&R trip.*

"Oh my God. She told you?"

You seem to take a lot of responsibility for things you can't control. Don't you?

"Maybe, but you trusted me to keep an eye on her. I felt I had betrayed that trust."

You're only human. Diane was older and should have known better. Besides, making a few mistakes along the way is what life's all about.

"I've always tried to avoid mistakes. It's just that this one was huge."

Listen, your loyalty to me has never been in question. Haven't the past forty-five years of keeping my spirit alive made up for any of the guilt you've carried?

"I hope it has, Rich."

Thanks for telling me. Now that you got that topic out in the open, can you forgive yourself? Cause I sure have, and so has Jesus.

Forgiveness. What a wonderful blessing from Rich.

Chapter Seventy

I passed through a town called Virgin and saw a sign "Zion National Park, 14 miles." I drove through Springdale, entered Zion's south entrance and stopped at the Visitor's Center for canyoneering information. Then, I followed the Loop Road until it ended at a parking lot for the Narrows Trail. I knew that a hike and fresh air would do me good. Before getting on the trail I engaged in a ritual I had followed in every national park I've visited this summer. The first thing I did was stuff essentials from my cooler to my day bag and threw it over my shoulder. Next, I put one foot on the bumper and tightened my boot laces; then the other. I couldn't venture down a trail without first getting oriented, so a map was essential. I squeezed one into my day bag. This trail would be different, so I put my iPhone inside a dry pouch and looped the shoulder strap over my neck. I sat on a bench at the trailhead and opened Rich's journal to where I had left off,

Day #35, July 25, 1970 (Zion National Park, Utah)
Zion means the City of God. I wonder if Isaiah was ever here to witness this magnificence. It's not a city. It's a spirit! All who come to Zion become people of God.

What the hell? Did Rich and Ginny just pass my bench wearing shorts, tee-shirts and leather sandals? I guess Rich left his Moses robe in the van because most of the trail involved walking in the river. I followed them on the first segment that meandered alongside the Virgin River. The water gurgled quietly across countless rocks in its inevitable journey south to join the Colorado. When we arrived at the Temple of Sinawava, Rich looked up while turning in a circle. "Only God could create such splendor." The Temple of Sinawava wasn't just one peak. It was the entire northern section of the canyon. We stood beside the river, surrounded on three sides by a natural amphitheater comprised of sheer cliffs.

Ginny pointed to the origin of a waterfall at the summit of a cliff. "Look at that!" A stream of water gushed from a crevice high in the rocks, cascading down hundreds of feet, turning limestone from orange to red. The trail dead-ended after a mile and merged into the river. Tall graceful maples and cottonwood trees grew along its banks, creating a ribbon of green.

Rich spotted a long branch on the ground and picked it up. "This'll make a good walking stick. I'll get one for you, too." He found another and handed it to Ginny.

"People must leave these behind when they return from their hike," she said. "They're still wet; probably just been used."

"I guess this is where we get wet, too. It's time to walk up the river." Rich stepped into the cold flowing water, beginning his assault against the knee-deep current.

I picked up a discarded walking stick and trailed them. Our progress was slow; often difficult as we searched for footholds among slippery river rocks and stones. We navigated around boulders and often stopped to stand in reverent silence at the natural beauty all around us. It seemed like we had been walking for hours. Rich glanced at the trail map, then put it back in Ginny's backpack. "They call that big boulder up ahead Floating Rock." It was a huge smooth rock in the middle of the river; it's mass diverted the water's flow around it. It could easily accommodate eight to ten hikers standing on its surface.

Soon after we passed it, Ginny said, "Look at those massive walls."

"They're awesome," said Rich. "This area is called Wall Street."

It gave the trail its name—The Narrows—being the narrowest and most dramatic section. Its 1,500 foot walls enveloped us. The river ate away at the shoreline as side walls got closer and closer until the span between them was a mere twenty-five feet and the emerald green water flowed up to our knees.

"Whoops!" Ginny yelled as she slipped into chest high water, almost losing her balance and her right sandal. She faced Rich and me walking behind and bounced up and down slapping the surface.

"What happened?" Rich shouted.

"This must be where the river runs deep."

Rich stepped into the high water, pushed his hands along the top until he reached Ginny to give her a big hug.

"Thanks. I needed that."

"Hey. Do you know what? This is a wonderful place to be baptized. What do you think?"

"I think you're a bit crazy. Babies wouldn't like to be in the midst of all this motion."

"I don't mean babies; I mean us. Cleanse us of our sins."

"Ohhh. Us. Sure."

Standing face-to-face, Rich made the sign of the cross on Ginny's forehead. "This is a symbol that you believe in Christ, and it's a reminder that he loves you."

Ginny repeated Rich's words, making the same gesture on his head. She followed Rich's ritual, mirroring both his words and actions. They held hands, looked into each other's eyes and when Rich nodded they immersed themselves. First Ginny, then Rich surfaced, goosebumps ran down their spines. They smiled at each other as they shook water from their hair.

"Your sins have been forgiven," said Rich. "You're one of God's children. Go in peace, and spread His words of love and salvation."

"I will." Ginny repeated the same words to Rich.

I watched and beamed as if I was the best man at Rich and Ginny's wedding. I was happy he had found someone who shared his values and was as committed as he was to living a spiritual lifestyle. I only wished that the two of them had found peace and lasting happiness.

Chapter Seventy-One

It was late afternoon when a peal of thunder rocked the canyon, followed by a torrent of rain. The Virgin River began to rise above their knees. Rich took out the trail map. They had reached Big Spring, the turn-around point for bottom-up hikers like them. Arriving at the landmark meant they had traveled five miles; four of them within water ranging in depth from a few inches to over four feet. As the water continued to swell Rich took Ginny's hand as they dragged themselves to shore. They rested on two small boulders, and I sat on one beside them. I was at a loss trying to find the source of the spring; searching for telltale bubbles that breeched the surface. Then I looked high into the canyon and saw that walls on the other side of the river were soaked from pathways of water flowing down. One more of Mother Nature's mysteries I'd never understand.

"We're supposed to turn around here. It's getting late, the river is rising. We don't' want to be in the middle of a flash flood," said Rich.

Ginny hugged Rich and whispered in his ear. "I'm tired and scared. What can we do?"

"There's a camping area nearby for hikers taking the top-down route. It's called High Camp and should be worth a try."

"We don't have our sleeping bags or tent. I'm hungry," said Ginny as the storm clouds began to scatter.

Rich stuffed the map in his back pocket. "We'll just have to pray for the best." He felt a cramp in his calf but willed his legs to keep moving. He reached out to Ginny who held his hand for the last hundred yards.

Ginny stood next to Rich in the middle of a stand of maple and Douglas fir trees. "It doesn't look like a campground."

"It's not a camp ground. It's a camp site—just a high spot to sleep for the night."

They walked across a soaked bluff large enough to accommodate a half-dozen tents and approached two broad-shouldered guys hunched over their backpacks.

"Hello. It's good to see other people out here on the river."

"Hi." The dark haired one began to connect a flexible backbone for his tent. "I'm Joseph."

"Hi Joseph. I'm Rich and this is my girlfriend, Ginny."

"You don't look like you planned to stay the night."

"We didn't count on it. It looks like we're going to have to. We're worried about the storm and way too tired to head back now."

"Luckily the storm is clearing. Though, it's a smart idea to stay put. Too many hikers get hurt trying to keep going when they're exhausted," said the blond-haired guy who called himself John. "It looks like you don't have a tent or any sleeping bags."

"Nope. We left them in the van," said Ginny. "Thought we'd only be out for the day."

"You're in luck. We'll be happy to share what we have with you. We're seminary students, the Lord's servants."

"Praise Jesus." Rich glanced up at the sky. "Thank you Lord for bringing us to your faithful followers."

"It's supposed to be a warm night, so there's no threat of hypothermia. You should change into dry clothes though," suggested John.

Rich shrugged his shoulders. "We would if we had any."

Joseph reached into his backpack and offered Rich and Ginny a few articles of clothes.

"Dry clothes. Something else to be thankful for."

"You two can get changed in my tent," said Joseph. "In fact, why don't you use it and my sleeping bag. It's not big enough for two, but you can at least sleep on top. I'll sleep under the stars tonight."

"Bless you, Joseph and John," said Ginny. "I don't know what we would have done without you."

"We're all God's children," said John. "He's brought us together for a reason."

"What might that be?" asked Rich.

"Who knows? How about breaking bread with us after you've changed. Perhaps we'll find out."

As Rich and Ginny stepped inside the tent to change, I rummaged through my backpack for dry clothes and some snacks. Sitting on a fallen tree, I put on a fresh pair of shorts and a sweatshirt, then propped myself up against a branch to observe Rich, Ginny and their new friends. Rich stepped out of the tent, wide-eyed with amazement when he saw John and Joseph sitting cross-legged around a poncho laden with trail food.

"Come join us," said John. "It's not much. But its sustenance."

"It looks wonderful." Ginny sat down, patted the ground and nodded at Rich.

Rich sat beside her. "Wow! We're blessed to be in this heavenly canyon with such generous souls."

They held hands as each of them gave a blessing for their food, asking Jesus for continued guidance. Joseph poured hot water into two small aluminum cups and passed them to Ginny and Rich. "I hope you don't mind sharing a teabag?"

"I can dig it, man. Hot tea in the middle of this trail is far out."

"When you're done, we'll pour some for ourselves," Joseph said as he refilled a small pot with water, placed it on the single-burner and lit the flame.

"That's some contraption."

"It's called a micro stove. It fits into my backpack and heats anything as long as it isn't more than a cup."

"Cool," said Ginny. "It looks like you guys have brought enough food for a picnic."

"We brought along a lot of lightweight protein—food that doesn't use water or have to be cooked. The upside is its energy food," said Joseph. "The downside is its cold."

"This will be our second and last night camping after hiking over twelve miles," added John. "The more we eat tonight, the lighter our load will be tomorrow. Help yourselves."

"We hiked five miles today. But, it felt like fifteen. Especially when the water was up to our chests in those deep sections," said Rich.

"Traveling against the current didn't help either," added Ginny.

"That's what an outdoor adventure is all about. Isn't it?" said John.

"Guess so."

Rich looked over the spread, nabbed a few saltines, the jar of peanut butter and a spoon. "This glass jar must have been heavy to carry?"

"It was, but there's nothing like peanut butter on a cracker after a long hike."

Rich arched his eyebrows as he looked at Joseph and scooped peanut butter from the jar to his crackers.

"Would you like GORP on top?"

"GORP?" asked Rich. "I know what GROK is. Never heard of GORP?"

"Good ole raisins and peanuts. They'll add crunch and sweetness to your crackers."

"Sounds good to me." Rich cupped his hands while Joseph poured the fruit and nut mixture into them.

"And for dessert there's a Snicker's bar for each of us."

"Are you sure you won't need them?" asked Ginny.

"No, we only have five more miles to go. It'll all be downhill," said John. He grinned and looked at Ginny.

"I'm going to save my candy bar for the trail tomorrow," said Rich.

"Me too," said Ginny. "Thanks."

The sun poked through the clouds and faded beyond the cliffs. Rich leaned on his elbows and looked up. Half of the sky was obliterated by a canopy of uninterrupted branches and leaves from the bluff to the water's edge.

"Waa. Waa. Waa."

"What's that?" Ginny asked, pointing to the trees.

"Sounds like a Mexican Spotted Owl," said Joseph. "Our guide book said Zion has the largest concentration of them in the state. They seem to love the high narrow slot canyons."

"Cool," said Rich. The background sound of crickets was interrupted once again by the call of an owl. Night settled in and a faint breeze roamed through the canyon.

"Time to build a fire." John lit kindling in the middle of a fire ring; damp leaves and branches smoked, then ignited, emitting a yellow flame. He added a few more pieces of wood as the flames flared into a campfire.

Ginny watched the fire crackle and flicker. "Just enough warmth to keep the chill away."

"I can feel the spirit of Jesus in those flames," said Rich.

"He's all around us," said Joseph.

"I've come closer to him this summer than ever before. God created the natural cathedrals of the West, and Jesus gave me hope and courage to explore them. I didn't know I'd find my soul along the way."

"Sometimes we have to venture deep into nature, stop everything, breathe and listen within," said Joseph. "That's what I love about the outdoors."

"Let's do some of that now," said Rich.

They sat close together in a circle, held hands and stared into the flames.

"Just breathe," said Joseph.

Rich looked at the stars twinkling like thousands of fireflies. "You can feel God's presence in this canyon wilderness. He's all around us."

"Yes. He's here with us. Just focus on your breathing," said Joseph.

"Breathe in; hold it, breathe out. Breathe in; hold it, breathe out," Rich whispered as he stared into the flames. "I can feel Jesus within me."

"He's within all of us," said John.

"What else can I do to worship him?" Rich asked.

"There are many ways to worship and serve Jesus. Follow your heart and act as if you are one of his disciples," said John.

"I thought I already was a disciple."

"Maybe you are. How did you come so close to Jesus, Rich?" John asked.

"I got religion fast in 'Nam. My Bible and faith in Him got me through it. I did so many evil things every day, then asked Jesus for forgiveness every night. I hope he heard my pleas."

"I know he did," said John. "You were blessed by Christ's compassion and infinite grace during your time of crisis in 'Nam."

"He was my salvation."

"Each of us is on our own journey of discovery and salvation, seeking to understand how our faith can uplift our spirit. Especially during our darkest hours when we think we're alone."

"I'm a seeker. How do I know if I'm on the right track?" asked Rich.

"As the path goes, you'll find it."

∞

Did John's statement relate to just Rich? Or, both of us? Rich had indeed found his own path, one that allowed him to explore new territory with like-minded spirits. Maybe he had even found a way to change the world and knew it began with changing himself first. Then, through his example he'd influence others. Who knows what his actions might yield someday. *After all, isn't that what Jesus did; lead by example?*

Of course John's words related to both Rich and me. Though, I hoped to soon find out if I had found my path.

Chapter Seventy-Two

I got up at sunrise to take advantage of as much daylight as possible. By noon I was driving along another monotonous segment of interstate. It could have been anywhere between Utah and New Mexico. My mind took flight with the wind flowing through the butterfly window. *Why did I leave one of the longest segments of my trip for today?* Here I was driving on Route 89, this time going south and retracing my path from a few days ago. *Where have I been going? What have I been trying to prove? Who was I trying to prove it to? Would anyone care if I succeeded or not?* I would and hoped I'd soon find out. I had been at this for too long—since the late 70's.

I had been working for a few years at my first professional job, gotten married and bought a small home at the Jersey Shore.

Seems like you were on your way.

"I was, but, I regretted not stopping in Corrales, New Mexico during my cross-country trip in '72. It had been less than two years since Mom got Ginny's postcard and I thought you set out in another direction."

You did what you did that summer. There's no going back.

"I know I can't undo something that's already been done. It would be like trying to get all the tape back into the BB King cartridge—impossible."

Rich leaned over and rummaged under the seat for the broken cartridge. *"The Thrill is Gone" was one of my favorite songs on that 8-track. Are you sure we can't rewind it?*

I looked over at him. "There's no hope for that tape."

∞

So, in order to ease my guilt about not stopping in Corrales, in the mid-70's I tried to contact Rich by letter. It seemed simple enough to pay a database company for address labels to over 100 Richard Duffy's living in the US. I remember Mom and me folding and stuffing my letters with Rich's description and the circumstances of his disappearance. I even included a stamped, self-addressed return envelope, hopeful that one of my letters would reach the "right" Rich. Within the next few weeks, I received dozens of responses. One of them sent a brochure—Duffy Yachts. Another included a prayer card about seeking peace and tranquility. Everyone wrote personal messages about how they empathized with my search. None of them were from my brother Rich.

Weeks passed, and I found myself consumed with other daily matters—starting my Master's Degree, fixing up my home and my job as a college administrator. One Saturday afternoon I was working in the yard when I heard the phone ring. I ran inside, reached around the kitchen door and picked up the receiver. I stood against the door jamb catching my breath. "Hello."

"This is your brother Richie. Did you think I was dead?"

I was stunned and immobilized as if I had been sucker-punched in the jaw. I don't recall exactly what I said. My response was probably more stammering than anything resembling communication. It certainly wasn't the reply I should have given, but I hadn't planned for this. *Why hadn't I thought this through in advance? What would I say if Rich ever called me?* I know my response should have been a resounding, "Yes. We haven't heard from you in years. We thought you were dead!" Instead I mumbled something like, "Not really." *Not really? What the hell was I thinking?*

Then I heard, "Is this Joe Flannigan?"

I never heard of anyone named Joe Flannigan. So, I said, "No."

"You're not Joe Flannigan? I guess I have the wrong number. Bye."

I don't know why I didn't simply say, "This is Dan Duffy. Is it really you, Rich?" The moment I had prayed for seemed to have come, and I blew it. I hung up the receiver. My knees buckled, and I collapsed on a kitchen chair. *Was that Rich? If it was, why hadn't I recognized his voice?* But, he said his name was Richie. I never called him that. I always called my brother Rich. *If it were him, why didn't I give him the proper cues?* I sat by the phone repeating, "Please call back. Please call back." No such luck. Tears began to stream down my face. I wiped them off with the sleeve of my shirt and walked outside.

My wife asked, "Who was that?"

"Wrong number," I said. I couldn't tell my wife how stupid I'd been. For weeks after, I made sure I was home on Saturday afternoons hoping he'd call again. But, he never did.

The phone call had lasted a mere instant, but with infinite consequences. I shudder to think that my reaction may have pushed him further away, convincing him that no one in his family cared. I'll never know for sure. What I had been hoping for seemed to be more out of reach than ever before. I never told anyone about my blunder. *How could I?* So, I kept this my secret, the burden I've carried. It's haunted me for over forty-five years.

∞

Rich jerked forward in his seat, tilted his head back as his cheek pressed against the windshield. *Look at those rays of sunshine poking through the clouds.*

"Do you want me to pull over to get a better view?"

No. I'm just amazed seeing God's grace. It looks like he's pointing from above, showing us the way.

Maybe he is showing me the way. What a hypocrite I've been judging Rich by asking if his future would have been different if he had thought through consequences before doing something? All this time, the question was more relevant to me. Look what I had done. Unfortunately, there was no way I could undo it.

Out of the corner of my eye, I saw Rich beside me, shaking his head. *You know, I've been trying to figure you out ever since you opened the garage door and sat your ass in the driver's seat of my GTO. Why are you the only one in the family who ever seemed to give a shit about me?*

"That's not true. I'm not the only one. We all cared about you."

Maybe, but you've done something. Remember what we said about our ole man? You could tell what was important to him by how he spent his time? Well, in your case, it's not just all the time you've spent trying to find me. It's that you've kept memories of me alive all these years.

"It's made me feel closer to you."

And, another thing. I've been thinking about that phone call. It really don't matter if the call was from me or not. What's such a bummer is you chose to believe it was me and beat yourself up about it ever since.

I turned to him and nodded. "I guess so."

Rich looked me in the eyes and placed his hand on my shoulder. *Hasn't forty-five years been long enough?*

I reached up, touched the scar tissue on the back of his hand and looked back at him. "Maybe, Rich, maybe, but, it brought me here with you, didn't it?"

Sure did. I'm blessed that we've had this time together. But, now it's time to let it go bro'. Do you hear what I'm saying? Let. It. Go.

Maybe control really is an illusion. After all, I had no influence over Mom deciding to leave my father. I was unable to change Rich's behavior that eventually got him sent to war. I couldn't stop Diane's decision to leave him or prevent him from moving out west. And, for certain, I had no part in his disappearance.

I took a deep breath and exhaled, then, another. I whispered, "Just let it go, Dan. Just let it go." I turned on the radio and Michael Parks was strumming his guitar and singing his country tune, "Long, Lonesome Highway." The lyrics made me think of Rich's decision to live life according to his own terms.

Chapter Seventy-Three

I exited I-40 for gas and something to eat in Winslow, Arizona. I found myself on a section of the West's most famous east-west highway, historic Route 66. The original "Main Street of America" and "Mother Road" spanned 2,400 miles and linked Los Angeles and Chicago. After filling the tank, I sat outside on the patio of *Las Marias*, eating a chicken chimichanga and munching on taco chips dipped in six types of salsa. I mixed three together to create a version I called, "Take It Easy," which was exactly what I wanted to do even if it would only last a few minutes until I was back on the road. One downside to the café was that they didn't serve margaritas.

Grey clouds drifted across the sky for as far as I could see. I put up the top and followed Route 66 east for a couple of miles where it merged again with I-40 east. A few hours later, the highway traversed the Petrified Forest National Park. I wanted to stop and explore it but there wasn't an interchange for miles in either direction. Just outside of Gallup, New Mexico I saw a sign, "Continental Divide." What I knew about it from a college Geography course was that precipitation which landed on its western slope would drain to the Pacific while moisture on its eastern flank would eventually end up in the Atlantic. Those were long distances for something as ephemeral as rain to travel.

It was 4:00 p.m. by the time I entered Albuquerque's city limits. I turned off I-40 and was on a different segment of historic Route 66, downtown's Central Avenue. I crossed a bridge over the Rio Grande River and pulled behind a slow moving VW bus with a psychedelic peace sign painted on its rear hatch door. When I saw the New Jersey license plate, I knew it was Rich and Ginny. They made a quick left on Rio Grande Boulevard and a right onto Plaza Street. I followed them until we parked in front of Old Town Plaza. It was a ten block historic area comprised of adobe buildings housing art galleries, restaurants and shops. It even had a Rattlesnake Museum that I hoped they weren't interested in visiting.

Rich stepped out of the van, yawned and tightened the rope belt of his Moses robe. "I have to stretch my legs."

"Me, too," replied Ginny. "The map says there's an outdoor sculpture garden. Let's go see."

They held hands as they entered the plaza and strolled past San Felipe de Neri Church. They entered the sculpture garden and ambled through the natural desert hardscape, stopping to gaze at a group of larger than life bronze sculptures. The figures depicted the plight of Pioneers: several men riding horseback using ropes to pull a covered wagon stuck in a ravine, others pushing from behind.

Rich chuckled. "That reminds me of the time my mom got our car stuck in the sand."

"No kidding?"

"That was a long time ago."

Ginny pointed above the trees. "Look at all those colorful hot air balloons!"

"Let's go get high."

I trailed Rich and Ginny as they got back on I-40 east and took the turn for I-25 north. There were still a few hours of daylight left when we arrived at Balloon Fiesta Park. We left the van and GTO on a grassy field and joined a few others waiting in line for the next available ride. A short distance away, dozens of vivid colored orbs blossomed into a floating flower garden as they ascended into the sky or returned to earth. Soon, drifting before us was an enormous fabric globe with yellow and blue striped panels encircling its sphere.

A man in a yellow fleece clipped a carabiner, then another into two rings anchored in the ground. "Next," he shouted.

We ran to a guy standing in a wicker gondola wearing a similar colored fleece with the words "We Take You Higher" embroidered on it. The pilot took Ginny's hand. She lifted her legs over the side and squeezed beside him.

"Welcome aboard! It's a little tight."

Rich held onto a guy wire and boosted himself into the basket. I slipped in beside him.

"I'm Jim. Just relax and enjoy the flight." The man's face and hands were tanned, perhaps wind burned from the dry desert air. He pulled on both sides of his baseball cap until it was snug on his head. An embroidered replica of his balloon adorned its crown. He signaled to his friend on the ground who unclipped the carabiners, then he pulled a metal ring above his head. "Whoosh!" A massive blue flame shot straight up into the middle of a "Hoola-Hoop" size opening at the base of the fabric. Nothing happened. The pilot pulled once more. "Whoosh!" The flames bellowed and the craft began to slowly rise. We floated in silence, interrupted by the occasional "Whoosh!" of flames emitted from a salad bowl size nozzle mounted on a bar above our heads.

The Rio Grande River meandered below us. The pilot pulled on a cord, and the balloon levitated, then slowly began its descent. The river widened as we got closer and closer. When we were thirty feet above the water, we heard another "Whoosh!" We drifted down and the basket briefly touched the surface before rising once again. "Whoosh! Whoosh!" We sailed higher and higher and moved with the wind. I hummed The 5th Dimension's sunshine pop hit, "Up, Up and Away" until we were over an undeveloped barren area.

Jim pulled the cord again beginning our slow descent to earth. Down, down, we floated. He waved to his chase driver whose van kicked up a cloud of dust as it crossed the sandy desert. The gondola bounced once, twice before being dragged and settling into the sand. We scooted over the side of the basket as the balloon deflated and rested on the ground.

"Thanks," said Ginny. "That was a great way to get high."

"Come again. We get high every Saturday afternoon."

∞

Daylight surrendered to dusk as the sun sank below the crest of a nearby mountain. A chill settled in the air. I rolled up my window and watched from the driver's seat as Rich and Ginny drove away. I was sad thinking it would be the last time I would see them in their VW bus because they were only a few miles from their Corrales commune. *Could it really have been over two months since I began my cross-country trip?*

Rich held his fist in front of him and pumped it in my direction. *We've seen it all. Haven't we?*

Scenes of my travels with Rich flickered before me. "I've witnessed more than I ever dreamed possible."

Me, too. What's your favorite memory?

"They're all favorites."

Come on, pick one.

"Let me think. I'm sure a song was playing when I experienced it."

Rich raised his hands palms up and looked at me. *What? You mean you've had a soundtrack playing in your head for the past eight weeks?*

"Guess so. Our trip really has been my very own motion picture. Of course it would have a film score."

There was something special about the day I sat in the car outside the Cody Diner. Some of my memories of Rich made me happy and others pissed me off. By the time I pulled out of the lot for Yellowstone, "Break On Through" by The Doors was playing. I listened to the lyrics and understood that I needed to break through a barrier that was holding me back. I had to let go of my view of Rich from the past.

Didn't that set you free?

∞

It seemed the whole trip ending with the command of the song had wiped the slate clean between us and our past. It wasn't just the song though. It was my whole experience clarified by the song. It opened my mind to accept Rich for who he was, not someone I had wanted him to be.

The last pickup truck pulled off the massive burnt grass field with the fabric from a hot air balloon crammed inside a huge nylon bag. Its wicker basket gondola hung over the tailgate. Other than my presence, Balloon Fiesta Park was deserted. I now saw its enormous dimensions. The grounds could accommodate four football fields, side-by-side and still have room for vehicles.

I erected my tent and camp chair beside the GTO and set up my tabletop grille on the ground. I lit the charcoal and when it glowed red, I put on a few burgers. After I ate, it became so dark I couldn't see my hands when I held them in front of my face. I sat in my chair, flipped on the light from my headgear and opened Rich's journal to his last entry,

Day #62, August 22, 1970 (Corrales, New Mexico)
Praise the Lord! We're finally home!
We've traveled many miles...
Our journey's just begun...

The night was tranquil. Zipped inside my sleeping bag, I drifted off and felt like I was floating on an endless sea. Hours passed before I was awakened by bright light. *Had I slept through the night?* I slipped through the front panel of my tent to see. Balloon Fiesta Park was illuminated by a luminous full moon hung high in the heavens. I hoped it was a good omen for tomorrow's visit to Rich's commune.

Chapter Seventy-Four

I was awakened at dawn as the first truck drove across the ballooning grounds and guys began unloading cargo. I crawled out of my sleeping bag and tent when I heard a propane burner ignite, "Whoosh!" Another day of festivities at the park had begun.

With no milk or yogurt in the cooler, I sat in my chair and ate a breakfast of dry granola right out of the bag. I washed it down with several gulps of OJ. I knew that today would be an important day because I had traced Rich's tracks over 5,000 miles from New Jersey to New Mexico. I was so close to Corrales where he and his kindred spirits engaged in communal living. I knew that the trip had been worthwhile. *But, would I finally discover what happened to Rich?* I couldn't wait to find out. I packed my gear, put the top down and drove off to see what was in store for me today.

My path took me over the AMAFCA North Division Channel which redirected flood water from the Rio Grande. It was an empty concrete lined arroyo that paralleled I-25. In a short distance I drove across the Alameda Lateral, another dry, but smaller stream bed. I turned onto St. Francis where the road turned from tar to dirt.

I was transported back in time when I pulled into a driveway and saw Ken's VW camper in the side yard. Its tires were flat, the rear engine access door was open and weeds sprouted into its wheel wells. I watched as Ken stepped out of the van's side door, bare chested, wearing boxers and carrying a blanket. Sally tailed him, her long brown hair askew and breasts visible through a clinging tee-shirt that ended just above her panties. They walked toward a backyard fire pit ringed with stones. It was next to a pile of seasoned split logs.

Nearby were two-foot sections of trees and an old stump with an axe wedged in it.

I heard humming, rhythmic clapping and drumsticks tapping to the beat of Cream's, "I Feel Free," as it blasted from the van. Rich clapped and sang along as he bopped down the back stairs. Ginny followed holding his rope belt in one hand and a straw basket filled with fruit in the other. Ken and Sally unwrapped the blanket and stretched it on the ground. Ginny tied the rope around Rich's waist. They hugged each other, sat cross-legged and formed a tight circle. Ginny passed the basket and then each took a piece of fruit. They held hands, closed their eyes and waited for Rich to begin. "Thank you Jesus for another beautiful morning. You have graced us with the freedom to live, love and worship. Amen."

They rested their elbows on their knees, placed their hands together in a prayer position and began chanting, "Aum. Aum."

Later that afternoon, I saw Rich standing under the shade of a makeshift canopy suspended by ropes tied between two trees. A piece of lumber was balanced on two saw horses as he measured and sawed off the end. He placed the board on the ground, turned it on edge and wedged it between two others. Then, he drove two screws into each end, completing the bed frame.

Ginny stood from tending her garden and shouted, "It's shaping up!"

Rich looked her way and waved. "I still have to screw eyelets all around and weave the rope before we can put the mattress on top."

"I can't wait to try it."

"Me, either."

Ginny got on her hands and knees and dug close to her tomato plants to loosen, then pull out the weeds. Her tomatoes, string beans, green peppers and cucumbers were ripe. She might pick them later and toss them in a garden salad. She'd can whatever they couldn't eat from her harvest: tomato sauce, dill pickles and string beans would be needed and delicious during the winter.

All afternoon I had been relaxing on the front porch rocking while reading one of Rich's books, Jack Kerouac's *On the Road*. In many respects Rich had followed a similar journey along an open road abounding in blissful exploration and experimentation. It was almost dinnertime and there was at least an hour before sunset when I walked through the front door. I heard footsteps above me. Ginny floated down the stairs in a yellow flowered dress. Her hair smelled of daisies as she passed through an open area divided into living, dining and cooking space. A *Desiderata* poster was mounted on the wall behind two sofas. Next to a farm table with six chairs hung a *Woodstock* movie poster. It featured a cluster of festival photos with captions: peace, people, love, grass, music and America.

Centered along the back wall was a black antique cast iron stove with raised letters: Glenwood. It had a large oven door and a smaller one to access the wood burning compartment. Four metal disks defined the range top with two built in warming shelves behind them. The stove exuded a sense of self-sufficiency as well as functionality for heating, cooking and baking. Hanging from a beam were bunches of colorful dried flowers: indian paintbrush, chrysanthemum and hibiscus. Beside them were clusters of dehydrated herbs. I heard Simon and Garfunkel singing "Parsley, Sage, Rosemary and Thyme" from car speakers hooked up to an 8-track tape deck.

After dinner, I sat in my camp chair and joined Rich and his friends around the fire pit as flames flickered from the fire. Ken propped Jensen car speakers in the window. The hushed tone of The Turtles began their catchy tune, "Happy Together."

Rich took a drag from a joint and passed it to Ginny. "This will make you happy."

"I'm quite happy with you." She took a toke, held her breath and gave it back to him.

Ken tossed Rich his calf skin bota bag. He twisted off the nozzle, compressed the sack and a stream of wine flowed into his mouth. He nodded to Ginny; she opened wide and he squeezed again.

Rich spoke to no one in particular. "It was far out yesterday tripping beside the Rio Grande."

Ken gave Rich the peace sign. "Next time you should take the van so you can play music."

Rich raised his hands, thumbs up. "I can dig it. Led Zeppelin and The Doors. Sometimes when I'm tripping I can see right through to the other side."

"What's there?" asked Ken.

"The Promised Land. Last week, I saw a stairway rise out of the river and soar above me all the way to heaven. It disappeared before I could climb it. If it appears again I'm gonna take it."

Ginny put her arm around Rich. "Don't leave without me."

Rich pulled her close and kissed her forehead.

∞

Hours passed as stars made their nightly procession to the western horizon. I was overcome by the stillness all around me, interrupted only by a single engine Cessna as it flew low over the yard. It roused me from my reverie beside a now smoldering fire, its embers glowed from orange to red as it was fanned by puffs of wind.

Chapter Seventy-Five

I experienced another sense of déjà vu and wondered if my mind was telling me that I had come to the end of Rich's journey. And my own, too. I erected my tent in Rich's backyard and pounded stakes into the compacted rock filled soil. I put together my table top charcoal grille beside the fire pit and roasted a few hot dogs. I washed them down with a couple bottles of Blue Moon. By 9:00 p.m. the air was nippy, and my eyelids were heavy. I yawned so much that a gnat flew in my mouth, stuck to the back of my throat and I gagged. I flushed it down with another bottle of beer and knew it was time for bed.

I drifted into a spaced out state of slumber. Shadows of Rich in his Moses robe wavered against the nylon wall of my tent. I heard him jabber, "Jacob had a dream. He saw a stairway to the clouds. Angels were floating all around. It was the gate to heaven."

That reminded me of something. I retrieved Rich's journal and leafed through it until I found a poem on the backside of the last page. I didn't remember reading it but somehow knew it was there.

Jacob's Ladder
When I imagine the World ending,
I'll be halfway to heaven
Naked beside the Rio Grande
With acid flowing through my mind
I'll climb Jacob's Ladder
Countless steps one by one
Until I reach the city of love

I became absorbed in a three-dimensional presentiment of Rich's poem. Yet, it was a glorious sunny afternoon under crystalline autumn skies, a veritable Indian summer. The cottonwoods were at their peak and absolutely gorgeous. In this central New Mexico flood plain, the river was placid—flowing smoothly and unencumbered—no longer an upriver wild and untamed threat. I sat cross-legged beside the Rio Grande. Rich and Ginny were lying on a blanket beside me on that fateful day in 1970. They were two twenty-year olds, oblivious to the consequences of their impending actions. Blind Faith's "Can't Find My Way Home" was blaring from their van on the gravel road behind them.

"Do you really think you should be taking so much acid, Rich? Why not one or two tabs—like me."

Rich smiled at Ginny. He took a swig of apple wine and tossed a handful of acid tabs into his mouth. "This is going to be a far-out trip. Should be the best ever! I'll see you on the other side." He handed the bottle to Ginny.

Ginny kissed Rich, dropped two tabs on her tongue and swallowed them with a sip of wine. They took off their clothes and held hands while lying side-by-side on the blanket—waiting for the acid to blow their minds.

"What's that?" Rich said. He watched as a magnificent staircase emerged before him—shimmering over the water like a mirage. As each stair appeared, it sparkled and vibrated a chaotic array of color—random light waves in violet, green and gold. Each step overlapped another and ascended into an infinite sky. He heard a spectrum of sound emanating from each color. The images became a cacophony of pulsating wavelengths of light and sound—triggering the stairway to begin stirring before him, moving upwards. He heard the opening guitar licks and then flutes play Led Zeppelin's "Stairway to Heaven." The song beckoned him to rise, and he did.

"Rich!" Ginny cried out. "Why are the trees so angry?"

Ginny's mind was scrambled; everything was unintelligible. She was supposed to be a dreamer in a fantasy. Instead, she was held captive on a bad trip, trapped as if within an evil wizard's nightmare. The trees and grass bent over and taunted her. They stared through her with raging eyes. She hung her head down and clasped her hands together in a prayer position. She tried to concentrate on her breathing—anything other than witness the madness all around her. She took a deep breath, held it and slowly released it. She did it once again.

She thought she saw Rich smiling at her and waving as he floated by. "Stay calm," she whispered. "This too will pass." She focused on her fingers. How serene they appeared, interlaced one within the other. She clasped her hands together and they formed a small opening. It got bigger and bigger as she raised them to her face. She imagined she was inside her cupped hands—protected and safe. When she gently touched her nose she closed her eyes and prayed, "Please, God, help me though this. I won't do this ever again."

The sun was setting when she awakened, slowly becoming conscious and aware of her surroundings. She was naked on a blanket, curled into a fetal position and sucking her thumb. She shook her hands, and flexed her fingers trying to regain feeling in them. She looked to her side for Rich but he was gone, his Moses robe and sandals abandoned beside her.

"Rich!" she yelled. "Rich! Rich! Where are you?"

She continued shouting for Rich as she put on her jeans and tee-shirt. She clutched her sandals and ran downstream along the riverbank frantically calling his name.

It was dark and cold by the time Ginny returned to the van.

Is that it? Rich was here one moment and gone the next? Another time that there was nothing I could do to change the outcome. I ran to the GTO.

Chapter Seventy-Six

I slammed the door of the GTO and looked over to the passenger seat. "What the hell happened, Rich?" I held my breath and hoped to hear an answer.

I had to split that scene because I needed a new beginning. I didn't know how to say goodbye, so I floated downriver away from my life at the commune. Ginny and my friends were fine being one big happy family—sharing everything—money, drugs, work, food, music and sex. I wanted to live the way Timothy Leary told me to live that day he spoke in Golden Gate Park. I let the current take me away... I had to "Turn on, Tune in and Drop out."

"But, you didn't have clothes on your back. You were naked and alone."

At first all I needed was an army blanket and a Bible. Jesus was there with me ever since that night in 'Nam. I had faith that I was on the right path even if I had to leave my friends and girlfriend behind.

"But, how'd you live? What'd you do for money?"

My faith led me to everything I needed, and that's all I cared about. Remember Joplin's song? Well, I had nothing left to lose and felt free as I never felt before.

"You needed to lose everything to feel free?"

I read one of Ginny's books about Thoreau's life. I wanted to go into the woods and live alone in a tiny cabin, too. I didn't know how to do it until I was carried away by the Rio Grande. It's amazing that you can live off the land in solitude. That day I floated away I was reborn a second time. All I cared about was getting closer to Jesus.

274

"I've read Thoreau too. But, reading *Walden* didn't motivate me to get lost in the wilderness. I can't imagine how you chose to do such a thing."

I thought we already had this talk. It wasn't your life to lead. It was my life. You chose a different path, remember? That made all the difference in your life. I'm glad for you. But, I made my own path.

"Was it worth it?"

You're not getting it are you? It's called rebirth. I shed my skin so I could grow another, just like a Jersey blue claw crab. I saw a chance to take a different path. There aren't many times in life you get a do-over. Would you have the same questions if I had become a monk?

I thought about what Rich had said and looked at him. "Probably not. Though, a monk lives in solitude within a community, you know, brotherhood and all that."

Think of my new life as becoming a monk without the brotherhood. It was selfhood. I stumbled out of the river naked, headed south and just kept walking. I lived alone, loving peace and tranquility. I'd do it again if I could turn back time. How about you? Are you happy with the choices you made in your life?

I hesitated before replying. "Yes, I am. I don't think I have any regrets. Maybe there are a few things I'd do a little differently. But, generally speaking I'm happy with the way I've lived my life."

Isn't that all that matters? After all, we're not in our bodies for long, are we? We had to find our own ways, even if we didn't walk side by side. It didn't make us any less brothers.

I let his comment percolate in my mind for a few minutes. "No. It didn't. But, it would have been terrific not to have to wait 50 years to spend time together."

Sometimes your prayers are answered in ways you can't even imagine. Did it ever occur to you that maybe I wanted to disappear?

I heard Rich's words but couldn't imagine that he would have wanted to have a complete disconnection from his family, friends and loved ones? Was his brain so fried from drugs that he just wasn't able to manage living collectively with others? Even Thoreau had a sense of community as he wrote, anticipating that others throughout the world and across time would someday read his words, thereby, establishing a link of communication with them from his cabin in the wilderness to readers.

I didn't care about returning to the society I had known before 'Nam. It was made up of crazy people who forced me to do things I didn't want to do—kill innocent people. Why would I want to rejoin them? I had to search for a part of me that was missing ever since that damn war. When I couldn't climb that stairway to heaven, I figured God had another plan for my life.

My time with Rich helped me understand why he possibly did what he did. "You had to find yourself."

I sure did. Just because I roamed didn't mean I was lost. I hoped that when the world turned upside down all the sinners would fall off, and I'd be left in peace.

I didn't know how to respond to his comment about the world ending. What I could make out was that Rich was striving to live in a world only he could imagine. A world that allowed him to live in peace and harmony with nature. A chance to begin to love himself again.

That's right. I created a new life and could never go back.

I thought about what Rich had said and knew it didn't relate to me. Maybe he could never return home. But, I sure could and knew it was time to get back on the road.

Chapter Seventy-Seven

It had been days since I turned onto I-40, heading east, but not for home. A force was guiding me to our nation's capital. Images of stone pathways beside the Mall and a Reflecting Pool flashed through my mind. I didn't know what I'd do when I got there and the subject couldn't be discussed with Rich. He hadn't been in the passenger seat beside me since I left Albuquerque. A palpable silence hung in the air, growing wider as I approached my destination. I sensed that our time together was coming to an end. Yet, didn't want to or know how to say goodbye.

It was late afternoon by the time I parked the car on Constitution Avenue. I wasn't sure what I was looking for but found myself walking along a gravel pathway beside the Reflecting Pool, heading toward the Lincoln Memorial. As I approached it, I imagined standing with young people at another time, listening to Senators Eugene McCarthy and George McGovern voice their opposition to the Vietnam War.

A mallard duck landed in the pool beside me. I shook my head and looked around. Scenes of civil disobedience dissolved before me, and I was alone. My eyes followed the duck as it took flight, joining several others high in the air before separating from the flock. I watched it lower its feet and spread its wings in graceful descent. I followed it until it landed on the grass beside the walkway at the west entrance to the Vietnam Veterans Memorial.

"The Wall," as it's called by veterans and citizens alike, contains the names of over 58,000 men and women who were killed in action; 1,200 of them are memorialized as Missing in Action or Prisoners of War. June 5, 1968 came to mind as the date Rich told me his radioman Truman McManus became

DAN DUFFY

MIA. *Maybe that's why I'm here?* To honor Rich's Marine Corps buddy. I flipped through a binder containing information on how the wall was organized: by names and dates of those honored. I grabbed a few pieces of paper and a pencil to make a rubbing of Truman's name.

I descended deeper into the landscape as I followed the walkway beside the wall which gradually rose taller on my left. I passed panel after panel with hundreds of names on each before stopping at 60W. It represented those killed or missing from June 3rd to June 8th 1968. Starting at the top, I scanned across each name from left to right. Two-thirds of the way down, in the middle of line twenty, I saw his name. I placed the paper on the wall and began rubbing the pencil until TRUMAN J McMANUS emerged. I stepped back and looked at my pencil rubbing.

When I glanced back at The Wall, I saw my reflection and brother Rich's as he stood in front of me. He looked nineteen years old, like he did that day in the bathroom mirror. But, this time I stood behind him—no longer the naïve and gullible thirteen-year old I was back in '64. I was in my sixties now and was the older brother. He leaned back into me and I gripped his shoulders. My vision blurred with tears as we stood gazing in silence at our reflection. Yet, our spirits soared connecting us as one. We had bridged many gaps and traveled far both in time and space these past six-months.

Even though Rich's name wasn't on The Wall, I knew how war had profoundly changed his life—and mine, too. I knelt down, placed another piece of paper against the polished black granite wall and held the pencil in my hand. This time as I rubbed the name Richard E. Duffy appeared, and I knew it was his way of saying good bye.

"OK, Rich. I'll say goodbye for now but you'll be with me forever," I whispered.

Of course I will. Isn't that where I've been all along?

I let go of the flawed impression of Rich I had for most of my life. Living his story had transformed me.

I exited the walkway to the east of The Wall and soon entered The Three Serviceman Statue Plaza where a life size depiction of heroic soldiers stood next to a granite stone and looked on in silence as I read the inscription:

"IN MEMORY
OF THE MEN AND WOMEN
WHO SERVED IN THE VIETNAM WAR
AND LATER DIED AS A RESULT
OF THEIR SERVICE
WE HONOR AND REMEMBER
THEIR SACRIFICE"

I already missed Rich and hoped that he felt the same about me. I returned to the GTO, put the top down and inserted Buffalo Springfield's album *Last Time Around* into the tape player. I turned up the volume and began singing along with Neil Young: "On the Way Home."

One more thing...

I hope you enjoyed my book. I'm thankful you invested time reading my story about me and my brother, Rich. I am hopeful that you received something of value from reading it.

If you believe your friends would enjoy this book, I would be honored if you would post your thoughts and also leave a review on Amazon.

Best regards, Dan Duffy

Sign up for announcements of paperback discounts and to receive my newsletter here: www.danduffyauthor.com Leave your email address and I will never sell or share it with others.

About The Author
www.danduffyauthor.com

If my life had a theme it would be, "Evolving as a Lifelong Learner." I've always enjoyed a challenge as an opportunity to grow and develop. An important value to me has been that education was a pathway to my future. My thirty-five year educational career resulted in the completion of an Associate of Arts (A.A), Bachelor of Arts (B.A.), Master's (M.Ed.) and Doctoral (Ed.D.)degrees.

My education served me well throughout more than 25 years of my work career where I assumed leadership positions in community college educational administration, private industry and business management. My positions varied from being Director of Training and Management Development within one of America's fastest growing companies to serving as Vice-President of Student Affairs during a period of strategic redirection and organizational renewal.

Since retirement my wife Helene and I shared the common fantasy that most retirees have of someday owning a B&B. Our dream became reality in May 2011, when we bought the Beech Tree Bed and Breakfast in Rockport, Massachusetts, but that's another story... Although Innkeeping is a demanding endeavor, New England winters and long nights provide me with time to pursue my other passion—writing. I've given much thought to the events that shaped my life, growing up as the middle-child of a single mom struggling to raise five kids. In the absence of my father I wanted to be just like my older brother Rich. Although this changed over the years, I am still trying to understand the impact he had on my life.

His disappearance forty-five years ago has baffled and haunted me. I've been motivated to put pencil-to-paper to transform my memories into a memoir; mostly truth, part fiction, about "our story."

Acknowledgements

While my brother's story has haunted me since his disappearance, I committed to begin "My Writers Journey" three and a half years ago. I am grateful to many individuals who engaged me along my journey, some urged me on from ahead, and others exhorted me from behind, but most accompanied me by my side. This metaphor of a mutual excursion serves as an important reminder of why people set out to explore new horizons and traverse unfamiliar territory in the first place. David Whyte says it is "because beyond the edge we have established for ourselves lies the unknown." Writing has allowed the unknown to become known to me.

I am grateful to my fellow Rockport Innkeeper friends, Ted and Jen Rassmann for countless discussions about my story and for assisting me in identifying *Brother, Brother* as an appropriate book title.

I have gained immeasurably from participating in programs offered by the Gloucester Writers Center www.gloucesterwriters.org. Thanks to Annie Thomas and Henry Ferrini, Co-Directors for their leadership in such a worthwhile endeavor. I'd also like to extend thanks to Ann McArdle for facilitating a "Works in Progress" workshop, as well as to my fellow workshop participants: Casey Breton, Richard Buck, Jim Masciarelli, Karin Peterson, Wendy Pierson, Ed Powers, Joe Snowden and Judy Spurr.

The GWC Open Mic monthly program has motivated me for the past three and a half years. Thank you to Amanda Cook, Facilitator and all those fellow writers who have shared their words and listened to the words of others.

I have benefitted greatly from my affiliation with a talented and caring group of writers known as "The Finish Line" writers group. Their critique of my writing and specific recommendations have provided me with valuable insight.

Thank you to Barbara Boudreau and Sandra Williams for your support and assistance in reading and critiquing my manuscript. Thanks also to Stacey Dexter, Cindy Hendrickson, Jane Keddy, Sue-Ellen Kresh, John Mullen and Cindy Schimanski.

Special thanks to my Beta Readers

My Siblings: Ray Duffy, Eileen Haney and Sue Kelly.

Toms River (NJ) Friends: Andrea Abramowitz, Darlene Asay, Pat Wagner Michaud, Anthony Parisi, Gail Parisi, Larry Perlberg, Laurie Perlberg, Skip Piakowski, Stu Schrier and Jack Wilkerson.

Other Beta Readers: Ellen Benowitz, Law Hamilton, Tina Krautheim, Lois McNulty, Pat Mandell and Terry Sawma.

Brother, Brother Playlist/Soundtrack

Chapter #3: Me and Bobby McGee, Janis Joplin

Chapter #7: On the Road Again, Canned Heat

Chapter #8: Déjà Vu, Crosby, Stills, Nash & Young

Chapter #9: Woodstock, Crosby, Stills, Nash & Young

America, Simon & Garfunkel

People are Strange, The Doors

Chapter #10: What's Going On?, Marvin Gaye

Chapter #13: Magic Carpet Ride, Steppenwolf

Strange Brew, Cream

Sunshine of Your Love, Cream

Chapter #22: On a Threshold of a Dream, The Moody Blues

Bad Moon Rising, Creedence Clearwater Revival

The Age of Aquarius, The 5th Dimension

Chapter #44: Break on Through, The Doors

Chapter #45: Closer to Home, Grand Funk Railroad

Chapter #46: I Want to take you Higher, Sly & Family Stone

Spirit in the Sky, Norman Greenbaum

Chapter #47: I Stand Alone, Al Kooper

Chapter #49: Going up the country, Canned Heat

Chapter #50: It's a Beautiful Morning, The Rascals

Piece of my heart, Janis Joplin

Chapter #52: Fortunate Son, CCR

Chapter #53: Mr. Lonely, Bobby Vinton

Chapter #54: Evil Ways, Santana

Chapter #55: In a White Room, Cream

One, Three Dog Night

Hey Joe, Jimi Hendrix

Chapter #57: With a Little Help From My Friends,

Joe Cocker

Chapter #58: Mr. Tamborine Man, The Byrds

Does Anyone Really Know what time it is?,Chicago Transit Authority

Eli's Coming, Three Dog Night

Up on Cripple Creek, The Band

Chapter #59: Born to be Wild, Steppenwolf

Only the Beginning, Chicago

A Whiter Shade of Pale, Procol Harum

White Rabbit, Jefferson Airplane

Goin Up the Country, Canned Heat

Easy to Be Hard, Three Dog Night

Chapter #60: Are You Experienced?, Jimi Hendrix

In-A-Gadda-Da-Vida, Iron Butterfly

Chapter #61: Purple Haze, Jimi Hendrix
Turn, Turn, Turn, The Byrds

Chapter #62: Good Times, Bad Times, Led Zeppelin

Live for Today, The Grassroots

Chapter #63: Freedom, Richie Havens

Pinball Wizard, The Who

The Fish Cheer, Country Joe McDonald

Find the Cost of Freedom, Crosby, Stills & Nash

Chapter #64: For What It's Worth, Buffalo Springfield

Chapter #65: Sugar Magnolia, The Grateful Dead

Truckin, The Grateful Dead

To Lay Me Down, The Grateful Dead

Chapter #66: I feel like I'm fixin to die rag, Country Joe McDonald

Chapter #65: Jumping Jack Flash, The Rolling Stones

Chapter #68: Grazing in the Grass, The Friends of Distinction

Everyday People, Sly and The Family Stone

Chapter #72: The thrill is gone, BB King

Long, Lonesone Highway, Michael Parks

Chapter #73: Up, Up and Away, The 5th Dimension

Chapter #74: I Feel Free, Cream

Parsley, Sage, Rosemary and Thyme,
Simon and Garfunkel

Happy Together, The Turtles

Chapter #75: Can't Find My Way Home, Blind Faith

Stairway to Heaven, Led Zeppelin

Chapter #77: On the Way Home, Buffalo Springfield

Reading Group Discussion Questions

Do you think it's possible for two people to transcend time and place?

The '66 GTO and cross-country trip provide the framework for the story. What might these elements represent in Dan's memoir?

The late '60's and early '70's were both turbulent and formative times in America. If you grew up during this era, which historical events were most troubling to you? Which ones gave you hope for the future?

What are your thoughts about Dan's integration of fiction within his memoir? What other authors can you think of who may have blurred the lines between fact and fiction? Do you think it's possible to write a memoir strictly based on "the facts."

What was Dan's initial reaction to finding Rich and his belongings? What motivated him to be willing to retrace Rich's route?

Do you know of anyone, like Rich, who may have said and done what he did? "Changing my life was easy. I turned left, not right and kept on going until my past was out of sight."

Why do you think Dan held onto the loss of his brother for over forty-five years?

Do you think Rich's transformation into a Jesus freak helped him cope with his circumstances? What about the conflicting nature of Rich following Jesus, yet using illegal drugs?

Do you think Rich personified his religious beliefs and principles in his everyday life?

How does Dan's journey transform him?

At times Dan looks at the world through Rich's eyes and body. What benefits could you identify if you had the ability to experience life from someone else's perspective?

Why would Rich hold himself responsible for death and destruction "all the way from the hamlet along the river to his bunker door?"

Do Rich or Dan change or mature by the end of the story? Do they have a clearer sense of who they are and why they did what they did growing up?

What passage(s) strike you as insightful?

Is the ending satisfying? If so, why? If not, why not?

If you could ask the author a question, what would it be?

NOTE: Feel free to contact Dan via email at:
danduffyauthor@gmail.com

Made in the USA
Monee, IL
24 August 2020

39243724R00177